Alpena Co. Library
211 N. First Ave.
Alpena, MI 49707

# Philanthropy in the 21st Century

# Philanthropy
## in the 21st
# Century

THE FOUNDATION CENTER'S 50TH ANNIVERSARY INTERVIEWS

Mitch Nauffts, Editor

## About the Foundation Center

Established in 1956, and today supported by hundreds of foundations, the Foundation Center is the nation's leading authority on organized philanthropy. It maintains the most comprehensive database on U.S. grantmakers and their grants, conducts research on trends in foundation growth and giving, and operates education and outreach programs. Thousands of people visit the Center's web site each day and are served in its five regional learning centers and its national network of Cooperating Collections located in every state and Puerto Rico. For more information, visit foundationcenter.org or call (212) 620-4230.

---

We are grateful to the following 50th Anniversary Sponsors who provided support to the Foundation Center for *Philanthropy in the 21st Century:*

**Contributor**
Carnegie Corporation of New York

**Patrons**
Altman Foundation
William R. Kenan, Jr. Charitable Trust
The New York Community Trust
The Whitehead Foundation

**Supporters**

| | |
|---|---|
| Achelis Foundation | J.C. Geever, Inc. |
| Bessemer Trust | Independence Community |
| Bodman Foundation | Foundation |
| The Buhl Foundation | Christian A. Johnson |
| Fannie Mae Foundation | Endeavor Foundation |
| FJC - A Foundation of | Sid W. Richardson |
| Donor Advised Funds | Foundation |

**Regional Supporter**
The Community Foundation for the National Capital Region

*The ideas expressed in this publication are those of the authors alone and do not necessarily reflect the opinions of the funding organizations.*

---

Copyright © by the Foundation Center, 79 Fifth Avenue, New York, NY 10003.
All rights reserved. A catalog record for this book is available from the Library of Congress.

ISBN 1-59542-163-7

To order additional copies, visit our web site: foundationcenter.org/pnd/21century/

Printed and bound in the United States of America.

# Contents

*Foreword* _____ v
    **Sara L. Engelhardt, President, The Foundation Center**

*Introduction*
    The Foundation Center: Fifty Years On _____ 1
    **James Allen Smith, Waldemar A. Nielsen Professor of Philanthropy,**
    **Georgetown Public Policy Institute**

**1** Philanthropy and the Rockefeller Legacy _____ 13
    **David Rockefeller, Chairman Emeritus, Chase Manhattan Bank**

**2** Philanthropy in an Interdependent World _____ 25
    **Stephen B. Heintz, President, Rockefeller Brothers Fund**

**3** Creating Change Through Informed Philanthropy _____ 37
    **Melissa Berman, President and CEO, Rockefeller Philanthropy Advisors**

**4** Donors and Philanthropic Intent _____ 47
    **Adam Meyerson, President and CEO, Philanthropy Roundtable**

**5** Spending Out as a Philanthropic Strategy _____ 63
    **Vincent McGee, Former Executive Director, Aaron Diamond Foundation**

**6** Building Nonprofit Capacity Through Challenge Grants _____ 81
    **John E. Marshall III, President/CEO Emeritus, Kresge Foundation**

**7** Expanding Opportunity for All Californians _____ 93
    **James E. Canales, President and CEO, James Irvine Foundation**

**8** Building the Field of Social Entrepreneurship _____ 105
    **Sally Osberg, President and CEO, Skoll Foundation**

**9** Working to Catalyze Social Change _____ 119
    **Emmett Carson, Former President and CEO, Minneapolis Foundation**

**10** Nonprofits, Philanthropy, and the Democratic Process _____ 133
Rick Cohen, Former Executive Director, National Committee for Responsive Philanthropy

**11** Philanthropy and the Next-Generation Web _____ 147
Daniel Ben-Horin, Founder and President, CompuMentor

**12** Governance, Accountability, and the Charitable Sector _____ 163
Diana Aviv, President and CEO, Independent Sector

**13** Philanthropic Leadership in a Changing World _____ 175
Steve Gunderson, President and CEO, Council on Foundations

**14** Fifty Years of Promoting Foundation Openness and Transparency _____ 187
Sara L. Engelhardt, President, The Foundation Center

**15** Philanthropy as Social Incubator _____ 203
Vartan Gregorian, President and CEO, Carnegie Corporation of New York

Index _____ 215

# Foreword

Sara L. Engelhardt
President
The Foundation Center

The Foundation Center marked its 50th anniversary year in 2006. While the past fifty years give us much to celebrate, the future offers *countless* opportunities to work with our many colleagues across the sector to magnify the impact of philanthropy on our changing world. Thus, throughout 2006 we designed a number of programs, projects, and initiatives using the overarching theme of "The Future of Philanthropy."

In this spirit, during 2006 Mitch Nauffts, publisher and editorial director of the Center's online *Philanthropy News Digest* (PND), conducted fifteen special 50th anniversary interviews of leaders in the field, which we made available in the Newsmakers feature of PND. This book assembles the series of interviews in a printed volume. Together the interviews weave a rich tapestry of experience, critical analysis, and aspiration that will undergird the future of philanthropy.

We asked Jim Smith, a historian who holds the Waldemar A. Nielsen Chair in Philanthropy at Georgetown University and who has deep knowledge of the foundation field over the past century, to write the introduction for the volume. He has done an excellent job of exploring the past as prologue to the recurring themes in the interviews and of looking to the horizon ahead, as many of those interviewed do, to consider what today's ongoing debates and the fast-changing environment foretell about the future of philanthropy.

We are indebted to many people for their help in creating this enduring memento of the Center's 50th anniversary year. First and foremost, we thank the busy leaders of the foundations, organizations, and associations whom we interviewed for marshalling their thoughts and putting in the serious time that these interviews reflect. We are most grateful, as well, to our 50th Anniversary Sponsors who supported this project. (A full listing appears at the front of this volume.) Finally, we offer our thanks to the diverse community of stakeholders in philanthropy who steadfastly turn to the Center for insights into the state of the sector. We hope that the wisdom assembled on these pages will provide new insight into where philanthropy is heading in the 21st century and will sharpen your own speculation about philanthropy's contributions to our future as a society.

# Introduction

## The Foundation Center: Fifty Years On

James Allen Smith
Waldemar A. Nielsen Professor of Philanthropy
Georgetown Public Policy Institute

Anniversaries inspire us to look forward. They also prompt us to reflect. In this book fifteen leaders of the foundation and nonprofit world take the pulse of contemporary philanthropy. As they do so, their collective gaze is focused most intently on present conditions, with brief glances toward the future by some and occasional autobiographical reminiscences by others. In contrast, I have been asked to offer a bit of historical perspective, looking back and trying to recover something of the world of the Foundation Center's founders. By recalling the worries and hopes of foundation leaders a half century ago, we might be able to locate philanthropy's fast-racing pulse at the very moment of the Foundation Center's inception — a pulse surely elevated by a lingering bout of McCarthy-era fever. Through two sets of eyes, past and present, we can ponder how far the Foundation Center's half-century journey has taken us. Fifty years on, how different does the philanthropic sector look?

When the Foundation Center (born as the Foundation *Library* Center) was first conceived, there were some 5,000 philanthropic foundations in the United States, according to the best available estimates. Aggregate assets were calculated at about $4.9 billion and annual foundation grants totaled approximately $300 million, roughly 4.5 percent of the $6.65 billion in total income received by America's charitable organizations for 1954. The numbers were as solid as F. Emerson

Andrews, who would soon leave his post at the Russell Sage Foundation to become the Foundation Center's first president, could make them.

Since the 1910s and 1920s several attempts to collect and publish data on foundations by the Twentieth Century Fund and the Russell Sage Foundation, where Andrews toiled for nearly thirty years, had met with only varying success. Research inquiries were regularly rebuffed or ignored by foundations. Financial data, when provided, was inconsistent. In fact, federal reporting requirements were introduced only in 1943. And even then, public access to tax data, though it had been made easier with the passage of the Revenue Act of 1950, was still very difficult. The work remained arduous even after the Foundation Center's creation, as foundation 990 forms were accessible only through visits to sixty-four separate IRS district offices.

What had become abundantly clear by the mid-1950s was that foundations were growing exponentially in number and size: from 505 foundations holding approximately $1.8 billion in assets in 1944 to more than 1,000 in 1950 holding over $2.5 billion. With the arrival on the national scene of the Ford Foundation (established in Michigan in 1936 but operated only locally and regionally during its first decade), no one could be sure how the philanthropic future would unfold. The sale of a large block of Ford Motor Company stock in January 1956 made Ford the nation's first billion-dollar foundation, its assets dwarfing those of the venerable Rockefeller Foundation and Carnegie Corporation. It was not at all clear how Ford would ultimately choose to value its remaining portfolio, much of it still in company stock. Valuing all its stock holdings at market prices would make it a $3.4 billion foundation. With that hefty infusion of capital added to the corpus, aggregate U.S. foundation assets would reach $7.7 billion. Moreover, Ford's decision in 1955 to appropriate the exceptional sum of $500 million for grants payable over a two-year period to private colleges and universities, medical schools, and voluntary hospitals would nearly double total foundation grantmaking in the United States in those two years.

**By the mid-50s . . . foundations were growing exponentially in numbers and size. . . .**

Foundations were emerging as an increasingly powerful and much more visible force in American society. The need for better information about them was apparent to many people inside the nation's largest foundations. Demands for sounder data and improved public understanding had already begun to intensify, as foundations came under critical scrutiny in the late 1940s and early 1950s. The Revenue Act of 1950, which made portions of foundation tax filings open to public scrutiny and imposed taxes on nonprofits' unrelated business income, had been preceded in 1947 by House Ways and Means Committee investigations of business enterprises owned and operated by tax-exempt groups. In New York State a legislative inquiry into so-called "charity rackets," which is to say fundraising and other corrupt charitable practices, had also gotten under way. These early warning signals of policy makers' growing concern about foundations and charities — their wariness of specific charitable practices and their apparent eagerness to find regulatory remedies — were soon overshadowed by two congressional investigations. Some Americans were questioning their patriotism and, more profoundly, the democratic legitimacy of philanthropic foundations.

F. Emerson Andrews watched what he termed the "strange malady" that swept across America during the McCarthy era, a populist contagion from which foundations would find no immunity. Representative Eugene Cox, a Georgia Republican, presaged his inquiry into foundations with several fire-breathing speeches in 1951. Cox spoke of "the tragic misuse of foundation money" and resources that had been allocated for "un-American and subversive activities or for purposes not in the interest or tradition of the United States." Pursuing a torturous chain of logic, he blamed the deaths of American soldiers in the Korean War on Rockefeller grantmaking that over several decades had built schools and colleges in China. He also asserted that the foundation's grantmaking had somehow swayed the Chinese intelligentsia to embrace Communism.

> . . . early warning signals of policy makers' growing concern about foundations and charities . . . were soon overshadowed by two congressional investigations. . . .

The fact that the Cox Committee's subsequent investigation into foundations did not degenerate into a witch hunt — unlike its sordid and at times comic investigative sequel under Tennessee Republican B. Carroll Reece — is due both to responsible work by the committee's own research staff and to the constructive role played by Andrews and

Donald Young, the Russell Sage Foundation president, who took on the burden of educating policy makers about the role American foundations had played since the turn of the century. Through the last six months of 1952, they worked closely with the Cox Committee's general counsel Harold M. Keele, an even-tempered and fair-minded Chicago lawyer. Keele, in turn, submitted a lengthy "voluntary" questionnaire to foundations prior to the hearings. Andrews and Young then persuaded most of their foundation colleagues that it would be prudent to answer the committee's queries, burdensome as they were. Some ninety questions were asked of the larger foundations in the long-form questionnaire, often requiring hundreds of pages in response and countless hours of foundation staff time in reviewing all grants made since 1935 for their possible links to specific individuals and organizations under investigation by the House Un-American Activities Committee.

Many foundation executives expected Cox's public hearings to turn from an inquiry into an inquisition. But the congressman's opening statement proved to be remarkably conciliatory, even enlightened. The first day of testimony was devoted largely to Andrews' painstaking research on foundations and to his conclusions from reviewing the questionnaires. (His many years of observing foundations would later yield the pioneering volume *Philanthropic Foundations,* whose fiftieth anniversary this year should also be noted.) In his testimony Andrews echoed the view of many foundation colleagues that rather than restrictive new legislation there should be a registry of all foundations and more detailed reporting of financial and programmatic activities, presumably on what was then known as IRS Form 990-A.

**In his testimony Andrews echoed the view of many foundation colleagues that rather than new restrictive legislation there should be a registry of all foundations and more detailed reporting. . . .**

From the opening moments of the hearings, Andrews sensed that "the policy of cooperation had been wise." Cox and his staff were respectful, giving time for all the foundation representatives to provide an accurate and detailed picture of foundation accomplishments. Cox seemed especially impressed with the testimony of the Ford Foundation's Paul Hoffman. "You preach a fine doctrine," Cox told him, "and it is something which ought to be carried to the firesides and the homes of people. . . . You have made a very fine case for the Ford Foundation. As a matter of fact, you have made a fine case for all the foundations." On balance, Andrews assessed the Cox hearings favorably: "Too hurried and not without flaws, they have supplied a rich storehouse of information and opinion concerning foundations in the early 1950s, and set a pattern for fairness and objectivity that might better have been followed in the several more recent 'Hearings' to which foundations have been subjected." (Writing in the 1970s, he was alluding to the hearings that preceded the Tax Reform Act of 1969.)

The Cox hearings produced an abundance of information about foundations (unlike the sloppy, rudely abbreviated Reece Committee fiasco which followed in 1954). In their wake there was no obvious way for researchers or the public to benefit from what had been learned, nor was there any organization responsible for continuing to undertake research or to shed routine light on the ever-increasing scope of foundation activities. Over the next two years a vague idea for a foundation data-gathering and information bureau began to take shape. Andrews and James Perkins, vice president of Carnegie Corporation, discussed what they began to call a "Central Information Agency on Foundations." (The name and its inauspicious acronym were soon dropped.) They talked about the need for more extensive and systematic foundation reporting and seemed especially concerned that only 28 of the 77 foundations with more than $10 million in assets were issuing annual or biennial reports.

The public still had little understanding of what foundations were doing and, no doubt, many popular misconceptions still hovered malodorously in the air following the congressional inquiries. Andrews was especially worried that the Reece investigations had done damage to foundations among the "headline reading public," although he and other foundation leaders did not foresee any new and more restrictive legislation on the horizon. Flagrant abuses, they thought, had been adequately curbed by the Revenue Act of 1950.

But foundation leaders remained uneasy; their institutions still seemed vulnerable to popular misunderstanding. James Perkins, who would become the Foundation Center's first chairman, acknowledged that the idea for the center emerged directly out of concerns raised during the congressional investigations. Many years later, in an oral history, he said, "It was quite clear that there was not a responsible place that the public at large could go to get information about foundations, and that without that center there was a lot of unnecessary mystery, and whatever seems mysterious is sometimes feared, and we thought that one way to clear up the mystery would be to collect all the information we could about foundations and have it available in some central spot, so that anybody who really wanted to find out would not have to get lost in the stacks or lost in government files. That was one impulse [for the Foundation Center's creation]."

> . . . whatever seems mysterious is sometimes feared, and one way to clear up the mystery would be to collect all the information we could about foundations. . . .

Perkins convened a meeting in New York of several foundation leaders, some of whom advocated what he characterized dismissively as a "public relations project." Later he said, "That was abandoned, I think happily abandoned, in favor of a more neutral repository of information." Calling it a library was a calculated stroke, in his view. The name "wouldn't frighten people. . . . [W]e were all concerned that this would look like the foundations combining to force their will on the unsuspecting scholar and the unsuspecting public, but nobody would ever think that a library would be dangerous."

The other impulse was the longer-term goal of improving foundation accountability and, perhaps, ultimately of prompting some form of self-regulation. With the rapid expansion in the numbers of foundations in the 1940s and early 1950s, there were growing concerns among the leaders of the older and better-established foundations that some new foundations did not understand the need for openness; they feared that additional financial abuses might come to light, ultimately leading government to intervene. Perkins remembered the vivid phrase that Carnegie Corporation chair Russell Leffingwell had often used. Foundations ought to have "glass pockets," he said. In the end, both Andrews and Perkins believed that some form of foundation self-regulation and professional standard-setting would be necessary to prevent abuses within the ranks of the newer and smaller foundations. The Foundation Center would be one important pillar as a framework for greater accountability was constructed.

After a long luncheon conversation with Perkins in May 1955, Andrews began to put their ideas on paper, saying in his first memo that they "thought an adequate national directory of foundations including appropriate financial and program information would serve useful ends and might be a substantial step toward self regulation." Andrews completed a full-fledged prospectus by October. Discussions with foundation leaders had also continued through the summer and fall because Perkins viewed the center necessarily as a "multi-foundation idea." No single foundation could or should move it forward or fund it. He had concluded in the wake of congressional investigations that "they were all anxious to dispel the notion that foundations were a mysterious group of institutions not necessarily working in the public interest. So the business of raising money for this turned out to be about the easiest money-raising venture I've ever been in." With an initial appropriation of $100,000 from Carnegie Corporation of New York, the Foundation Library Center opened its doors in November 1956. F. Emerson Andrews, America's self-styled "foundation watcher," would begin to build a permanent observation post for himself and other keen-eyed philanthropic observers.

> ". . . an adequate national directory of foundations including appropriate financial and program information . . . might be a substantial step toward self regulation."

Despite its benign and disarming name, the founders of the Foundation Library Center understood that they faced certain perils. As the center gathered information, the walls of privacy and secrecy behind which many foundations had carried out their activities were inevitably going to be breached. The center could not be certain what might be exposed. In collecting information from IRS forms 990-A, they knew they "would soon encounter some policing questions," as Andrews put it. He wondered whether they would be obligated to tip off the IRS to abuses whenever they discovered irregularities or learned about organizations that had simply failed to file returns. In the end, they foresaw that "such a service would expand into standard-setting functions, much as did the ostensible pension fund of the Carnegie Foundation [for the Advancement of Teaching]."

The founders knew they were taking a necessary and decisive step toward improving foundation accountability. They wanted to lift the veil from foundation activities and assure the public that organized philanthropy would continue to enjoy a legitimate place in American society. Fifty years on, it is intriguing to speculate about how they might view current debates about philanthropy, a discussion which is no longer merely an American conversation but a global one. Some features of our early twenty-first-century discussion would be very familiar, resonant themes with only slight variations. Other topics could not have been foreseen by even the most prescient observers from their vantage point in the mid-twentieth century.

Forces similar to those at work a half century ago — rapid growth in the number of foundations, a quantum jump in philanthropic assets (Gates and Buffett now dwarfing older foundations just as Ford did in the 1950s), lingering concerns about congressional inquiries, worries about public misperceptions of philanthropy, distress about scandalous uses of foundation resources, and persistent hopes for improved self-regulation and standard-setting — still shape our contemporary discussions. But for all that seems familiar, much more has changed since the Foundation Center was established.

The annual report essays of the Foundation Center's earliest supporters — Carnegie Corporation and the Russell Sage, Ford, Rockefeller, and Kellogg foundations — are one way to delve into that very different world. Written by John Gardner, Donald Young, Henry Heald, Dean Rusk, and Emory Morris, their language is often eloquent and sometimes scholarly in describing specific programs. But fifty years ago the now routine and perhaps over-used word "sector" and its common descriptors, "nonprofit," "independent," and "third," were not a part of their lexicon. There was little sense of a "foundation field." The term "civil society," now on everyone's tongue, made not a single appearance in the essays of foundation presidents writing in the mid-1950s. At best, they possessed a loose self-perception of large foundations sharing a common and distinctly American tradition, but it is not at all clear that they saw themselves comprising a coherent philanthropic world or that they considered themselves to be part of a wider nonprofit sector. Our current language — indeed the very perception — of an independent or third sector would not emerge until nearly two decades

> . . . it is not clear that they saw themselves comprising a coherent philanthropic world or that they considered themselves to be part of a wider nonprofit sector. . . .

later. And the much older Enlightenment language of civil society would not be retrieved until the 1980s.

To delve into the mid-twentieth-century world of the largest American foundations is to find institutions and their leaders intimately, indeed almost exclusively, connected to the worlds of higher education and research. Their presidential essays bore such titles as "A Time for Decision in Higher Education," "The Great Talent Hunt," "How to Think About College," "The Crisis in Higher Education," and "Foundations and Educational Needs." In 1956, on the occasion of its twenty-fifth anniversary, the Kellogg Foundation asked in "Look to the Future" how academic knowledge might be applied to improve health and agriculture, while affirming the foundation's enduring "belief in the efficacy of advanced education for the training of leaders." Similarly, the Ford Foundation described itself as "essentially an educational foundation," explaining in its annual report for 1956–57 "that through education society can realize its fullest potential for material abundance, intellectual enlightenment, and moral growth." The Russell Sage Foundation devoted much of its program to improving graduate training in various professions by drawing on the insights of social science research.

Discussions in the nation's largest and oldest foundations converged around concerns for higher education, advanced professional training, and scientific research. The rapidity of scientific and technological advance, which all had witnessed during World War II, was transforming the American economy, and that, in turn, would generate demands for a far better-educated and more technically skilled work force. Demographic change — the post-war baby boom especially — would soon create new pressures on American colleges and universities, while population growth in the developing world would pose even longer-term research and educational challenges.

In the interviews that follow, it is not merely the awareness of a distinctive sector — whether termed philanthropic, nonprofit, independent, third, or civil society — that is noteworthy. That sectoral awareness, which has meant a growing self-consciousness and professional sensibility within the sector, was set in motion in the mid-1950s. The trend then accelerated more than three decades ago with the passage of the Tax Reform Act of 1969. Discussions about the sector have attained much greater intellectual coherence and precision through research and data-gathering initiatives that began with the Filer Commission and now continue in several think tanks and a dozen or more academic centers. The sector's sense of itself has been further reified by the many infrastructure organizations, from associations such as the Council on Foundations and Independent Sector to affinity groups and academic centers that now serve to link the full range of entities in the sector.

The Foundation Center stood virtually alone as an "infrastructure" organization in 1956. Today's foundation and nonprofit leaders are asking about the role of this infrastructure and whether it is under-funded, overbuilt, or in need of consolidation — questions that weren't contemplated a half century ago. And on the horizon are still newer questions, driven by information technologies and new philanthropic models. The familiar language that described a distinctive "sector" has already yielded to debates about entrepreneurship, venture philanthropy, new business models, and blurring sectoral boundaries. Perhaps it will soon give ground, as some in the interviews imply, to discussions of social webs and network effects.

> . . . Foundations are now compelled to operate in a vastly expanded universe of nonprofit organizations, with many implications for strategies and tactics. . . .

The interviews also reveal how philanthropic roles are changing. Foundations are certainly less wedded to research universities. They are now compelled to operate in a vastly expanded universe of nonprofit organizations, with many implications for the strategies and tactics foundations have at their disposal. Older discussions of strategic philanthropy, coupled to the concepts of venture philanthropy and social entrepreneurship in the 1990s, have propelled a robust give-and-take about outcome and impact measures, theories of change, and quantitative tools for assessing philanthropic effectiveness.

Many of those who are interviewed in these pages also take note of structural changes within the grantmaking world; there are new philanthropic mechanisms such as donor-advised funds and new means of pursuing social benefit that no longer presume nonprofit status. For better or for worse, there is more competition. In the following pages, most seem to celebrate cross-sectoral collaboration and to welcome whatever there is to learn from the worlds of business and finance.

Relationships with government and assumptions about the role of the state have also clearly changed over the decades. Now and for the foreseeable future, foundations must assume that government resources will be severely constrained. This poses new challenges, too, as foundations think about public-policy advocacy. It suggests that the rhetoric of social change, still central to philanthropic discourse, will be either tempered or employed with more precision. It also suggests that ideological debates about liberal and conservative philanthropy — labels that were rarely used fifty years ago — will continue unabated.

Some issues remain constant. The need for accountability and transparency is still keenly felt, focused on both standard-setting and government's capacity to investigate and enforce the law. If there is a difference between then and now, it is that present-day leaders see how much more complicated a system of accountability is and how interrelated public and private mechanisms are. Above all, the concern about financial resources persists. There are perpetual worries that even as assets mount — and public attention always focuses on the grandest gifts — the capacity of philanthropy will never be up to the scale of the challenges society faces. Philanthropy, despite its past accomplishments and continuing promise, must temper public expectations and clarify what can and cannot be expected of it. Indeed, it is striking that fifty years after the creation of the Foundation Center — and with more than one hundred years of organized philanthropic activity as a benchmark — foundation leaders still lament that their work is misunderstood by policy makers and the public.

> **Philanthropy, despite its past accomplishments and continuing promise, must temper public expectations and clarify what can and cannot be expected of it. . . .**

The lament and the rejoinder to it have been remarkably consistent across the decades. In John Gardner's words, foundations were endowed with society's "free funds," provided with its "risk capital." They were (and are), he said, "a new source of support for innovation — a source specifically designed to further creativity." The description of philanthropic assets as "social venture capital" is not at all new. Indeed, as long ago as 1953–54 a Sloan Foundation report observed that "this phrase, or some variant, has become quite popular in the lexicon of foundation trustees and executives." It is still popular. The debate is always about how such assets can be used in venturesome and creative ways, and whether those who control the "free funds" are up to the challenge of creative risk-taking. The contours of that perennial debate are drawn in the pages that follow.

# Philanthropy and the Rockefeller Legacy

David Rockefeller
Chairman Emeritus
Chase Manhattan Bank

*Sixteen-year-old John D. Rockefeller landed his first job, as a bookkeeper in the booming metropolis of Cleveland, Ohio, on September 26, 1855 — a date Rockefeller would celebrate the rest of his life as "Job Day." Thrifty, punctual, and industrious, the young Rockefeller, according to his biographer Ron Chernow, was "a fervent adherent of the gospel of success." Devoutly religious, he also believed that work and charity were two sides of the same coin. "I was trained from the beginning," he told William O. Inglis, a New York newspaperman, more than half a century later, "to work and save. I have always regarded it as a religious duty to get all I could honorably and to give all I could."*

*Rockefeller succeeded spectacularly at both. By the mid-1890s, when he began in earnest to step back from his responsibilities at Standard Oil — the company he founded with his brother William and built into the most powerful and feared industrial concern in America — he was the wealthiest man in the country and its second most famous philanthropist, after Andrew Carnegie. Unwilling to settle for peaceful retirement, Rockefeller, according to Chernow, then did an extraordinary thing. With his wealth accumulating at "an astonishing rate," he set out, with the help of Frederick T. Gates, his chief philanthropic adviser, and his only son, John, to give that fortune away.*

*Spelman Seminary (later Spelman College), the University of Chicago, the Rockefeller Institute for Medical Research (later Rockefeller University), the General Education Board, the Rockefeller Foundation, the Rockefeller Sanitary Commission for the Eradication of Hookworm — the philanthropy of John D. Rockefeller was unprecedented in its scale, broad-mindedness, and imagination. It also created suspicion, for many years, among his critics, who viewed it as a thinly disguised vehicle for Rockefeller economic interests.*

*John D. Rockefeller did not give his fortune away, though not for lack of trying. By the 1920s, the Rockefeller Foundation was the largest grantmaking foundation in the world and Rockefeller, in Chernow's words, had "established himself as the greatest lay benefactor of medicine in history," having given $450 million — out of a total of $530 million given during his lifetime — to institutions active in the field. Instead, starting in 1917, he began to transfer his remaining assets, roughly $500 million (close to $10 billion in today's dollars), to his son John, who would spend the rest of his life working to extend his father's philanthropic legacy while creating his own.*

*Born into wealth and privilege and raised from birth to excel, the children of John D. Rockefeller, Jr. and his wife, Abigail — Abby (known as Babs), John, Nelson, Laurance, Winthrop, and David — leveraged their unique advantages into storied careers in business, philanthropy, politics, and the arts. And the Rockefeller family itself came to embody, as much as a single family could, the ambition, generosity, and genius of America in the twentieth century. As Joseph Persico, a speechwriter for Nelson and, later, his biographer, put it, "the seed capital that they planted in philanthropic endeavors gave them greater national and international influence than did their profit-making enterprises and was certainly more lasting in effect. . . . They were responsible enough, and wise enough, to underpin their own position by strengthening, through their giving, those institutions in society that they found worthy of perpetuation."*

*The Foundation Center's* Philanthropy News Digest *sat down with David Rockefeller, retired chairman of Chase Manhattan Bank, to talk about his father and grandfather's philanthropy, the origins and evolution of the Rockefeller Brothers Fund, the motivations behind his personal philanthropy, and his family's philanthropic legacy.*

*Mr. Rockefeller retired as chairman of Chase Manhattan in 1981 and served as a member of the International Council of JP Morgan until August*

*2005. In 1987, he stepped down as chairman of the Rockefeller Brothers Fund, a grantmaking organization founded in 1940 by Mr. Rockefeller and his brothers. He is, in addition, the former chairman of the Museum of Modern Art and continues to serve as chairman emeritus and life trustee.*

*Mr. Rockefeller has wide-ranging interests and involvement in the fields of international relations and civic affairs. He served as chairman of the Council on Foreign Relations from 1970 to 1985 and now chairs its international advisory board. He also was instrumental in creating the International Executive Service Corps (IESC), a volunteer group of retired people that provides technical and managerial assistance to private enterprise in developing nations, and helped found the Trilateral Commission in 1973, stepping down as its North American chairman in 1991 and now serving as honorary chair. In 1979, he co-founded the New York City Partnership, which is dedicated to economic development and effective governance in New York City through private-public partnerships.*

*He is also honorary chair of the Americas Society — which he served as chair from 1981 through 1992 — and the Council of the Americas, an organization which he founded to promote closer inter-American cooperation as well as better communication between the public and private sectors in Latin America.*

*Mr. Rockefeller graduated from Harvard and holds a Ph.D. in economics from the University of Chicago, where he is a life trustee. During World War II, he served as an intelligence officer in North Africa and southern France and was an assistant military attaché in Paris at the time he was demobilized as a captain in 1945.*

*He has two sons, four daughters, ten grandchildren, and one great-granddaughter. His wife of fifty-five years, the former Margaret McGrath, died in March 1996.*

---

**Foundation Center (FC):** Over five generations, the Rockefellers have made philanthropy a family calling. How do you explain your family's ability to keep that tradition alive and relevant?

**David Rockefeller (DR):** Well, it certainly started with my grandparents, Laura Spelman and John D. Rockefeller, both of whom were strong and ardent Baptists from an early age. In fact, Grandfather tithed regularly from the time he was a teenager. As he became a successful businessman beginning in the 1860s, he also maintained his charitable giving and expanded its scope well beyond Cleveland, Ohio, to include Baptist churches, colleges, seminaries, and missionary societies across the country. As a devout Christian, Grandfather believed, and even said, "God had given him his money." He did not mean this in a boastful way, but that he had been rewarded for his faith and was expected to use these resources wisely for the benefit of the broader community of which he and his family were a part. That is really the beginning of the Rockefeller tradition of philanthropy.

> [Frederick] Gates persuaded Grandfather to move beyond simple charity to find the root causes of disease, ignorance, hunger . . . and to do something about finding solutions. . . .

It was not until the late 1880s, however, that Grandfather began to consider supporting other organizations. And it was really the influence of Frederick T. Gates, whom he met during the effort to establish the University of Chicago — originally a Baptist organization — that made all the difference.

Gates was an ordained Baptist minister and a remarkable man. Among other things, he persuaded Grandfather to use the wealth he had accumulated more broadly for the benefit of mankind. Gates persuaded Grandfather to move beyond simple charity to find the root causes of disease, ignorance, hunger, all of humankind's afflictions, and to do something about finding solutions. That shift in emphasis and the embrace of science marked the transition to philanthropy. Gates was Grandfather's closest associate for more than thirty years, and his influence was enormous. But I think it's also clear that Grandfather was very receptive to the idea of using his wealth to help other people even before Gates arrived on the scene.

Grandfather established the Rockefeller Foundation in 1913, around the same time Andrew Carnegie started his foundations, and that began an entirely new era of philanthropy, both for Grandfather and, I dare say, for the country. It's interesting, isn't it, that two men who played such important roles in the development and economic life of this country — my grandfather and Andrew Carnegie — were also early leaders in philanthropy?

So, the family tradition of philanthropy started with Grandfather and was kept going by my father, John D. Rockefeller, Jr., and subsequent generations of the family. It's been part of our upbringing, the feeling that with opportunity comes obligation, and in a way that sort of summarizes the spirit behind all of it. Certainly, my father, who for a short time worked for the Standard Oil Company, soon came to the conclusion that he would rather devote his life to not-for-profit activities, and he did so. And my brother John, my oldest brother, pretty much did the same. I don't think he ever had another activity or interest that inspired him in quite the same way as philanthropy did, and he devoted his life to it.

As for the rest of us — my sister, my other brothers, and myself — while we've had many interests, we nevertheless made philanthropy an important part of our lives. In fact, we realized that individually our financial resources, including those we might devote to philanthropy, were quite small compared to those that had been available to Grandfather and Father. Right before the outbreak of World War II, we got together to discuss ways in which we could cooperate to be more effective. One theme of our meetings was that it would be worthwhile for us to focus on areas where we had common interests, and one of them was the field of philanthropy — not least because, in more than a few instances, we were being asked to make contributions to the same institutions. It made sense to find a way to collaborate, especially in the case of organizations where we lived — here in New York City, in Tarrytown, up in Maine, and so on.

That was the origin of the Rockefeller Brothers Fund, which was founded in 1940. I think the concept of the Brothers Fund made a lot of sense at the time, and it's become a very useful organization that still has ties to the family and continues to be supported by new generations of Rockefellers, even though it has a life of its own apart from the family.

**FC:** Your grandfather, along with Andrew Carnegie and Frederick Gates, more or less invented modern philanthropy. What do you consider to be his greatest philanthropic achievement? And what was his greatest philanthropic innovation?

**DR:** Well, the Rockefeller Foundation was the first foundation that purposely looked outward to the world and had global objectives. Grandfather, working with Dr. Gates and, later, other people, felt his business interests were global in nature and that therefore he had a philanthropic responsibility on that level. I think his recognition of that fact has to have been one of his greatest contributions to the field.

> . . . the Rockefeller Foundation was the first foundation that purposely looked outward to the world and had global objectives. . . .

At the same time, he understood that his philanthropic activities needed to be organized and that, even though his understanding of people and the world was impressive — despite never having gone to college — he needed to have people with a broad understanding of the world to help him. Of course, as time passed, he felt less and less of a need to be involved in the day-to-day details of grantmaking, and he was happy to let his associates handle the specifics.

But in some respects, it was my father, under Grandfather's tutelage, who really turned the foundation into a force to be reckoned with. Father chaired the foundation for more than twenty years and participated in the creation of its major program areas — supporting the development of the hard sciences, extending work in public health around the world, and applying the emerging knowledge of the social sciences to the problems of poverty around the world. He left a lasting imprint not only on the Rockefeller Foundation, but on American philanthropy as well.

**FC:** Did your father discuss his philanthropic activities with his children?

**DR:** Oh, yes, very easily and broadly. Not that he thought he had to discuss every detail, but he was very open in his interests and his discussion of them. Of course, a lot of his philanthropy related to the trips he took, and for me that's one of the interesting aspects of what he did. When he would go on trips — and he often brought us along — he would see things that needed to be done. For example, on our first trip out West, we spent six weeks traveling around and, of course, stopped to see the redwoods in northern California. At one point, we visited a spot where lumber companies were cutting down these enormous trees that had been around for two thousand years. Well, Father, while he recognized the importance of timber as an industry, felt it would be a tragedy if all those trees were cut down. So he gave $1 million — which at that time was a lot — to buy a huge stand of redwoods in northern California, and today that stand is called the Rockefeller Grove.

Similarly, when Father visited Versailles in France for the first time — again with his children — he discovered that this unbelievable monument was not being taken care of, either by the French government or the French people. The roof was leaking and some of the interior walls and even furniture was damaged. So he got an architect friend of his to work with the French government to replace the roof, and he followed that up with a lot of other improvements. Those are just two illustrations. He did that in many parts of the world, and I think it's one of the interesting aspects of his philanthropy: He simply wanted to help where he saw a need.

> . . . I think it's one of the interesting aspects of [my father's] philanthropy: He simply wanted to help where he saw a need. . . .

**FC:** When you and your brothers established the Rockefeller Brothers Fund in 1940, did you have specific philanthropic goals in mind? Or did your goals and objectives evolve over time?

**DR:** To a large extent they evolved over time. On the other hand, a similar kind of thing happened with us. For example, when President Magsaysay of the Philippines was killed in a plane crash in 1957, it was a major disaster for the country and for Asia. We immediately decided that it would be desirable to do something in the region based on his legacy, and so we established — and it still exists — the Ramon Magsaysay Awards Foundation, which has recognized the courageous efforts of many individuals — including the Dalai Lama — to bring positive change to the nations and people of Asia.

As time went on, of course, the RBF built up its staff, which increasingly became responsible for the direction and activities of the fund. But even today, younger members of the family — my nephew Steven, my son

Richard, who just became chairman of the board, and many other cousins and members of the fifth generation — are very involved in the fund and in philanthropic activities in general. Richard is a medical doctor and has long been interested in responding to the HIV/AIDS crisis in sub-Saharan Africa. My daughter Peggy started an organization called Synergos, which is doing socially related work all over the world. She became great friends with Nelson Mandela and his wife, Grace Machel, the widow of President Samora Machel of Mozambique, who was killed in a plane crash in 1986. So, the interest of the family in philanthropy and in international causes is alive and well.

**FC:** Your brothers and sister were known to have strong personalities and varied interests. In terms of the RBF, did that make it difficult to reach consensus on specific programs or areas of interest?

**DR:** There were lively discussions, and we didn't always agree, but I don't think we disagreed on the basic principles. We might disagree about a particular project, but I think we were in general agreement about the broad areas we wanted to support. The remarkable thing, I think, is the degree of harmony in those conversations rather than the fact that occasionally we disagreed.

I also think it's remarkable that to this day members of the family continue to have their own interests, as well as shared common principles. For example, I've set up a foundation of my own called the David Rockefeller Fund that focuses its activities in places where I live, mostly in Maine and in Tarrytown. It's relatively small, but I've used it to give to institutions that are important in those communities and that need support. It's also a way to get the next generation, my grandchildren, involved. I have so many children and grandchildren — sixteen, not counting spouses — that we developed a process by which they rotate on and off the board at three-year intervals. I also made it possible for each of them to have responsibility for giving away a certain amount to causes or organizations that interest them. It's a wonderful way to encourage them to think philanthropically, and I think they've found it to be useful.

**FC:** Have you made a conscious effort over the years to connect your own philanthropy with your strong interest in international affairs? And has your personal philanthropy differed at all from the family's approach to philanthropy over the decades?

**DR:** My personal philanthropy flows out of the family interests to which I've been exposed. Certainly, there are some areas I've been more interested in than others, but that doesn't mean there has been conflict among my interests. It merely means I've concentrated on specific issues and areas and, as a result, have had more of an interest in them than other members of the family. For instance, I have been involved with the Rockefeller University for more than sixty-five years as a trustee, chairman, and chairman emeritus. I find RU's scientific work into the causes of disease, molecular biology, and now genetics to be of enormous significance for the world. It is the principal reason why I donated $100 million to RU last year.

On a more personal basis, my interest in international affairs has been expressed through my involvement in organizations like the Council on Foreign Relations and the Americas Society. These organizations attempt, and largely succeed in my view, to inform Americans about what is going on in the broader world, and why it is important to remain engaged globally. This is philanthropy of a different kind, but it is just as important in its own way as the work of Rockefeller University or the Museum of Modern Art or any number of other organizations. An informed citizenry is the key to maintaining a free and open society — that is what both the council and the Americas Society do.

> **My personal philanthropy flows out of the family interests to which I've been exposed. . . .**

**FC:** The list of organizations you've been involved in and chaired over the years is, well, long. [Laughter.] But it's illustrative, I think, of your belief — a belief shared by your father and grandfather — in the importance of institutions as a stabilizing force in society. Are you worried that forces such as globalization and rapid technological change are undermining the influence and stabilizing role of institutions in society?

**DR:** No, not at all. I think, in a way, the existence of those institutions is one of the means by which we're better able to cope with the very problems you mentioned. If they didn't exist, I think we'd be in much more trouble than we are.

**FC:** Today, the endowments of the Rockefeller Foundation and the Rockefeller Brothers Fund are larger, in nominal terms, than they've ever been. But as a percentage of total philanthropic assets and gross domestic product, they're quite modest. Do private foundations like the Rockefeller Foundation and the Brothers Fund have the same ability today to promote new ideas and influence civic life that they had in your father and grandfather's day? And what, if anything, can private foundations do to preserve their unique role in American society?

**DR:** Well, one of the encouraging things that has happened in this country is that many other wealthy families have seen what our family has done and felt it was worthwhile — most recently and notably, of course, with Bill and Melinda Gates and Warren Buffett. In fact, at the event in New York City this summer at which Mr. Buffett made his announcement, he referred to the fact that in many ways he was inspired and influenced by the Rockefeller Foundation and what the family had done philanthropically. I am very proud of the fact that others have followed our lead and, in many cases, have created foundations that are substantially larger than the Rockefeller Foundation. That is excellent, and we couldn't be more pleased.

> **I am very proud of the fact that others have followed our lead. . . .**

**FC:** If American philanthropy is the child of American capitalism, how likely is it that philanthropy in this country will change in the coming decades as capitalism itself changes in response to global economic forces?

**DR:** I do think philanthropy is a particularly American institution, in the sense that from the earliest days Americans tended to believe they had broader responsibilities than just making money. And while there are examples of successful and important foundations in other countries — in Europe, Latin America, and elsewhere — for whatever reason, philanthropy seems to be something that fits Americans to a tee.

On a personal note, I couldn't be happier that my children and grandchildren share my interest in philanthropy. At the event in New York, Warren Buffett made a point of saying he was especially pleased he had been able to pass his values and interest in philanthropy on to his children. It is cause for optimism that people like Buffett and the Gateses and many, many others care about the world around them, are joining with others to try to find solutions to the challenges that confront us, and are passing on those values to their children and grandchildren. The world is a better place for it.

**FC:** And do you think fifty or a hundred years from now, someone from *Philanthropy News Digest* will be interviewing one of your great-great-grandchildren about the Rockefeller philanthropic tradition and the remarkable achievements of American philanthropy?

**DR:** I hope so. But I also hope that many of the problems we have been discussing will have been solved long before our successors meet for the interview! Certainly, philanthropy is important, but we should not lose sight of the fact that philanthropy is an instrument designed to find enduring solutions for the afflictions of humankind. It would be wonderful if they had nothing to talk about at the meeting.

**FC:** Well, thank you for speaking with us today, Mr. Rockefeller.

**DR:** It was my pleasure.

*Mitch Nauffts, editorial director of* Philanthropy News Digest, *spoke with David Rockefeller in October 2006.*

## 2

# Philanthropy in an Interdependent World

Stephen B. Heintz
President
Rockefeller Brothers Fund

*For an ever-larger portion of the world's population, globalization — the increasing economic integration and interdependence of countries around the globe — is a fact of life. As* New York Times *columnist Thomas Friedman writes in* The Lexus and the Olive Tree: *"Globalization is not the only thing influencing events in the world today, but to the extent there is a North Star and a worldwide shaping force, it is this system."*

*But while the system may be new, power politics, clashing civilizations, and chaos are as old as Adam. The drama of the post-Cold War world, writes Friedman, is the interaction between the new system and all the old passions and aspirations. From factory floors in the Midwest, to the back alleys of Karachi and Kabul, to the studios of Al Jazeera and the bond pits of the Chicago Board of Trade, it's a drama whose first act has raised more questions than it has answered and whose second act is still being written.*

*The Foundation Center's* Philanthropy News Digest *spoke with Stephen B. Heintz, president of the New York City-based Rockefeller Brothers Fund (www.rbf.org), about the role of philanthropy in an increasingly interdependent world, risk and the concept of failure in a philanthropic context, and the importance of leadership in a time of rapid change.*

*Before joining the Rockefeller Brothers Fund in 2001, Heintz, whom* Philanthropy News Digest *first interviewed in September 2000, served as founding president of Demos: A Network for Ideas & Action, a public policy research and advocacy organization working to enhance the vitality of American democracy. Prior to that, he served as executive vice president and chief operating officer of the EastWest Institute, where from 1990 to 1997 he lived in Eastern Europe and worked on issues of economic reform, civil society development, and international security. He began his career in the mid-1970s with a series of key assignments in Connecticut state government — first as chief of staff to then-state senate majority leader Joseph I. Lieberman (1974–76) and later as commissioner of the state's Department of Income Maintenance (1983–88) and Department of Economic Development (1988–90).*

*A magna cum laude graduate of Yale University, Mr. Heintz has published articles in the* International Herald Tribune, *the* Washington Post, *the* Wall Street Journal Europe, *and several books and journals. He lives in New York City.*

---

**Foundation Center (FC):** Stephen, we had the opportunity to speak with you in the fall of 2000 as you were preparing to leave a New York City-based organization called Demos to become the president of the Rockefeller Brothers Fund. Did you have certain expectations, as you were getting ready to make the move, about the Rockefeller Brothers Fund and what you might be able to accomplish as its president? And if so, have those expectations been met?

**Stephen Heintz (SH):** I knew the Rockefeller Brothers Fund by reputation, as well as through direct experience as the president of a grantee organization that had enjoyed the fund's support for a number of years, so I had a pretty good sense of what this place was like. Among other things, I knew it to be a dynamic, professionally led institution with a superb staff and a deep commitment to the highest aspirations of what philanthropy should be. And I'm happy to say that my sense of what the RBF was has been confirmed since I've been here. In fact, in some ways, much of my experience here has exceeded the expectations with which I arrived.

**FC:** Has anything failed to meet your expectations or been different than you thought it would be?

**SH:** The most important difference, as it turns out, is that I've learned it's much more difficult to manage philanthropic assets in an excellent fashion than I thought it would be. I think those who work in the grantee community and struggle to raise funds and meet a budget year after year, as I did at Demos, often dream about working at a foundation, thinking that it must be easy to give away money. But it isn't. In fact, what I've learned over the last five years is that to give away money, and to do it strategically, effectively, efficiently, and transparently, is a lot more difficult than one would imagine.

> . . . to give away money, and to do it strategically, effectively, efficiently, and transparently, is a lot more difficult than one would imagine. . . .

**FC:** I can imagine some people hearing that and thinking, Really? How hard could it be? What are some of the challenges a foundation like the RBF must contend with as it tries to be strategic, effective, efficient, and transparent in its grantmaking?

**SH:** Finding high-impact points of entry in a given field, leveraging additional resources, and evaluating results.

**FC:** About nine months after we spoke with you in the fall of 2000, New York City and Washington, D.C., suffered major terrorist attacks that resulted in the loss of almost three thousand lives. In the weeks and months after 9/11, it became fashionable for people to say that the attacks had changed everything. Do you believe the 9/11 attacks changed everything?

**SH:** I don't think they changed everything. I understand why people felt that way at the time. The shock of the experience, especially for those who live in New York or in Washington, D.C., was quite traumatic, even for those of us who did not face the tragedy of losing a family member or a friend. So I understand why people expressed that view at the time. But I do think the attacks changed a lot of things. They certainly changed our self-perception as a nation. Before 9/11, we essentially saw ourselves as being invincible, and now, I think, we're much more aware of our vulnerabilities. The attacks also changed, rather dramatically, our politics, especially with respect to our relationships with friendly countries and multilateral institutions around the world.

In fact, we've seen some profound changes in our politics since 9/11, and not all of them have been for the better.

On a more reassuring note, there have been things that haven't changed. Americans continue to be an optimistic people. New Yorkers, who were most directly affected by the attacks, continue to go about their lives, almost as if nothing had happened. The city itself remains popular with tourists and people who love the opportunity and excitement it provides. That resiliency and optimism about the future is part of the American character, and I don't think that has changed.

> **. . . we really haven't formulated a new approach to U.S. global engagement that is appropriate for the conditions and challenges of the twenty-first century. . . .**

The other thing I would say is that some things haven't changed enough. For example, we, as Americans, haven't changed how we think about the role of our country in an increasingly interdependent world, and we really haven't formulated a new approach to U.S. global engagement that is appropriate for the conditions and challenges of the twenty-first century, terrorism being one of those challenges. So, I guess I would say that the post-9/11 period has been an interesting mix of some things that did change, some things that maybe should have changed that haven't, and some things that have remained more or less the same.

**FC:** Global interdependence is a concept that you and your colleagues have given a lot of thought to — so much so, in fact, that you've incorporated it into a new tagline for the RBF: "Philanthropy for an interdependent world." In your view, what are the most critical challenges philanthropy should focus on in an increasingly interdependent world?

**SH:** Before I answer that, let me just say something about the tagline itself. When I came aboard in 2001, the RBF didn't have a tagline. Our visual identity was pretty traditional, in part because we had the word *fund,* rather than *foundation,* in our name, which leads many people, when they first hear about us, to think, Oh, it's an investment fund, or a hedge fund, or something like that. They don't know we have something to do with philanthropy. So the tagline became an important way of quickly alerting people to the fact that we are a *philanthropic* institution.

And as we were struggling to come up with something that, in a few words, described what we're about, this notion of interdependence just popped to the surface and was more or less immediately adopted by our staff and board as an accurate expression of our approach to philanthropy.

Now, in terms of the kinds of issues I think should be at the top of philanthropy's agenda as a result of the phenomenon of global interdependence, clearly global warming is a high-priority issue, and it's also one of our top priorities. In fact, I'm pleased to be able to say this morning that last week our board of directors approved our budget for 2006, and the single largest increase in that budget is for the work we are doing on global warming.

Second, the whole twenty-first-century set of challenges to international security and peace is another major reflection of growing global interdependence. In previous centuries, going all the way back to the Treaty of Westphalia in 1648, international security was thought of in terms of relations between nation-states. But here at the beginning of the twenty-first century, we're seeing that nation-states, while continuing to be important actors on the global stage, are not the only actors on that stage. Over the last fifty years or so, we've witnessed the emergence of many new non-state actors that have the potential to help create the conditions of greater security and peace — multilateral institutions like the United Nations, the European Union, the World Trade Organization, and so on. But we've also witnessed the emergence of non-state actors, including global terrorist networks like al-Qaeda, that are intent on undermining existing international security arrangements. And how we address the continuing emergence of non-state actors and the threats they pose to international peace and security is something that philanthropy must be involved in.

> . . . how we address the continuing emergence of non-state actors and the threats they pose to international peace and security is something that philanthropy must be involved in. . . .

The third challenge I would mention is the whole issue of equity in terms of globalization, economic development, and trade. We're seeing enormous economic gains in many formerly impoverished countries thanks to the acceleration and deepening of globalization. But we're also seeing many countries and tens of millions of people sinking deeper into poverty and being left even further behind. And unless we, in the developed world, collectively decide that there are better ways to manage globalization — ways that will create greater equity and opportunity and environmental sustainability in less developed countries — I think we're going to face major challenges and see a growing backlash against the economies and institutions perceived to be driving the process of globalization.

**FC:** The scope of the challenges you've outlined is, well, global. You and I both know that institutional philanthropy represents a relatively small percentage of the dollars available to address any issue, let alone issues that require action and cooperation on a global scale. Given the relatively limited resources at its disposal, what role, in your view, should philanthropy play in addressing these kinds of challenges?

> **One of the things philanthropy can do is to promote research, education, and advocacy to help the general public understand these issues and their implications more fully. . . .**

**SH:** There are a variety of appropriate roles where the limited philanthropic resources you have noted can achieve significant impact. The first would be in the areas of education and advocacy. One of the things philanthropy can do, and already does fairly well, is to promote research, education, and advocacy to help the general public understand these issues and their implications more fully, to create a sense that there are solutions, and to highlight our collective progress in tackling them. That's a critical function that philanthropy can and should play.

The second thing has to do with philanthropy's role in helping to shape public policy and the public-policy debate. Ultimately, many of these kinds of global challenges will only be solved by changes made at the public-policy level, and one of the things philanthropy can do in this regard is to help develop the ideas for change. It can fund demonstration projects and new policy models, it can disseminate learnings from those projects and models, and it can help take the most successful of those projects and models to scale, so as to broaden their impact. We all know that the resources required to solve these problems will have to be provided through public-private partnerships. But philanthropy can be the leading edge of those investments, in the sense that it can help steer bigger players and deeper pockets into new fields and approaches to solving these enormous challenges.

Last but not least, I think it's up to philanthropy to really take risks as it tries to address these kinds of problems. There are experiments begging to be funded in all the areas I've mentioned, and, let's be honest, we don't know what the results of any of them are going to be. Unfortunately, it's increasingly difficult for business to fund these kinds of experiments, and government, which has always been risk-averse in some respects, has become even more so on account of the polarization of our politics. Yet we know that experimentation is a major driver of human progress. All of these things put more pressure on philanthropy, in my view, to embrace a greater level of risk, to fund more experimentation, and to disseminate the results and lessons of that experimentation to others.

> . . . we probably have become more risk-averse as a field than is appropriate, given the kinds of problems we face. . . .

**FC:** Are you suggesting that philanthropy may have lost some of its appetite for risk?

**SH:** There are all kinds of philanthropies, and some are more risk-averse than others. Generally speaking, though, I would say we probably have become more risk-averse as a field than is appropriate, given the kinds of problems we face and the growing aversion to risk we see in the private and public sectors. At a minimum, it's something philanthropy needs to examine. Here at the RBF we've asked ourselves: What is our risk profile, and do we need to recalibrate it? Partly as a result of that conversation, I think we have become willing to assume a higher level of risk, in a way that is prudent and careful but also appropriate to the times and challenges we face.

**FC:** Philanthropy's profile in the media and the public mind is higher today than it has been in decades, maybe ever. With that higher profile, however, has come heightened scrutiny of the field, which in turn has led foundations increasingly to value outcomes and measurement as a way of demonstrating impact and effectiveness. Is the growing emphasis on outcomes and measurement within the field a healthy development?

**SH:** It's good that we're all thinking more seriously about how we evaluate our impact; that's a very healthy thing. But I'm not entirely convinced that quantitative measures are the best way to evaluate impact in philanthropy, and they're certainly not the only way. I'm reminded of something that Albert Einstein once said: "Not everything important can be measured, and not everything that can be measured is important." In the rush to quantify things, I think people sometimes end up measuring things that don't really tell them whether they're having impact or not. At the Rockefeller Brothers Fund, we ask ourselves whether there are aspects of a given program that can be measured, and if so, whether they're likely to tell us something meaningful. If the answer to both those questions is yes, we'll go ahead and measure them.

> **In the rush to quantify things, I think people sometimes end up measuring things that don't really tell them whether they're having impact or not. . . .**

But we also ask what else we should be doing to evaluate a program's impact, and we're continually looking for ways to improve our capacity for qualitative evaluation, both internally and through the use of external assessments and third-party consultation. For example, for the last two years we've commissioned the Center for Effective Philanthropy to survey our grantees about their experience with the RBF, both positive and negative. We've also commissioned CEP to survey some of our unsuccessful grant applicants in order to get a better understanding of their experience; to survey our own employees as a way to identify internal management and organizational culture issues we might want to address; and to survey our trustees on a range of governance issues. All those surveys and the effort to acquire qualitative information about our policies and practices is in support of a key goal we have set for ourselves, which is to be a center of philanthropic excellence, in everything we do. In our grantmaking we want to strive for excellence in our relationships with our grantees, and we also want to be excellent in the way we manage our assets, treat our employees, and govern the work of the foundation. It's a big ambition, but one well worth pursuing.

**FC:** Do you plan to commission grantee perception reports from CEP on a regular basis?

**SH:** We do. I could see us commissioning a survey every three or four years. They really have provided us with valuable baseline information, and we've already used the results from the first survey to change some of our practices in terms of how we communicate with the grantee community, which was an area where we did not do as well as we might have hoped. In fact, we've hired a wonderful new communications officer to help us improve in that area, and we've also used the results in internal performance evaluations. So I do think conducting those surveys on a periodic basis will serve us well and will help us in our efforts to achieve continuous improvement.

**FC:** You've spoken eloquently in the past about the concept of failure in a philanthropic context. Are foundations as comfortable with the concept of failure as they should be?

**SH:** Well, obviously, nobody wants to fund failure. But I do think foundations have to be open to the notion that, if they are going to operate with an experimental disposition — which, as I said earlier, is something philanthropy should do — that in itself suggests there will be instances of failure. What's more, foundations need to embrace and learn from those failures. I'm a firm believer that failure can teach you as much as success. I believe that if we are not failing some of the time, we are not living up to our mandate; it means we're not pushing ourselves enough, experimenting enough, taking enough risks. So let's embrace failure when it happens, as it inevitably will.

To that end, there are a couple of things we can do. One is to just be open about it, to talk about it in the way we're talking about it right now, and to have people understand that we're going to fund some things that may fail, but we're going to fund them anyway because we think they're worth trying. Living up to our principles is also important, as is being transparent about our failures; that's absolutely essential — both in terms of acknowledging failure and in our willingness to disseminate lessons that may come out of it.

> . . . if we are not failing some of the time, we are not living up to our mandate; it means we're not pushing ourselves enough, experimenting enough, taking enough risks. . . .

**FC:** What's the role of leadership in all of this?

**SH:** I'm a big believer in leadership. I'm a believer in both the importance of individual leadership, and in collective leadership. I believe that every person in an organization has the opportunity to be a leader in his or her sphere of activity. As the leader of an organization, what I want to try to do is enable the people who work for me to be the best leaders they can be and, in doing so, create an organization that rewards individual performance and impact. That's very, very important.

**FC:** What did you think of *Time* magazine's recent selection of Bill and Melinda Gates and U2 frontman Bono as Persons of the Year?

**SH:** I think it was refreshing that *Time* chose individuals who earned their fame in other arenas and recognized their philanthropic contributions as the major reason for their selection. That's good. Anything that draws more attention to philanthropy and philanthropists is a good thing. One of the things I've learned in my time here is that there's a real lack of understanding among the public about what philanthropy is, how it operates, and the challenges it faces. Anything that helps to educate the public about the role of philanthropy in society and about the good work people in this sector are doing is a good thing.

**FC:** Media pundits have been busy the past few weeks eulogizing the John M. Olin Foundation, which closed its doors after fifty years of grantmaking. Conservative pundits, in particular, have used the occasion to celebrate the role of the foundation in mainstreaming the conservative movement. Would you agree that Olin and other conservative foundations — I'm thinking of the Lynde and Harry Bradley Foundation, the Scaife foundations, the Smith Richardson Foundation, and others — have been important players in the success of the conservative movement over the last quarter-century? And if so, what can foundations with a more progressive bent learn from the example of their conservative peers?

> **One of the things I've learned is that there's a real lack of understanding among the public about what philanthropy is, how it operates, and the challenges it faces....**

**SH:** I do think Olin and other foundations that share its philosophy have played a significant role in the political success of the conservative movement, although some of the pronouncements about Olin in recent weeks have overstated the case. Let's not forget, however, that there are other factors that have contributed to the rise of the conservative movement and its current position in the public policy arena.

As you probably know, the encomiums to Olin speak directly to an interesting debate under way in the mainstream foundation community about whether there's a need to invest in or create a group of avowedly progressive foundations to serve as a counterbalance to some of the conservative foundations. In fact, a number of efforts are already under way to organize that kind of philanthropy, including something called the Democracy Alliance, which is seeking to create a donor collaborative of wealthy individuals who work together to fund progressive infrastructure, progressive nonprofit organizations, and to develop, organize around, and advocate for new ideas with regard to various policy challenges. I think that's a good thing. I'm all for pluralism in philanthropy. I think it's one of the great strengths of philanthropy, and I think it's one of the reasons why philanthropy is important to the health of a vibrant democracy. Philanthropy should be part of the development and exchange of ideas in a democracy. But I also understand that there are lots of foundations that don't want to be pigeonholed as either conservative or progressive, that want to approach tough issues in a less ideological way, and that want to continue working on issues in a framework with which they're comfortable. And that, too, is entirely appropriate.

> . . . philanthropy is important to the health of a vibrant democracy. Philanthropy should be part of the development and exchange of ideas. . . .

**FC:** In our conversation this morning, you've given us a picture of a philanthropy that is outward-looking, inclusive, and committed to social change. You've also described a number of formidable challenges that, in your view, the field must come to grips with over the next decade or so. What would be the consequences if philanthropy failed to rise to those challenges?

**SH:** It would mean significantly less progress on the key global issues we've been discussing. I don't want to overstate the case. As you noted earlier, philanthropy is a relatively modest component of the resource base available to support work on major domestic and international challenges. But it's an important one, and it's one that has the capacity, both intellectually and financially, to leverage other resources. In fact, the real consequence of philanthropy's failure to rise to these challenges just might be the lessening of that leverage. If we don't improve our effectiveness, if we don't work in a more collaborative manner, if we avoid risk and forgo the lessons that failure can teach us, we will not exercise the kind of leverage we have the potential to exercise, and, as a result, we'll see less progress on some of these extraordinarily significant challenges than we would otherwise. And that will not only be a loss for philanthropy, it will be a loss for the global community.

**FC:** Well, Stephen, thanks very much for your time this morning. It was interesting, as always.

**SH:** Thank you. It's been a pleasure.

*Mitch Nauffts, editorial director of* Philanthropy News Digest, *spoke with Stephen Heintz in January 2006.*

# 3

# Creating Change Through Informed Philanthropy

Melissa Berman
President and CEO
Rockefeller Philanthropy Advisors

*Over the next three or four decades, new technologies, globalization, the growing ethnic and cultural diversity of American society, and an intergenerational transfer of wealth estimated at between $6 trillion and $40 trillion will combine to dramatically change charitable giving in the United States. New and growing demands on society — at home and abroad — will create new and greater expectations for philanthropy. Failure to meet those expectations, in turn, will result in ever-greater consequences, social as well as political. To meet the challenges of the 21st century, philanthropy will need to be smart, flexible, open, and bold.*

*The Foundation Center's* Philanthropy News Digest *spoke with Melissa Berman, president and CEO of Rockefeller Philanthropy Advisors (www.rockpa.org), a full-service philanthropic advisory firm, about the changing philanthropic landscape, the link between information and effective philanthropy, and the likelihood of regulatory change in the field.*

*Berman has led Rockefeller Philanthropy Advisors since January 2001. Prior to that, she was senior vice president for research and program development at the Conference Board, a business research organization, where she oversaw the organization's research and publications on management practices, global corporate citizenship, and governance.*

*A frequent speaker, she has been profiled in the* New York Times, *and her ideas and views have been featured in the* Wall Street Journal, BusinessWeek, *the* Financial Times, USA Today, Town & Country, *the* Boston Globe, *and the* Houston Chronicle.

*Berman holds degrees from Harvard and Stanford, and serves on the boards of City Harvest and the Foundation Center, as well as on advisory panels for the Ron Brown Award for Corporate Leadership and New Ventures in Philanthropy.*

---

**Foundation Center (FC):** What are the origins of Rockefeller Philanthropy Advisors?

**Melissa Berman (MB):** Our roots go back to the 1890s when John D. Rockefeller engaged a gentleman named Frederick Gates, who was both a businessperson and a minister, to help him make decisions about the myriad philanthropic requests he was receiving — in part because Mr. Rockefeller had come to realize that he needed to make decisions at what he called the wholesale, rather than retail, level. Ever since then, the Rockefeller family's business office has included individuals who help family members with their philanthropy. In 2001, the family decided that because of the growing interest in philanthropy, it would be a great time to spin that group out of the family office and turn it into an independent nonprofit advisory service for donors around the world. And that's what we did, in January of 2002.

**FC:** What kind of services does RPA offer?

**MB:** We help donors plan their philanthropic program and do research on their behalf about giving opportunities and strategies. In a way, we serve as a sort of outsourced foundation staff, helping them put together program guidelines, conducting site visits, soliciting proposals, preparing dockets, monitoring grants, and so on. We also have a donor-advised fund under our aegis that can be used for both international and domestic giving, as well as to house special projects and initiatives related to philanthropy.

**FC:** Do you and your colleagues have a working definition of philanthropy, and if so, how is it reflected in your work?

**MB:** We think of philanthropy as a process whereby a donor thinks about how to use his or her resources to make change happen — everything from the kind of change, to the resources needed to make that change happen, to how you measure success. We believe that every donor who comes to us should be able to answer those kinds of questions, and it's our job to help him or her develop a philanthropic program that reflects their values and beliefs.

> **We think of philanthropy as a process whereby a donor thinks about how to use his or her resources to make change happen. . . .**

**FC:** In your work, you place considerable emphasis on helping clients become effective philanthropists. What are the hallmarks of effective philanthropy?

**MB:** For us, effective philanthropy means that a donor has thought through the end results he or she would like to achieve and how they plan to get there. That's what we mean when we say "fund the solution, not the problem." Let me give you an example. A lot of people are interested in ending poverty. Some people think the key to ending poverty lies in economic empowerment programs such as microcredit financing initiatives. Others think the key to ending poverty is education. Now, those are both terrific answers to the problem of poverty, and very few people would say one is right and the other is wrong. But rather than just focusing on the problem and looking around for organizations that work to end poverty, an effective philanthropist will ask, What approach to ending poverty makes the most sense to me? Which organizations have adopted that approach, or one like it? Which organizations within that group are doing work that already demonstrates some effectiveness? In my opinion, some people jump too quickly from fixing on an abstract noun like education or poverty to choosing a specific organization to fund, without ever really developing a sense of what their options are.

**FC:** Does effectiveness imply a certain level of "engagement," in the sense that venture philanthropists use that word?

**MB:** At a minimum, donors need to be engaged in a thoughtful process. Whether they participate personally or not is up to them. For many donors, anonymity is a moral issue, and the anonymous donor can be just as effective, in my view, as the philanthropist who is hands on and out front. But, again, the important point is that donors need to be engaged in thinking through their choices. It's worth putting some thought into understanding how much time you want to, and can, devote to your giving; to how you'd like to spend that time; to what resources besides money you can and want to commit; and to how you will know whether you're achieving your goals.

**FC:** Are the high-net-worth individuals who come to you for help better informed about philanthropy and their philanthropic choices than their parents and grandparents were?

> **The reason we see disaggregation of [philanthropic] resources is because people continue to grapple with how to frame the problems philanthropy is trying to solve. . . .**

**MB:** Thanks to cable television and the Internet, all of us are better informed than our parents and grandparents were. But we're often better informed in a superficial way, by which I mean that while we have access to a great deal more information, we don't necessarily have access to a great deal more meaning. Without a framework to structure the information, it's just a barrage of anecdotes — about problems, solutions, great work, or terrible waste. Intimidation and inertia are often the results.

**FC:** The number of foundations and nonprofit organizations has increased dramatically over the last twenty years. In the same way that information overload contributes to ever shorter attention spans, has the effectiveness of the nonprofit sector been hampered by the disaggregation of philanthropic assets among so many different organizations and types of charitable vehicles?

**MB:** If we had absolute, definitive proof that there was a right size for a grantmaking or philanthropic vehicle, as well as absolute, definitive proof about the most successful approaches to solving problems on the grantee side, then I think we'd start to see more concentration of philanthropic resources. The reason we see disaggregation of those resources, in my view, is because people continue to grapple with how to frame the issues and problems philanthropy is trying to solve, as well as how to assess the impact of those dollars.

**FC:** Are the tools we use to assess the impact of those dollars useful, or do we need to develop new ones?

**MB:** Although there's great work being done on this topic now, it's just not enough for the size of the nonprofit sector around the world. Think of what the business sector has: graduate schools of business filled with faculty doing research; independent research institutes; consultants who also publish; industry and trade associations that produce studies on improving performance. The public sector has a small fraction of that level of resources devoted to understanding how government is effective. And the nonprofit sector has a small fraction of the small fraction that the public sector has. So it's no wonder we have scarcely any good ways to identify or to replicate successful nonprofit initiatives. Our sector needs a real twenty-year plan to create and maintain the institutions that will have the scale and scope to answer basic questions objectively about outcomes.

> **. . . we have scarcely any good ways to identify or to replicate successful nonprofit initiatives. . . .**

**FC:** One of the more significant developments in the field over the last decade has been the emergence and growth of charitable gift funds. Have those funds been a plus for philanthropy?

**MB:** Sure. They've made it easy for many Americans to get more involved in philanthropy and charitable giving than they would have otherwise. They're a very effective, efficient charitable vehicle for many, many people.

**FC:** Should they be subject to greater regulation?

**MB:** I think the entire charitable sector needs to be more accountable than it has been, and that's true of all kinds of philanthropic vehicles. We need more of the transparency and accountability that have been demanded of the business sector in recent years. Which is not to say that one particular type of philanthropic vehicle is ipso facto better than another.

**FC:** Why have foundations and nonprofits received so much scrutiny, from both Congress and the media, over the last few years?

**MB:** Well, first of all, the not-for-profit sector is much larger than it ever has been. In fact, I believe it's the sixth-largest industry in the United States. When you're that big, people pay attention to you. But there's also a great deal of attention on philanthropy now because there's a great deal of hope riding on it. People believe — and we should take this as a vote of confidence in the work we do — that philanthropy has the potential to ameliorate some truly pernicious problems. When those hopes are disappointed, people become a little frustrated.

**FC:** Is that scrutiny of the sector likely to result in more regulation of the sector?

**MB:** I don't know if it will manifest itself in regulatory change. I think it will manifest itself, one way or another, in a higher set of standards and expectations around accountability and transparency, and that's a good thing.

> **There's a great deal of attention on philanthropy now because there's a great deal of hope riding on it. . . .**

**FC:** What does American philanthropy do well?

**MB:** American philanthropy is especially good at funding a diversity of organizations and approaches. It's especially good at responding quickly. And it's pretty good at institution building. We seem to have a fundamental belief that nonprofits play an important role — separate and distinct from government's role. And that's true regardless of whether you talk to liberal or conservative Americans. There's a strong link for Americans between the entrepreneurial spirit in the for-profit and nonprofit sectors.

**FC:** What could it do better?

**MB:** It could do better on the institution-building side — we may have created more now than our system can bear. It could do better in terms of focusing on the sustainability of the organizations it supports. We could be smarter about understanding what kind of operating costs are needed to run and report on superlative programs, instead of just looking to fund only "program activities." That's a kind of cost-shifting in the end. And, as I've said, it could do better in terms of funding solutions, not just problems.

**FC:** Does it take as many risks as it should?

**MB:** I think individual donors take risks all the time. Private philanthropy is often remarkably bold and creative, and many individuals — especially individuals with the kinds of business backgrounds that many of the newer philanthropists have — are very comfortable with the idea of risk. At the same time, they tend to be careful about having a working theory of change before they take a risk.

**FC:** Does risk-taking correlate to age? By that I mean, are younger donors more likely to fund something that's really out there than an older donor?

**MB:** Our experience at Rockefeller Philanthropy Advisors suggests that risk-taking correlates with two things. First is a person's general approach to life — his or her personality, philosophy, and mind-set. That's fairly stable over time. Second is the amount of time or resources a person has to devote to their funding. When you're informed, you're taking risk in a fundamentally different way. Taking risk doesn't have to be the same thing as acting on blind faith.

**FC:** Obviously, the notion of legacy is important in American philanthropy. How do you respond to those who argue that, given the pressing nature of challenges we face at the beginning of the 21st century, philanthropy should be more focused on addressing short-term needs and problems?

> . . . the jury is still out about whether more focus on the short term would help to bring about the kind of social change most of us would like to see. . . .

**MB:** I think the jury is still out about whether more focus on the short term would help to bring about the kind of social change most of us would like to see. There are no hard and fast answers as to whether it is better to be endowing foundations in perpetuity or using those resources up front. There are advantages and disadvantages to both approaches, and very little in the way of rigorous proof to support either point of view.

Ultimately, I think it's a matter of personal choice and assessment as to how one uses one's philanthropic resources.

**FC:** What seems to drive the high-net-worth individuals who come to Rockefeller Philanthropy Advisors for assistance?

**MB:** I would say there are two drivers acting on our clients today: one is a hunger for effectiveness, and the other is a strong desire to forge a deep and ongoing family involvement in philanthropy.

**FC:** Do gender and culture affect the way a donor approaches his or her philanthropy?

**MB:** Absolutely. People have different experiences in life that have a huge impact on the way they view the world. For example, we often find that women are more focused on the family implications of philanthropy. Similarly, different ethnic and nationality-based cultures often have their own traditions of giving, and those traditions often are reflected in an individual or family's philanthropic choices.

> **I think we should be encouraging more experiments that combine the best aspects of the for-profit sector with the best aspects of the not-for-profit sector. . . .**

**FC:** When you look out over the philanthropic landscape, do you see anything that really excites you?

**MB:** I find some of the experiments in social entrepreneurship, where you may have a nonprofit that's using business tools or a for-profit that has embraced a social purpose, to be interesting. In fact, I think we should be encouraging more experiments that combine the best aspects of the for-profit sector with the best aspects of the not-for-profit sector. I think that would be fantastic.

**FC:** The Republican-controlled Congress has been flirting with permanent repeal of the estate tax for a while now. Do you think that's likely to happen? And, if it did come to pass, what would be its impact on philanthropy?

**MB:** You know, that's a social experiment that has never been run in the United States. And the estimates of the impact vary tremendously, so I would say we simply have to wait and see what happens. The tax code clearly motivates people's behavior, but there are many people of wealth who have decided it's not helpful to succeeding generations to pass on everything. And there are also many donors who see philanthropy as a way to help shape the kind of world they want to live in.

**FC:** If John D. Rockefeller were alive today, what do you think he'd say about the state of American philanthropy?

**MB:** I think he would be encouraging more people to think wholesale, as he would put it, when it comes to philanthropy. I also think he'd be pleased to see many of the institutions that he was personally involved with still thriving — institutions like Spelman College, the University of Chicago, and Rockefeller University. Mr. Rockefeller was a huge believer in institutions and in defining institutional success in terms of longevity and sustainability. On that score, I think he'd be thrilled by what his philanthropy has accomplished.

> **Philanthropy truly is becoming a global phenomenon, and that's a very good thing. . . .**

**FC:** Philanthropically speaking, will we ever see the likes of a John D. Rockefeller or Andrew Carnegie again?

**MB:** We're already seeing their likes. Think of just a handful of the new philanthropic or social investment initiatives: the Gates Foundation, Ted Turner's commitment to the UN, the Omidyar Network, Google.org. And over the coming decades we'll also see the likes of Carnegie and Rockefeller in Europe, India, Russia, and China. Philanthropy truly is becoming a global phenomenon, and that's a very good thing.

**FC:** Well, thank you for speaking with us, Melissa.

**MB:** My pleasure.

*Mitch Nauffts, editorial director of* Philanthropy News Digest, *spoke with Melissa Berman in March 2006.*

# 4

# Donors and Philanthropic Intent

Adam Meyerson
President and CEO
Philanthropy Roundtable

*Whether their passion is public health, the environment, alleviating poverty, or reforming education, philanthropically minded individuals across the political spectrum are looking for novel ways to advance their goals and increase the effectiveness of their philanthropic dollars. As John J. Miller argues in the September 2006 issue of* Philanthropy *magazine, donors increasingly are interested in identifying successful models, best practices, and new ideas. "Their challenge," he adds, "is to build and sustain a set of enduring institutions that truly matter."*

*While that has always been true, what's different today is the eye-opening range of choices and giving vehicles available to the individual donor. As Adam Meyerson, president of the Philanthropy Roundtable, a national association of donors, foundation trustees and staff, and corporate giving officers, notes, there has been "an entrepreneurial explosion of new service providers, some for-profit, some nonprofit, offering advice, information, and investment opportunities" to donors. And what is especially significant about these new services and vehicles is that they empower and leave the individual donor in charge as never before.*

*The Foundation Center's* Philanthropy News Digest *spoke with Meyerson about his organization's efforts to assist donors in achieving their philanthropic intent, calls for greater regulation of the charitable sector, the success of conservative foundations in the public policy arena, and the role of competition in the marketplace of ideas.*

*Meyerson joined the Roundtable (www.philanthropyroundtable.org) as president in October 2001. From 1993 to 2001, he was vice president for educational affairs at the Heritage Foundation, where he coordinated the conservative think tank's civil society projects, its publications on the Founding Fathers, and its "No Excuses" work on high-performing high-poverty schools. Meyerson also was editor-in-chief of Heritage's magazine,* Policy Review, *from 1983 to 1998.*

*From 1979 to 1983, Meyerson was an editorial writer for the* Wall Street Journal *and editor of its "Manager's Journal" and "Asia" columns, and from 1974 to 1977 was managing editor of the* American Spectator *magazine, then based in Bloomington, Indiana. He is, in addition, co-editor of* The Wall Street Journal on Management, *a book published by Dow Jones-Irwin in 1985.*

*Mr. Meyerson graduated summa cum laude and Phi Beta Kappa from Yale University in 1974. From 1977 to 1979, he attended Harvard Business School and completed all requirements but the dissertation for a doctorate in international business.*

*He and his wife, Nina, live with their three sons in Washington, D.C.*

---

**Foundation Center (FC):** What is the Philanthropy Roundtable?

**Adam Meyerson (AM):** The Philanthropy Roundtable began in the late 1970s as a small, informal network of grantmakers whose aim was to increase political and intellectual diversity within the philanthropic community. We also worked to promote greater respect for donor intent and for private voluntary approaches to improving communities and helping people to help themselves. Originally, we operated under the auspices of an organization called the Institute for Educational Affairs. The Roundtable became a free-standing organization with an independent board of directors, a small staff, and an expanded calendar of conferences and other services in 1991.

Today, our mission is to foster excellence in philanthropy and to help donors achieve their philanthropic intent, to protect philanthropic freedom, and to assist donors in advancing liberty, opportunity, and personal responsibility, both in America and abroad. We have an annual budget of more than $3 million, a staff of thirteen, and a membership of over four hundred and fifty philanthropic organizations and families.

**FC:** What kinds of things does the Roundtable do to help ensure donor intent is honored in the long-term administration of foundations and charitable trusts?

**AM:** The history of modern philanthropy is a story of one foundation after another violating and, in some cases, directly contradicting the most cherished values of their founding donors. For that reason, the Philanthropy Roundtable recommends to donors who care about the preservation of their intent that they give very generously while living and that they consider establishing a sunset provision for their foundations that kicks in, say, a generation or two after their deaths.

That said, we understand that many founding donors are interested in establishing foundations in perpetuity, and we are committed to protecting their freedom to do so. In those cases, we offer some suggestions to donors and future boards of directors that will make it more likely that the founding donor's intent will be adhered to.

**It is vitally important for the founding donor or donors to articulate and put into writing a clear mission statement for the foundation. . . .**

First, it is vitally important for the founding donor or donors to articulate and put into writing a clear mission statement for the foundation, preferably in its charter or trust document. Second, it is important for the founding donor to establish a long pattern of giving while living and to reflect on and record what he likes and dislikes in his giving. A knowledge of giving style, a time horizon for expected results, and a donor's likes and dislikes, as well as the principles that have formed his or her giving, can be a very important supplement to a mission statement.

Donors and boards can also establish outside review processes to enforce adherence to donor intent. One such process is to give legal standing to outside organizations to sue the foundation's trustees if they determine the foundation is not following its founder's intent. Another is to give independent analysts the authority to review the foundation's grants, say, every five years, and to make sure they comply with the founding donor's intent.

It's also important to choose trustees with the judgment and understanding to ensure adherence to donor intent after a new generation assumes leadership of a foundation. In many cases, family members are best for carrying out the founding donor's charitable objectives, but not always. Finally, there are three kinds of trustees to avoid at all costs: trustees with a world view that differs dramatically from that of the founding donor; trustees who will abdicate to staff the responsibility of setting the strategic direction of the foundation; and trustees who will ignore their fiduciary duties and think of the foundation's assets as their own money to distribute.

> **It's also important to choose trustees with the judgment and understanding to ensure adherence to donor intent after a new generation assumes leadership of a foundation. . . .**

Many of the violations of donor intent we see in foundation grantmaking can also be found in endowment giving. We recommend that donors be very cautious about endowing universities or other cultural institutions unless they are convinced that those institutions will continue to remain faithful to the values the donors cherish most.

**FC:** Are you and your colleagues guided by a specific theory of change when designing your activities and programs?

**AM:** Yes. In 2003, the Roundtable embarked on a new strategy designed to provide philanthropists with more in-depth service and greater opportunities for strategic collaboration. To that end, we established a number of specialized affinity groups. We call them breakthrough groups, and they have been a major source of growth for us. To date, we've established breakthrough groups in K–12 education, environmental conservation, higher education, and national security, and we are considering others. In establishing these groups, we ask two questions: First, is it an area where we can make a distinctive contribution not offered by other organizations? If another organization is addressing the issue as well as we can, we'll refer donors to that organization. And second, is it an area where philanthropy can help achieve dramatic breakthroughs in the next ten to fifteen years? As for our theory of change, let me illustrate that briefly with our K–12 education program.

Our primary objective with the K–12 program is to leverage philanthropic resources to help achieve breakthroughs in the education of low-income children over the next ten to fifteen years. We think that's possible because breakthroughs in that area have already been achieved on a small scale. And in many cases, philanthropists and the social entrepreneurs they have supported have been the drivers of those breakthroughs. We think it's possible to extend the improvements that have already taken place, and that philanthropists are key to making that happen. To that end, we are putting significant resources into working with donors across the political spectrum to solve one of the great crises our country faces, which is the miseducation of low-income children.

**FC:** I'd like to come back to that. But first, I want to ask you about a couple of technical issues. What's the Roundtable's position on estate tax repeal?

**AM:** We don't take a direct position on that issue, although we do hold that repeal of the estate or death tax may affect the form and timing of charitable giving. But it is not likely, in our view, to affect the scope and scale of philanthropy in general.

**FC:** I'm not sure I understand.

**AM:** The remarkable tradition of American philanthropy long antedates the establishment of the federal estate tax in 1916. Stanford University, the Chicago Symphony Orchestra, St. Patrick's Cathedral in New York City, and Massachusetts General Hospital are just some of the thousands of institutions that owe their origins to private philanthropy in the days before the estate tax, or, for that matter, other tax incentives for charitable giving were instituted. Moreover, for the last several decades, despite a variety of tax policies, overall charitable giving in this country has remained fairly constant at about two percent of national income.

> **. . . charitable giving is best increased not by specific tax incentives but rather by boosting economic growth. . . .**

51

This strongly suggests to us that charitable giving is best increased not by specific tax incentives but rather by boosting economic growth.

Now, just as the estate tax creates an incentive for giving on one's deathbed, it is possible that if it were repealed, bequests might decline. We might also see reductions in instruments such as charitable lead trusts, charitable remainder trusts, and charitable gift annuities, which offer tax advantages when transferring assets to younger generations. But the motivations driving most philanthropists — the desire to help cherished institutions, to assist the needy, to cure disease, to expand opportunity, to reform public policy — will not disappear with repeal of the estate tax. The most effective philanthropy on one's deathbed builds on the knowledge and habits gained from a lifetime of giving, and that wisdom will not be affected by changes in the estate tax. In fact, repeal of the death tax will likely encourage more giving by donors while they are living, which we believe will lead to greater thoughtfulness in philanthropy.

> The motivations driving most philanthropists . . . will not disappear with repeal of the estate tax. . . .

Instead, we believe the case for and against estate taxes should be made on other grounds than their influence on philanthropy. The central question to be debated is whether it is just and good for parents to be able to pass on their homes, their businesses, their farms, and other property to their children — whether inheritance is compatible with a free society and our ideals as a nation. If the answer is yes, estate taxes should be abolished, or at least limited. If it's no, than they should be retained, or perhaps strengthened. In either case, philanthropy will flourish.

**FC:** Does the Roundtable support the charitable reform provisions included in the 2006 Pension Protection Act?

**AM:** Historically, the Roundtable has not gotten involved in legislative issues. However, in January 2005 we established the Alliance for Charitable Reform as an emergency initiative to respond to legislative proposals on Capitol Hill that would affect private foundations and public charities. The mission of ACR is to offer commonsense solutions for abuses in the charitable sector while protecting the freedom of donors and foundations to use their best judgment in carrying out their charitable objectives.

For us, common sense starts with the proposition that government should vigorously enforce existing laws before announcing sweeping new ones. We recognize that new, narrowly targeted laws may be necessary to correct specific abuses not covered by current rules. But most of the transgressions in our sector that have caught the public's attention are violations of existing law. There is no need to rewrite the fundamental public policy framework governing philanthropy, which historically has given private philanthropic organizations wide discretion in how they use their resources to achieve their charitable missions.

> **Most of the transgressions in our sector that have caught the public's attention are violations of existing law. . . .**

We expect that the big battle over philanthropic freedom will take place in 2007. We will do everything in our power to resist requirements for foundation accreditation, five-year reviews of tax-exempt status, arbitrary limits on trustee and staff compensation, federal micromanagement of the boards of private organizations, limits on the compensation of family members who sit on family foundation boards, and other freedom-threatening measures that have been proposed in the last two years by Senate Finance Committee and/or Joint Tax Committee staff. As it becomes ever clearer that Sarbanes-Oxley has imposed significant costs on small-cap companies and is responsible for keeping new businesses from listing on American stock exchanges, it will become increasingly important to resist applying the Sarbanes-Oxley mind-set to charities and foundations.

As for the Pension Protection Act that passed this summer, we think that a number of its charitable provisions were quite sensible and that some could have benefited from more open debate. Some provisions now require technical corrections because the way the legislation was introduced did not allow for a full discussion of the issues, and a number of unintended consequences are now coming to light.

On a related matter, the Philanthropy Roundtable is opposed to formal industry-wide self-regulation as an alternative to congressional legislation. We believe that overreaching legislative proposals can and should be resisted on their own merits, without substituting a private, self-regulatory regime that could be equally overreaching and intrusive.

For instance, the Roundtable does not currently, nor do we intend to, set certain governance standards or codes of conduct as criteria for membership, as some of our sister philanthropic service associations are advocating. We believe it is consistent with the principles of a free society for private membership organizations to set eligibility standards if they wish. But we do not believe our membership would appreciate such a code, nor do we believe that it would be an effective way for us to improve foundation effectiveness. While foundations should be free to participate in voluntary accreditation or certification programs if they wish, the Roundtable is strongly opposed to any requirement that accreditation be a condition of tax-exempt status. An accreditation requirement could pose a very serious threat to independent thought in philanthropic foundations.

Moreover, accreditation simply isn't necessary for foundations. There is a public-interest rationale for accrediting hospitals or day-care centers, where health and safety issues are at stake. Public charities may also find it helpful to be certified or accredited on a voluntary basis in order to win the confidence of donors, and there are some very impressive models in that area, such as the Evangelical Council for Financial Accountability. Foundations, on the other hand, are not taking investments from others, nor are they entrusted with the safety of members of the public. Indeed, so long as they obey the law, foundations do not have to be, and should not have to be, directly accountable to anyone except their own donors and trustees.

> **So long as they obey the law, foundations do not have to be, and should not have to be, directly accountable to anyone except their own donors and trustees....**

**FC:** It's not uncommon these days to hear liberals suggest that conservative foundations — organizations like the Olin Foundation, the Bradley Foundation, the various Scaife foundations, the Smith Richardson Foundation — have, over the last twenty-five years, hijacked the political agenda in this country and have managed to do so at a cost of only $70 million a year. Are they correct? And if they are, how did conservative foundations manage to pull that off?

**AM:** Foundations across the political spectrum have had an influence on public policy over the last thirty years. On the liberal or progressive side, public policies such as campaign finance limitations, Head Start, racial quotas, the Public Broadcasting System, population planning assistance, medical marijuana initiatives, and many of our healthcare and environmental policies result substantially from the work of liberal and progressive foundations and philanthropists. On the conservative side, foundations have effectively pushed for K–12 education reforms, including charter schools, vouchers, and the standards and accountability movements; welfare reform; a renewed emphasis on serious constitutional interpretation in judicial decisions; deregulation of transportation, banking, telecommunications, and other industries; a renewed appreciation for the benefits of capitalism; and reforms in policing and sentencing, which have led to dramatic reductions in crime in New York and many other cities.

But whether one is liberal, conservative, or somewhere in between, there are certain approaches that foundations interested in influencing public policy follow, and I'd just like to mention a couple of them.

First, they know what they stand for and are deeply committed to clear principles that they will not compromise. Second, they influence public debate through ideas, strategic investments, and collection of the right data. Third, they think long-term and give long-term support to institutions that are well positioned to advance their public policy objectives. Fourth, while they're always looking to achieve measurable results in the short run, they keep their focus on the long term and are patient because they know public policy reform takes time. Fifth, they work to build broad-based coalitions, usually across party lines. Sixth, they are not afraid of controversy, although they do not seek it. As a funder, if you are not prepared to be criticized, you probably shouldn't be in the public policy business. Seventh, they study and work to establish models of success. These can include demonstration projects or field trials that illustrate the case for a broader reform agenda. And last but not least, they keep control of their own funding decisions. They're willing to work closely with other funders who share their principles and public policy agenda, but in the absence of long-term agreement on principles and strategy,

> **As a funder, if you are not prepared to be criticized, you probably shouldn't be in the public policy business. . . .**

they are cautious about formal collaboration with other private donors and about matching funds provided by public agencies.

**FC:** Are ideological labels useful when discussing philanthropy? Or are they a distraction from the real issues and work that needs to be done?

**AM:** There's enormous ideological diversity in philanthropy. Just look at the donors and foundations working for and against gay marriage, for and against school choice, for and against the decriminalization of marijuana, for and against the living wage, for and against the introduction of personalized Social Security accounts — this diversity is one of the glories of a free society. Our system of self-government assumes that citizens have the intelligence and initiative to make the important decisions that affect their lives, including how to direct their charitable contributions. Freedom of philanthropy, like freedom of the press, religious freedom, and economic freedom, is essential to the American experience, and the Philanthropy Roundtable is committed to defending the right of donors and foundations to determine their charitable missions. It's one reason why we plan to fight vigorously against accreditation requirements, five-year reviews of tax-exempt status, and other measures that could give government officials the opportunity to suppress political views with which they disagree.

**There is no one right way to improve our communities, our nation, or the world. . . .**

My favorite quote about philanthropy comes from the late Waldemar Nielsen, who said: "These strange and wonderful inventions [foundations] have a unique freedom from the dependency of other institutions on markets or constituencies that cripple their capacity to take the long view and to bring a competent and disinterested approach to the search for solutions to complex problems." Nielsen went on to say: "It is a waste of important potential if foundations do not make use of the special freedoms they have been given to take the long view; to back the promising but unproven idea, individual or institution; to take an unpopular or unorthodox stand; to facilitate change rather than automatically endorsing the status quo; . . . to act and not merely react; to initiate, even to gamble and dare."

If we take Nielsen seriously, and I think we should, we need to discourage the groupthink that characterizes much of the foundation world. There is no one right way to improve our communities, our nation, or the world. Instead, we should be pushing for more ideological diversity, not less; we should be pushing for more diversity in the strategies and approaches we fund, not less; we should be encouraging more, not less, diversity in our dreams and aspirations.

**FC:** I take it you believe there's a role for competition in philanthropy?

**AM:** Competition dramatically improves performance, whether one is talking about business, education, scientific research, sports, or most other areas of American life. At the Roundtable, we believe philanthropy would be stronger if there were more competition within the field. For example, there is no penalty today for mediocre performance in philanthropy. In highly competitive fields, mediocre performers have to adapt and improve or find a new line of work.

Having said that, there are three important elements of competition in philanthropy. The first is the competition among grantees for charitable and philanthropic dollars. The second is the competition among different visions of philanthropic effectiveness — something we try to encourage at our own conferences through vigorous debate and the exchange of ideas. And third, and perhaps most important, is the competition for the philanthropic imagination of new donors. As you know, there is an entrepreneurial explosion of new service providers, some for-profit, some nonprofit, offering advice, information, and investment opportunities to new donors. And it's partly because of this competition that new donors are providing so much of the vitality in philanthropy today.

Warren Buffett's "merger" with the Gates Foundation offers some interesting possibilities in this regard, and I predict that more donors will follow his example and choose to align themselves with an already established funder, or perhaps take more of a portfolio approach by giving through a variety of funders rather than a single one. If that happens, we could see a very interesting situation in which funders compete with each other for new philanthropic capital. It would be extraordinarily healthy for philanthropy, in my view, for funders as different as the Open Society

> **We could see a very interesting situation in which funders compete with each other for new philanthropic capital. . . .**

Institute, the Carnegie Corporation, the Bradley Foundation, the Robin Hood Foundation, and/or various community foundations to compete with each other over who has the most effective philanthropic strategy for addressing society's greatest challenges.

**FC:** Do we have adequate metrics to measure foundation effectiveness and/or the social benefit delivered by foundation resources?

**AM:** The study of philanthropic effectiveness is still in its infancy. In addition to quantitative analytic tools, it would be very helpful to develop a case study literature of great philanthropic achievements and failures, both in the academy, on the model of business school case studies, and in the philanthropic press. During the next decade or so, we are likely to see major advances in this area, as more and more business entrepreneurs, acting either as donors or as service providers for donors, apply their penetrating intelligence, understanding of strategy, and insistence on defining and measuring results to philanthropic questions.

**In a free society, different philanthropists will define the meaning of effectiveness differently. . . .**

I am not sure that it is possible or even desirable to develop general metrics of social benefit generated by philanthropy as a whole. This is because in a free society, different philanthropists will define the meaning of effectiveness differently. What we need is new analytical tools to help individual philanthropists to better define and achieve their objectives, not across-the-industry measures of net social benefit.

**FC:** Is philanthropic effectiveness a function of the amount of resources available to address a problem, the quality of the ideas behind those resources, or some combination of both?

**AM:** The quantity of resources and the quality of the ideas behind those resources are both important. The experience of the federal government certainly shows that money alone is not sufficient to achieve results. We spend $400 billion per year on public K–12 education, yet 40 percent of our fourth-graders cannot read at grade level. Similarly, there are some very large foundations that have made very little difference in the world.

On the other hand, you don't have to have bottomless resources to have impact. Small and medium-sized foundations can and frequently do exercise extraordinary philanthropic leadership by focusing their resources on finding breakthrough solutions to specific problems.

**FC:** Is it your view that private funding and initiative is always preferable to public sector engagement with an issue? And is there any issue that is simply too large or complex for the private sector to solve on its own?

**AM:** Advocates of limited government, in which we include ourselves, have always said that government has important responsibilities, including national defense, the administration of courts and our system of justice, the protection of public health and safety, and so on. In addition, many of the leading reforms pushed by some of our members — for example, Social Security reform or school vouchers — are really aimed at redirecting, not limiting, government spending. Moreover, regardless of what members of the Philanthropy Roundtable think, big government is a fact of life for the foreseeable future and almost every philanthropist today must determine his or her strategy in the shadow of massive government spending. To give you just one example, the National Institutes of Health spend $30 billion per year on biomedical research — almost as much as what all foundations combined give, to all causes and programs, in a year. Any philanthropist who wants to make a difference in the area of biomedical research would be foolish to replicate what NIH already does. Instead, many philanthropists are having an impact in biomedical research by focusing on a specific hypothesis or field of study or kind of research that is not funded by NIH.

> **In recent decades government funding has come to dominate many areas of American life that historically had been the province of private charity and initiative. . . .**

In recent decades government funding has come to dominate many areas of American life that historically had been the province of private charity and initiative. We think it would be useful to have a national debate about a number of government-funded programs and initiatives, including FEMA disaster relief, medical care for low-income families, the Legal Services Corporation, the National Endowment for the Arts, and so on, and to ask which of these functions could be delivered more effectively, more efficiently, and more compassionately through privately funded organizations.

**FC:** Since the 2004 election, there has been grumbling within conservative circles about the growth of federal spending and the size of the budget deficit. Has the conservative movement — and conservative philanthropy as a manifestation of that movement — reached a high-water mark in terms of its influence in the marketplace of ideas?

**AM:** We see enormous amounts of new energy pouring into philanthropy of all kinds, including conservative philanthropy. The field is being revitalized by successful business entrepreneurs who are applying their leadership skills, institution-building know-how, out-of-the-box entrepreneurial imaginations, passion to innovate and serve, and money to a range of charitable initiatives. Some are conservative and some are not. At the Roundtable, we see this as an enormously fertile period for philanthropy of all kinds.

**FC:** Globalization has brought any number of transnational issues, including climate change, nuclear proliferation, and the spread of infectious diseases to the fore. Partly in response to these challenges, philanthropy seems to be evolving from a field of independent institutions and individuals to one increasingly comprised of networks. Do you see that trend continuing over the next decade or so?

**AM:** I'm not sure I share your premise that philanthropy is moving away from independent institutions and individuals. On the contrary, we're seeing an extraordinary explosion of new services to help donors make wise decisions and achieve their charitable objectives. Some of these services offer high-level information and analysis about potential grantees. World-class business consulting firms and venture capitalists are also exploring how to apply their principles and techniques to philanthropic giving. Donor partnerships and networks are another service to philanthropists who want to achieve leverage with their grants.

One of the most exciting developments is the growth of intermediaries — public charities that themselves make grants and frequently provide management assistance to grantees. In many respects, they act like a kind of nonprofit mutual fund, providing two important services: first, they lower the information-gathering costs for each grant, increasing accountability for both donors and grantees. Second, by pooling the funds of a number of donors, they diversify the risk of any particular philanthropic investment by sharing financial responsibility. These intermediaries are especially important in international giving, where donors may not be confident they have enough local knowledge to make informed decisions on their own.

What is significant about all these new entrepreneurial services is that they leave the individual donor in charge: rather than replacing the donor, they empower him with more information, more choices, and more confidence in his giving program. And because the various networks, intermediaries, and other services compete for the dollars and — more important — the mental attention of the donor, the donor has a growing opportunity to receive high-level help in defining his charitable objectives and selecting the most effective philanthropic vehicles for achieving his objectives.

> **What is significant about all these new entrepreneurial services is that they leave the individual donor in charge. . . .**

**FC:** We've been talking about a field that has grown rapidly over the last decade or so and, increasingly, is celebrated as the best hope for incubating solutions to a long list of problems. Is the time ripe to have a national discussion about philanthropy and its role in American society?

**AM:** As a relative newcomer to philanthropy, I would say that I've been surprised by how little serious discussion there is of this amazingly vibrant and important sector. Outside of a few academic programs and the occasional scandal or an eye-opening announcement such as the Buffett-Gates merger, you don't see much attention paid to what foundations and philanthropists actually do. We don't have many observers of the field these days with the wisdom and insight and knowledge of someone like Wally Nielsen. Instead, the field is dominated by a kind of insularity and suffocating groupthink — in part, because philanthropic families and foundation trustees and staffers are regularly flattered and lionized by their grantees, to the point that they begin to believe their reviews. As a result, they rarely have to respond when their assumptions are challenged or their effectiveness as grantmakers is questioned. I think philanthropy would be a much stronger field if there were more debates, more and better watchdog groups, and more attention paid to the field by serious journalists, scholars, and experts in areas where foundations are trying to make a difference.

**FC:** Well, thank you for your time this morning, Adam.

**AM:** Thank you for your questions and the opportunity to share our views.

*Mitch Nauffts, editorial director of* Philanthropy News Digest, *spoke with Adam Meyerson in October 2006.*

# 5

# Spending Out as a Philanthropic Strategy

Vincent McGee
Former Executive Director
Aaron Diamond Foundation

*It's a classic debate: whether to endow a foundation "in perpetuity" or to "give while living," endowing a foundation only for a limited period of time. Proponents of the former argue that perpetual foundations are best able to put long-term money into solving long-term social problems, serve as a critical pool of risk capital for solutions to unanticipated future problems, and/or enable a donor to ensure the continuation of a family philanthropic tradition after his or her death. Those who favor limited-term foundations argue that it's irresponsible, even immoral, to keep large amounts of tax-advantaged wealth on the sidelines when present needs are so great and that limited-term foundations are the best way to ensure that a foundation's assets will be spent in accord with the founding donor's intent.*

*One of the best-known recent examples of a limited-term foundation was the Aaron Diamond Foundation, which awarded more than $200 million in grants as it spent itself down over a ten-year period between 1987 and 1996. Although active in the areas of education, arts and culture, and human rights, the foundation was most famous for its focus on and funding for AIDS research — and for the feisty leadership of its president, the late Irene Diamond. It was funding from the Diamond Foundation, for example, that made possible the establishment, in 1991, of the Aaron Diamond AIDS Research Center, under the direction of Dr. David Ho. ADARC subsequently pioneered the use of combination drug therapy to control the disease — a development that has helped reduce the death rate of*

*HIV in America and Western Europe to one-fifth of what it was in the late '80s and '90s.*

*The Foundation Center's* Philanthropy News Digest *spoke with Vincent McGee, the former executive director of the Aaron Diamond Foundation, about the Diamonds' decision to convert their family foundation into a limited-term foundation, the foundation's work in the field of AIDS research, Mrs. Diamond's role at the foundation, and some of the lessons McGee has learned over thirty-five years as an executive and consultant for nonprofits and foundations.*

*McGee served as vice president and secretary of the Irene Diamond Fund from January 1994 to March 2002 and as executive director of the Aaron Diamond Foundation from May 1985 to December 1996. Prior to that, he was executive director (1980–1985) of the Hunt Alternatives Fund, vice president for development (1977–1980) at the City College of New York, and executive director (1973–1975) of the DJB Foundation. He spent a year in jail in the early '70s for his anti-war activities, where he broke bread with the likes of Carmine DeSapio and Bobby Baker, and rubbed shoulders with small-time embezzlers, a two-star general, several high-level Mafia types, a group of Jehovah's Witnesses, and many other war resisters. "My higher education," McGee adds, "was enriched by working on the production line at Eastman Kodak while attending the University of Rochester during the mid-'60s racial struggles in that city and by working for a New York City law firm while attending Hunter College at night."*

*He continues to work and consult for a number of individual donors and foundations, including the Overbrook Foundation and the Atlantic and Epstein philanthropies, and serves on the boards of the Baker Foundation, the Balm Foundation, the Center for Philanthropy and Civil Society at CUNY, FoodChange, PATH, the Rockefeller University Council, and the Sister Fund.*

---

**Foundation Center (FC):** You've had an interesting career in philanthropy. What were some of the advantages — and disadvantages — to moving around and doing as many different things as you have?

**Vincent McGee:** Well, in fact I didn't move around as much as it may seem. I was at the Aaron Diamond Foundation and then with the Irene Diamond Fund for seventeen years, the bulk of my career. I started in philanthropy at the DJB Foundation in March of 1973. But I'd been doing work in the nonprofit world and with donors since the late 1960s. In those years I was the executive director of the six-thousand-member Business Executives Move for Vietnam Peace. I ran their operation in Washington, where I lobbied, gave speeches, and organized. People in the broader anti-war movement assumed that our group had a great deal of money, and they often came to us looking for funding. Sometimes, I was able to match their requests with business executives who had their own foundation or who were willing to give money out of their own pockets. After a few years, Carol Bernstein, the widow of one of those executives, Daniel Bernstein, hired me to help her and her second husband, W.H. "Ping" Ferry, with the DJB Foundation, as well as with their personal giving.

It was rich experience for me, and it helped me to look at life from a variety of perspectives. Among other things, I learned to avoid preconceived notions and labels, as well as how to meet people where they live and how to listen.

> **As I like to say, the business of philanthropy comes down to asking, saying no, and saying yes. . . .**

In the foundation world, there are certain power dynamics that people don't pay enough attention to. As I like to say, the business of philanthropy comes down to asking, saying no, and saying yes. Most of us on the donor side really don't appreciate how hard it is to have to ask all the time. In contrast, foundation board members, officers, and staff spend most of their time saying "no" — usually graciously, sometimes peremptorily or indirectly, and often after making the applicant wait longer than is necessary. Obviously, it's much better to say "yes." But common courtesy — answering the mail and returning phone calls — goes a long way to lightening everyone's load.

**FC:** How did you meet and become involved with the Diamonds?

**VM:** An attorney involved in Mr. Diamond's real estate business had been on the board of Amnesty International with me. He knew I did work with foundations and donors and he introduced me to Mrs.

Diamond in the fall of 1984, several months after Mr. Diamond had died, unexpectedly, of a heart attack. Earlier that year, the Diamonds, both of whom were in their seventies, had planned to activate the foundation they created in 1955 but had used mainly as a "pass-through." They did most of their giving directly, outside the foundation. But by 1984 they had decided to return a significant portion of the money Mr. Diamond made in real estate to institutions and people based in New York City, where he made that money. They also chose three areas in which to focus their giving — medical research, minority education, and culture — and decided that the foundation's endowment should be spent down within a decade of the death of either of them. Mr. Diamond also asked that his businesses be liquidated within five years of his death, the proceeds going to the foundation or to Mrs. Diamond.

**FC:** So it was his idea to spend down the foundation's endowment?

**VM:** They came up with the idea together. Mrs. Diamond seemed to support the concept when she and I first talked about it, but as the foundation began to ramp up its activities she became more and more convinced that spending down was the right thing to do. She subsequently included in her will a similar provision for her own wealth.

**FC:** Did you encourage her in that decision?

**VM:** I did. I had already been involved in a spend-down with the DJB Foundation and understood the rationale. Spending down is an attractive option for many people — though clearly not for every foundation or donor. The Diamonds liked the concept, and that was fine with me.

**Spending down is an attractive option for many people — though clearly not for every foundation or donor. . . .**

We had about a two-year lead time before we started the ten-year countdown, largely because of complications related to the liquidation of Mr. Diamond's estate. So there was a delay in those assets being released to the foundation, which gave Mrs. Diamond and me and her other advisors time to develop our program.

Even early on, we saw that AIDS was an area in which the foundation could have an impact. Irene Diamond was the farthest thing from homophobic, and she had enough interest in and knowledge of science to recognize that AIDS was a virus spread by blood, by sexual fluids, by dirty needles, and so forth. We were being advised by Lewis Thomas, the well-known essayist and former head of Memorial Sloan-Kettering. He told us to go for it and to learn as much as we could about the virus.

So we dug in. We didn't have preconceived notions about the role we might play. We simply saw ourselves as giving established researchers the resources necessary to get involved with the AIDS virus, hoping their work would produce results that might qualify for federal funding, in larger amounts and for a longer term than we could ever provide. The concept of the Diamond AIDS laboratory itself evolved from the observation that many institutions in and around New York City wanted to do AIDS work but didn't have the protected lab space and other facilities needed to work in a serious way with this kind of retro-virus. To make a long story short, we quickly found space in the Public Laboratory Building and devised a plan to have a private corporation lease the space. Stephen Joseph, then the city's Commissioner of Health, assuaged our concerns about working with a large city bureaucracy, and eventually the Aaron Diamond AIDS Research Center (ADARC) was incorporated. Funds to cover the initial planning and research costs came from the foundation. Funds to cover building renovation costs came from us and from the city, which leased the space to us for twenty years at $1 per year.

> **We didn't have preconceived notions about the role we might play. . . .**

**FC:** This was 1986, 1987?

**VM:** The foundation made its first AIDS research grants in 1985. The concept for ADARC took shape in late 1987, early 1988, and was formalized in 1989. The lab's doors opened in April 1991.

**FC:** Did you and your colleagues do anything special to educate yourself about the virus?

**VM:** Well, there wasn't a huge amount to read at first, so we learned as we went along, talking to researchers, working with Dr. Thomas and with our second medical advisor, Alfred Gellhorn. He had been dean of medicine at the University of Pennsylvania and was recruited by City

College, where he created the Sophie Davis School of Biomedical Education and where I first met him in the late 1970s. After I started working at the Diamond Foundation, I asked him if he would come in and meet Mrs. Diamond, and he agreed to help us. Later, both he and Dr. Thomas joined the board of the foundation, then the board of ADARC. They were the ones who interpreted the science into lay terms for the rest of us.

The more we learned, the more we realized there needed to be a significant AIDS research center in New York City that could work with different researchers and research institutions. New York had become the epicenter of HIV/AIDS in the United States and desperately needed a research effort that was focused and that cut through the institutional competition and red tape normal in the early stages of a new epidemic. The initial academic affiliation for the scientists at the lab was with New York University Medical School, but eventually ADARC settled in at Rockefeller University and its renowned clinical hospital.

> . . . we realized there needed to be a significant AIDS research center in New York City that could work with different researchers and research institutions. . . .

**FC:** One of your great successes was finding Dr. David Ho to head up the lab. Serendipity?

**VM:** Actually, no. It was the work of a search committee chaired by Dr. Edwin Kilbourne, an influenza expert at Mount Sinai, and comprised of Dr. Thomas and several senior scientists in New York City research institutions. Mrs. Diamond and I were on the committee *ex officio.* The committee went about the search in a very serious, methodical way, and as it narrowed down the field of candidates the main issue came down to whether we should choose a young person with talent and promise or a senior person with operational experience who could come in and get things going. Mrs. Diamond opted right from the start for the former — for a person, as she put it, "who's hungry for action." We were fortunate to find Dr. Ho, but it wasn't serendipity.

**FC:** With the foundation committed to spending down its assets in a relatively brief period, what, if anything, did you do about evaluation? Did you have goals and objectives from the start? Did you try to develop specific benchmarks beyond your broader goals over time?

**VM:** Mrs. Diamond was a quick study. She and I would meet daily. We were often joined by a scientist or a member of our staff; we had an excellent staff. Mrs. Diamond had been a script and talent editor in Hollywood — she worked with Hal Wallis for a number of years, and her claim to fame was finding the script that became *Casablanca*. At the foundation she saw herself as the boss with big ideas and me as the technical expert who did the work and ran the office and staff. Maybe it had something to do with working through the problems associated with the settling of her husband's estate, but for various reasons we learned to trust each other implicitly. That doesn't mean we didn't have our differences; sometimes we argued like cats and dogs! But our scrapping would always end with a laugh, and we'd be back on track quickly.

We also had a high-powered board that didn't micromanage our activities. In its formal meetings, which it held four times a year, the board would talk through new ideas, review what we had learned, and approve startup grants and various changes to the program. Remember, these were busy people, and to get them on the board in the first place and then to keep them focused on a highly technical, changing field required a lot of work.

> **Mrs. Diamond was not a fan of comprehensive and costly evaluations. . . .**

Mrs. Diamond was not a fan of comprehensive and costly evaluations. First of all, we had a ten-year time frame in which to accomplish something and we were learning as we went along. It wasn't unusual for us to make a small grant on a sort of trial basis and to increase support if the work bore fruit. Project leaders were encouraged to let us know early if problems materialized. In those cases, we would change the grant agreement and adjust the plan. We were also willing to provide general support, in addition to project support, on the theory that people who were scrambling for the latter shouldn't have to worry about how they were going to keep the lights on. In the case of some of the larger institutions we worked with, it wasn't unusual for us to fund as many as three different projects or programs in addition to providing general support. Later, as we moved into the wind-down phase, we intensified our work with technical assistance and management groups, and by using our power to convene — usually by bringing people together in our conference room — we did our best to ensure that there were multiple funding streams for many of the projects and activities we supported and to move work onto public budgets where possible. It turned out to be a very successful model.

**FC:** The Diamond Foundation was known for its pathbreaking work in HIV/AIDS. Did you have the same kind of success in other program areas?

**VM:** Yes, especially in education. Early on, some of our board members wanted to focus on increasing minority enrollment in prep schools and elite institutions of higher education. That was not Mrs. Diamond's interest, nor mine. Fortunately, with the help of several others on the board, especially Dr. Gellhorn, we began to explore how to make a difference in the basic quality of public education in New York City, from preschool on. Our thinking was that by doing something to improve the system, we could help many, many more students and raise the level for everybody.

As I said, we got some good advice and over time we helped to develop a number of effective programs. For example, we pioneered many of the things that are now known as the New Visions Schools, which the Gates Foundation, Carnegie Corporation, and others are putting hundreds of millions of dollars into around the country — breaking up big schools and creating smaller, themed schools where young people connect to a specific focus and get more attention. To make that work, we also helped start minority recruitment programs for principals and teachers and collaborated with Agnes Gund's Studio in a School and others to bring the arts, which had been eliminated from most public schools during the city's fiscal crisis in the mid-70s, back into the curriculum. Toward the end of the foundation, we also funded a survey of arts education in the city that laid the groundwork for a special Annenberg Foundation grant which prompted city funding for a restructuring of the arts curriculum in the schools.

> **We pioneered many of the things that are now known as the New Visions Schools, which the Gates Foundation, Carnegie Corporation, and others are putting hundreds of millions of dollars into around the country. . . .**

In the area of arts and culture, we developed a focus on performing arts as a career vehicle for young people in music and dance, with film as a smaller area of interest. Because of Mrs. Diamond's long-standing interest in free speech, personal liberties and human rights, we also developed programs in those areas. Mrs. Diamond also made large personal grants outside the foundation to expand the minority presence at Julliard and gave $30 million over fifteen years to Human Rights Watch.

And though we initially set out to keep the foundation's AIDS work focused on medical research, we quickly became aware of the problem of AIDS in other settings — for example, children having parents with AIDS or being infected themselves and how people living with HIV/AIDS were discriminated against at school and in the community. We discovered the importance of educating young people and teachers about AIDS, as well as the absence of AIDS in health education curricula, and so forth. As a result, we quickly moved AIDS as a focus into our education and, later, human rights work. When people began to recognize our work as being ahead of the curve, particularly when we started a program for AIDS education and condom availability in the public schools, Mrs. Diamond would say, "I'm a grandmother. We ought to be talking about this candidly. This is a disease that can be avoided, but people have to know how it's transmitted and they have to change their behavior based on the facts." The Aaron Diamond Foundation was seen as a model because there was a consistency and integrity across the spectrum of our program activities.

> **The board understood that this was a ten-year program and that their participation was very important — being a sounding board, generating ideas, and setting policy. . . .**

**FC:** Would the foundation have been as successful if Mrs. Diamond herself had not been as active and committed a donor as she was?

**VM:** No, she was the key. The other part was that she and I and the staff worked well together and the board respected what we were doing. They understood that this was a ten-year program and that their participation was very important — being a sounding board, generating ideas, and setting policy. They knew they were stakeholders in the foundation's success, but also that they had a different kind of ownership in that success. Almost all of our board members had an active interest in a nonprofit organization as an active volunteer or a founder, but they resisted pitching their own projects to us unless it clearly complemented work we were doing. That was crucial, and it made it easier for everyone; we were able to avoid the internecine power struggles that frequently develop whenever money, power, and influence are involved.

**FC:** Did Mrs. Diamond consider her involvement with the foundation a full-time job?

**VM:** Yes. She would come into the office four days a week, for five to six hours. And when she wasn't in the office, we were on the phone, or out and about meeting people or doing things in the evening. In the years I knew her, she became a vocal advocate for spending money while you are living with lots of her friends and associates. Some of them give her credit for getting them to think about using their resources to make a difference and having the satisfaction of acting philanthropically while still alive.

**FC:** Those ten years must have gone by quickly. Did you and your colleagues do anything that, in retrospect, you wish you had done differently?

**VM:** In a couple of areas we on the staff were sorry, as we got closer to the end, that we didn't stick with a few things for a longer term and argue more with Mrs. Diamond. She didn't like or have the patience for process and long learning curves. She once said to me, "Look, you have youth and time to talk about process. I don't. I'm the fire engine driving your process down the street!" That impatience was energizing, but at times it cut conversations shorter than they might otherwise have been. But you don't get to play the game over. We had an extraordinarily effective run that was characterized by a low level of acrimony and a lot of joy and satisfaction.

> **We tried, to the best of our ability, to walk in other people's shoes. We'd ask them to forget about what they thought we wanted to hear and to tell us what they needed. . . .**

**FC:** In the past, you've criticized foundations and foundation culture for being insular, overly cautious, and arrogant. With all of its success, how did the Diamond Foundation avoid those pitfalls?

**VM:** Well, we tried to listen, listen, listen, and learn. We tried, to the best of our ability, to walk in other people's shoes. We'd ask them to forget about what they thought we wanted to hear and to tell us what they needed. We had our focus and we kept to it mostly, although we made exceptions when the situation demanded it. We also made decisions quickly, especially when we had to say no, and we tried to give helpful suggestions when we did say no.

**FC:** As the foundation field has grown in size, assets, and diversity, do you think foundation culture has changed?

**VM:** In many ways, yes. But so has the culture around us. My critique of the power dynamic in foundations is similar to my critique of power in business and government: it's overly "top-down." People with power rarely take the time to listen and pay attention to people without as much power. Similarly, we rarely admit how little we know about reality for the underresourced. It's partly attributable to the shortness of attention spans in our culture, our tendency to "learn by sound bite." And, of course, people are all too willing to tell people in power what they think they want to hear.

> **To do philanthropy well, you need practice, you need humility, and you need to listen and learn new skills. . . .**

Listen, it's not easy to give money and resources, advice and counsel, effectively. Many foundations and donors feel that adequate staffing is a luxury, that having professionals around is a luxury, and that boards always knows best. Sometimes that's true, and sometimes it's not. I often ask business executives or lawyers who are on boards how they feel when those who don't have their expertise or training second guess their professional decisions. I ask them if they look to professionals and specialists when entering a new business or area of practice. I ask them whether they trust those professionals and how they use them effectively, without sacrificing the right to make the final decision.

There is a significant infusion of new money into philanthropy, much of it from younger entrepreneurs who have had brilliant success in specific industries and think this experience will automatically translate into nonprofit work. Many quickly discover that lots of money and time can be wasted learning how not to do philanthropy. To do philanthropy well, you need practice, you need humility, and you need to listen and learn new skills.

It's also true that those of us who work in foundations and nonprofits want to keep our jobs. We're careful not to rock the boat too much and often don't speak as candidly as we might or should. But while it is essential to speak candidly, timing and context are important; you need to wait for the right opportunity and have the right research or information at hand when you make your case. Only then will candor lead to positive results.

**FC:** Who should have the final say in deciding whether the results of a program are positive? The foundation or donor or the grantee?

**VM:** Foundations and nonprofits increasingly are being asked to demonstrate results, and more and more of them are using funding strategies and metrics to measure outcomes and publicize them. That's fine. In fact, it's important, because good work and resources can be wasted if people don't know how to budget or formulate strategies to plan for the future. There's a delicate balance, however, between who funds the process and who is responsible for making the decisions. Is the nonprofit doing something mostly because a donor or a foundation wants to fund it? Or not doing something because it might cause controversy or generate public scrutiny? Is it paying too much attention to a local legislator's complaints, to management consultants and advisory and foundation program staff who may not know as much about a subject area or the specifics of the nonprofit's work as they think they do?

It is very hard for nonprofits that need funding to say no to a donor, to push back with hard questions, or to say, "That's too much your strategy, your idea of what we need — and too much money. It will ruin us." The danger is what I call funder-sponsored mission creep, and you see it all the time — missions that keep changing to fit a funder's agenda or the shifting sands of public opinion. It's something nonprofits and foundations need to think more about: if you were established for a specific purpose but are continually morphing into something else, you're probably not going to be as effective as you could or should be. It's also fine to go out of business when a job has been accomplished, or to join forces with others to accomplish a goal or set of goals.

**FC:** The idea of too much money would strike most nonprofit executives as exactly the kind of problem they'd like to have.

**VM:** Too much money often creates a higher risk of failure than having not enough. If things are working well, more funding can usually be found. But you can't take money out of a project once it has been committed, even if the project is going off the rails. I also think there's value for nonprofits in having to go out into the marketplace to look for money from donors and the community and the public sector. Doing so is a good way to test your ideas against the competition. If you have more money than you need and are able to hire whomever and do whatever you want, things get taken for granted. You're also less likely to take advantage of a lot of the people and resources in a community that would benefit from participation in your project.

**FC:** Foundations often seem to be most comfortable working behind the scenes. Given the higher profile of philanthropy these days and increased scrutiny of the field, do you think it's appropriate for individual foundations to be less cautious about promoting their efforts and activities?

**VM:** Absolutely. So-called private foundations are actually a public trust — they're funded with tax-exempt money which otherwise would have largely gone to the government. We need to bc open and accountable as a field, we need to be less thin-skinned and more available to those who seek assistance, and we need to try more things in the hope that the public sector might fund them down the road.

> **We need to be open and accountable as a field, we need to be less thin-skinned and more available to those who seek assistance. . . .**

But it all has to be done carefully. I don't like situations where all of a sudden a foundation that has been active in a field decides it's not going to make grants for a year or two as it reevaluates its program. That can be very destructive, both in terms of the foundation's responsibility to specific projects as well as to the broader field. In situations like that, it's much better, in my opinion, to phase out a program gradually in parallel with open discussion and lot of consultation and transparency. It's important in change situations to listen and to pick the brains of the people you've come to know and trust. But don't take advantage of them. If you ask project people to do some serious thinking, give them adequate time and funding to do it well.

At the same time, it's important for foundations to stick with a focus for a reasonable period of time. Every field has a learning curve and it takes time to master the basics, to achieve something, and then have a wind-down that gives other funders or the public sector adequate time to pick up where you left off.

You're seeing more of that kind of thinking in the bigger foundations, where the foundation will commit a portion of its resources to a specific field or area over a fixed period of time. The idea is to see how it works and then, after ten years or whatever, to make a decision about sticking with it or moving on to something else. In either case, it's important to commit to a healthy investment of both time and money up front, as well as to the intellectual legwork that is part and parcel of any successful program, and to do everything humanly possible to make sure the lessons learned from the project are shared as widely as possible.

**FC:** Is it also important for foundations to communicate their failures?

**VM:** Again, absolutely. That's how everybody learns — from failures as well as successes. One of the first things I look at when considering a new proposal or project is the budget and the list of funders. My comfort level goes way up if I see foundations or individual donors whom I respect already giving support. If I have a contact, I'll pick up the phone and say, "I've just seen something from so and so, what do you think?" Or, "Why are you funding them — or why have you stopped funding them?" It saves you from having to reinvent the wheel. The same thing applies if you make a mistake. You have to ask, "Whose mistake was it? Did we really understand the proposal? Did we put in too much money? Were our expectations too high? Had we thought through our involvement going forward?" When something fails, you have to take the time to look for the positives and any lessons learned, and to at least consider how some amount of continued support can help the organization or the field learn something from the experience.

**FC:** Back in 1987 you suggested that restoring public faith in government and other institutions was a worthwhile challenge for philanthropy to take up. Do you feel as strongly about that today as you did twenty years ago?

**VM:** I feel more strongly about it. In the last five to ten years, particularly since 9/11, the confidence of Americans in their government and other institutions has sunk to historic lows, as has the confidence of the world in us. The mixed participation rate of Americans in the electoral process is just one illustration of the disillusionment and feeling of powerlessness experienced by many, many Americans. But how do people find the hope and optimism that would motivate them to participate? Foundations and nonprofits can do a lot about that. There is a growing appreciation, for example, of the importance of ethnic media and grassroots publications in minority and underserved communities. In California, more people get their news and commentary from ethnic media than from the mainstream media. San Francisco-based New America Media, for instance, has become a model for promoting minority voices nationally. Similarly, institutions of all kinds increasingly are perceived as being less responsive to the commonweal and more likely to serve the interest of big business. That's not a sustainable trend. If allowed to continue, it will ultimately destroy the fabric of this country and turn our friends into enemies. Philanthropy can and should play a much bigger role in documenting the influences of and changes in the global economy, in informing the public about transnational issues, in funding research and scholarship on solutions to transnational problems, and in leading the way with bold new ideas. There's a lot more we can do to step up to the plate.

> **Philanthropy can and should play a much bigger role in documenting the influences of and changes in the global economy. . . .**

**FC:** In terms of specific problems or issues, where do you see the best chance for philanthropy to make a breakthrough over the next decade or so?

**VM:** I would say continuing to play a leading role in coming up with solutions to public health crises, to ending malnutrition and hunger, to addressing looming water shortages, and to mitigating global climate change. It's a tall order, in that it will mean doing things to change the activities of not just the U.S. government and corporate America, but governments, businesses, and citizens around the globe.

It also means working in a more focused way to change the climate of opinion in the United States and elsewhere through research and the dissemination of objective research findings. And it means working to influence the media to see problems differently and to help shape the development of new media forms that are available to the masses. We can do that, in part, by developing cheaper laptops and providing Web access in remote areas of the globe. I mean, if you can have a hand-cranked radio, why can't you have a hand-cranked laptop that can connect to the Internet?

In the last decade, thanks to the Web, we've seen whole communities, regions, and even countries leapfrog a hundred years of expensive landline infrastructure, with tremendous results. At the same time, it has opened a Pandora's box of hopes and expectations. Private philanthropy can do a great deal to develop models and document ways that government can connect to this new global, digitally savvy generation. Who knows, maybe it can even figure out a way to change the conversation about taxes and distribution of wealth? I mean, it's crazy to think we can pay less and less in taxes and still live in a fully functioning society, let alone remain a global power and leader. Philanthropy, unlike other sectors, can play a role in changing perceptions of our actions and motives without being inappropriately political; it has much more potential than it realizes to influence and speak from a position of authority.

**FC:** If you were advising a new donor today, what two or three things would you recommend that person do in order to be an effective philanthropist?

**VM:** One, get involved sooner rather than later in your giving and try to learn as you think it through for the long run. Two, learn how to listen and do periodic hard-nosed appraisals of your own expertise as well as your tolerance for change and experimentation. Three, try to be relaxed and open about what you're doing. Talk about it with your spouse and your children and family. Be sure to tell them why you're interested in doing something and try to involve them in your activities. And four, learn from the world around you and don't allow yourself to believe you're the only one who can change it.

There is a great diversity of ideas in philanthropy and great freedom to learn and experience different perspectives. But it's also hard work and requires discipline. Done well, the results can be very satisfying and uplifting. Those of us with a say in the allocation of philanthropic resources have the opportunity to make a significant difference in this world. Having that responsibility and how well we handle it is both a privilege and a challenge. But at the end of the day, you couldn't ask for more interesting or rewarding work.

**FC:** Well, thanks for speaking with us today, Vinny.

**VM:** Thank you.

*Mitch Nauffts, editorial director of* Philanthropy News Digest, *spoke with Vincent McGee in November 2006.*

# 6

# Building Nonprofit Capacity Through Challenge Grants

John E. Marshall III
President/CEO Emeritus
Kresge Foundation

*Over the last century, certain foundations have become identified with specific causes or innovations: Carnegie and children's programming for public television, Rockefeller and the Green Revolution in food production, Mott and the growth of community foundations, Gates and global public health. And then there's the Kresge Foundation (www.kresge.org), which, since its establishment in 1924 by S.S. Kresge, the founder of the S.S. Kresge Company (later known as Kmart), has embraced a type of support — the challenge grant — and transformed it into a powerful, multi-faceted tool designed to build the capacity and effectiveness of its nonprofit grantees.*

*The Foundation Center's* Philanthropy News Digest *spoke with John E. Marshall III, Kresge's longtime president and CEO, about the evolution of the challenge grant at the foundation, the importance of effective board leadership to the success of nonprofit organizations, the role of foundations in helping society adapt to disruptive change, and the foundation's new "green" headquarters building in Troy, Michigan.*

*Marshall joined the foundation as vice president in 1979, was named president in 1987, became a trustee in 1991, and was promoted to CEO in 1993. Prior to joining the foundation, he served as executive director of the Rhode Island Foundation (1975–79), as associate director of development at Brown University (1972–75), and as advertising manager for U.N. Alloy Steel Corporation in Boston (1968–70).*

*An alumnus of Brown ('64), he serves or has served on the boards of the Detroit Downtown Partnership, the Health Foundation for the Americas, the Detroit 300 Conservancy Endowment, City Year Detroit, New Detroit, and the Association of Hole in the Wall Camps Foundation. He also is a member of the Community Foundation for Southeastern Michigan's GreenWays Initiative Leadership Advisory Committee and the Detroit Riverfront Conservancy board, and serves as co-chair of the Panel on the Nonprofit Sector's Working Group on Self-Regulation and on the Council on Foundations' Working Group on Stewardship Principles for Independent Foundations.*

*Mr. Marshall stepped down as president and CEO of the foundation on June 30, 2006.*

---

**Foundation Center (FC):** You've described the Kresge Foundation as the most misunderstood foundation in America. In what way is it misunderstood?

**John Marshall (JM):** I think most people see our main interest as being in the built structures we support. We're known for capital funding — nobody does it as extensively as we do, and so people often think that's our primary interest. But it isn't. Actually, we take a very hands-off approach to the capital projects presented to us, in that we really don't intrude that much on individual boards and staffs with respect to the planning of a project. People think we do, that that's how we add value, whereas we like to think we do that by using a capital campaign as an opportunity to engage with a nonprofit when it is focused on trying to accomplish something that will move the organization forward. If we can get to the organization early enough, we feel we can help it build on its existing capacities in a variety of ways, in addition to having a building at the end of the process.

**FC:** Is that what you mean when you describe Kresge's role as that of a catalyst rather than a funder?

**JM:** Yes. If the building of a building by definition requires a lot of people to work together, our view is that the process can and should be used to achieve something bigger than the sum of its parts. I'm talking about obvious things like the ability to offer improved or expanded programming or to develop a stronger base of support. The difficulty comes in measuring something like that. The way we do it is to look for evidence of growth in the number of new gifts, in larger gifts from existing funding sources, in a board of directors that has engaged with and invested in the process and reaffirmed their commitment to the organization, in executive directors who have a new set of milestones or benchmarks against which to measure the development of their organizations, in higher organizational visibility, and so on.

**FC:** Kresge is famous for awarding challenge grants. Has the challenge grant always been an important instrument in the foundation's toolkit?

**JM:** Yes, almost from the beginning. I think the origin of the challenge grant here was based in a desire to make the application process manageable for both the applicant organization and the foundation, which in the early days was just a small group of officers of the S.S. Kresge corporation. In business terms, I think Mr. Kresge — who was a businessman, after all — wanted to know that people who received money from his foundation would use it to accomplish two things: raise the rest of the money they needed to build the building they wanted to build; and two, to sign a contract with a builder so that everyone could be reasonably sure the building would be built. What we've done with those two simple expectations is to fold them into a much more elaborate capacity-building process that pushes a nonprofit to achieve some of the other growth milestones I mentioned. And the challenge grant helps to drive that because it creates both an opportunity and a deadline that requires people to work against a carefully conceived plan if they hope to make it happen.

> . . . a Kresge challenge grant creates both an opportunity and a deadline that requires people to work against a carefully conceived plan. . . .

**FC:** You mentioned the importance of effective board leadership to the success of nonprofit organizations. Have you and your colleagues developed metrics to measure board effectiveness in a nonprofit context?

**JM:** Carrying a project such as the ones we fund to a successful conclusion requires leadership. In fact, we will not engage with a nonprofit unless it is able to demonstrate leadership at the board level.

If an organization comes to us with directors that have not committed their own personal gifts to the project in question, or that have not agreed to work within the campaign structure to help bring the project to the attention of others, we simply don't see it as an opportunity to build capacity and are unlikely to fund that project. We also expect that an organization will come to us with several of the larger gifts needed for a successful campaign already committed, as well as with a campaign organization already in place and functioning in terms of securing gifts from individuals outside the organization.

> . . . we will not engage with a nonprofit unless it is able to demonstrate leadership at the board level. . . .

**FC:** Do you have those expectations regardless of the size of the organization?

**JM:** The expectation that boards will commit their own funds and that they will provide leadership? Absolutely. We realize that some organizations do not have boards that are populated by people of great discretionary income or wealth, so in those cases we want to see leadership by participation — essentially, show us that your board members have given according to their ability to give.

**FC:** What do you do in situations where a board and staff are prepared to lead but the community being served is challenged in its ability to support an organization?

**JM:** In those situations, we inquire as to the incremental growth that is planned, realizing that transformational change is a step-by-step process, and we hope to learn from their experience.

**FC:** Is it your view that growth and success are synonymous in the nonprofit world?

**JM:** Not growth for growth's sake. But an organization that is able to support its programs with ever-increasing donated and volunteer support obviously has more options than an organization that can't. Remember, in much of the nonprofit sector, where operating costs are largely supported by contracts, reimbursements, and earned income, the role of internal stakeholders in governance and program origination can be overwhelmed by the needs and agendas of funders. In my opinion, the nonprofit that has a healthy, alternative stream of support from a committed donor base is more likely to innovate in its programming and do a better job of serving the community whose mission it is to serve than an organization that has to rely on contracts and outside funders.

**FC:** Earlier this year, you and your colleagues unveiled a newly renovated "green" headquarters building. Can you tell us what's special about the building? And how did a Midwestern foundation like Kresge get into the sustainable design business?

**JM:** We got into sustainable design because we were starting to hear about it from lots of different people. Finally, at our last board-staff planning retreat, we asked ourselves whether, as a funder of capital projects, we should take a position on sustainable design. As I said earlier, we try not to intrude in the project-selection process, but with a new technology paradigm emerging we felt it was time to ask whether we should encourage nonprofits to be part of the workout of some these strategies and approaches. And the answer from our board and staff was yes.

So, we developed a three-part program. Part one focuses on educating nonprofits, which we do through an area of our Web site and two very informative pamphlets that explore sustainable design and green building techniques. Part two is centered around planning grants, which we offer to qualified organizations — in part because we've learned that truly integrative green design is more costly than traditional design. At the same time, the earlier in the design process an organization explores its sustainable design options, the more money it's likely to save over the long haul. And the third part of the program revolves around bonus grants to organizations that go through our normal challenge grant process and decide to have their projects certified under the U.S. Green Buildings Council's LEED Program. The idea is that we can use those grants to reward nonprofits for having been early adopters and for calling attention to the fact that nonprofit organizations are successfully adopting green building practices.

> **. . . the nonprofit that has a healthy, alternative stream of support from a committed donor base is more likely to innovate. . . .**

Not surprisingly, we've had a good response to the program. We've exhausted the planning-grant fund twice and replenished it both times, and the bonus grants . . . well, it takes a year after a project has been completed to be certified under the LEED program, so we've paid out only one or two of those. But we've committed to a good number of them, and the education component of the program is very popular. We're seeing lots of traffic to the Web site, and we've been doing some orientation meetings around the country in conjunction with the Nonprofit Finance Fund in New York.

> **. . . we can use those grants to reward nonprofits for calling attention to the fact that nonprofit organizations are successfully adopting green building practices. . . .**

Now, you also asked what's special about our building. For us, the really special aspect of it is that we have combined a stone farmhouse built in 1850 with a brand-new structure that employs many of the new approaches and techniques we've all read about — everything, that is, except solar and wind power. For most people who visit us, the elements that are really interesting are the geothermal closed-loop well system for heating and cooling the building, the use of so-called green roofs on a limited basis, and the way the building is sited, which allows us to shade the building's interior spaces from the most intense effects of the sun but also, through the use of light shelves, to bounce sunlight off the ceiling, thereby greatly reducing the need for conventional lighting. The building also has a raised-floor HVAC system, which means that only the first six feet of the vertical interior space need to be conditioned, instead of all the way up to the ceiling, which is the norm with conventional HVAC systems. And we divert rain runoff from the parking lot through a special paving application and from the roofs into retention ponds and a cistern. The collected rainfall is partly used for irrigation of the green roofs, but mostly it is simply absorbed naturally so as not to overcharge the municipal storm sewer. All of these systems are up and running and are being monitored, and we've taken steps to integrate the whole site into an educational component of the program. For example, nonprofit leaders who visit us — and we have four hundred to five hundred appointments a year with agencies that are seeking funding — are introduced to these concepts. We have also pledged to report our findings, in terms of what worked and what didn't, to the broader public.

**FC:** I grew up in the Midwest and know that it's cold and cloudy for a good part of the year. Are you saying that green building design and green concepts can be adapted to any environment and climate, even cold and cloudy ones? And is that message being heard by nonprofits in sun-challenged regions of the country?

**JM:** More and more so, yes. We talked ourselves out of solar and wind power, but some of the simplest things you can do are the most effective in terms of keeping a building light and open-looking without letting a lot of solar radiation in and putting a tremendous load on the HVAC system to cool the building.

**FC:** Do you think Kresge will be funding sustainable design a decade from now?

**JM:** That will depend on the experience of our grantees and our own project.

**FC:** While we're on the subject of the Midwest, do you despair of the region's economic future? And if not, what do you see as potential catalysts for its economic recovery and long-term viability?

> **History teaches us that every economy goes through periods in which it has to adjust to disruptive change — we're not going to get a pass on that. . . .**

**JM:** The industrial Midwest is certainly challenged these days, and everyone is aware of that. But people in Detroit and other metropolitan areas in the region are used to a cyclical economy. Sometimes the local economy is in sync with the rest of the country, and sometimes it isn't. People in this part of the country have lived through booms and busts in the past, and so they're not inclined to adopt a sky-is-falling mentality. That said, the current downturn is deeper and probably has lasted longer than previous downturns, and that has everyone concerned.

On the plus side, the region possesses a wealth of engineering and design talent, and if down the road there is less demand for that talent on the automotive and auto supply side, it stands to reason that those talents could be applied to related or even unrelated industries. History teaches us that every economy goes through periods in which it has to adjust to disruptive change — we're not going to get a pass on that. The economy of this region was once driven by timber, then metal fabrication, principally for use in building stoves, and then the auto industry. So, change is inevitable, and change will come. The second-largest industry in Michigan is agriculture, which would probably surprise most people. We also have a concentration of major health centers and universities in Michigan, and those are areas, along with information technology and the finance and knowledge-related businesses, that show promise and are likely to help drive our economy in the future.

> . . . perhaps our greatest contribution is in working to make the region a place where people want to live and build a future. . . .

**FC:** Do foundations have a role to play in helping the region navigate that transition?

**JM:** Well, we certainly do in terms of supporting nonprofits that are engaged in supporting that process. The Kresge Foundation has had a special program in Detroit for the last thirteen years through which we have committed about $140 million and which, in turn, has generated in excess of $1 billion in project development funding, a lot of it bricks and mortar but some of it for endowment and program. But perhaps our greatest contribution, and the area where other foundations are most likely to have an impact, is in working to make the region a place where people want to live and build a future. Before people will do that, they need to be assured that the quality of life a region has to offer — from its schools, to its arts and cultural opportunities, to its healthcare systems — lives up to their expectations. I don't think you can underestimate the importance of that.

**FC:** Helmut Anheier and Diana Leat, the authors of a new book about philanthropy, have written that, "The potential of foundations is largely unfilled due to a low-key malaise affecting the foundation sector." They further suggest that this malaise is not about money or governance or debates about payout; it's about "a lack of awareness of what is possible and the largely unrealized potential of foundations." Do you agree? And are foundations doing the best they possibly can in what is a rather challenging environment for nonprofits?

**JM:** Well, I can't presume to know what evidence they would point to from just that quote. But remember, the foundation field is extremely diverse and full of people and organizations working on lots of different problems from lots of different directions. You have everything from small family foundations that were set up two or three generations ago and are still operated by family members as a family activity, to very large staffed foundations with relatively high administrative expense ratios, to operating foundations that create and run their own programs and grantees. Here at Kresge, we take the position that if you find a mechanism that strengthens an organization and find people that are eager to go through your application process and value your grant not as the be-all and end-all, but rather as a useful tool in a toolkit full of useful tools, you have a good chance of strengthening that organization and, in the process, strengthening the community or communities it was created to serve. We also take the position that there is more talent and innovation in our community of nonprofits that is waiting to be released than probably can be imagined or prototyped by any group of staff members or trustees. We certainly acknowledge that foundations have been responsible, directly or otherwise, for great breakthroughs in science and for the development of pioneering social models. Yet, behind most of those breakthroughs are groups of committed people, volunteers and paid staff, who created a platform from which those discoveries could be made and implemented.

**FC:** Do you worry that foundations are too wedded to twentieth-century models and practices to remain relevant and/or have impact on the problems of the twenty-first century?

**JM:** Every field needs to be prodded by individuals and entities willing to take a different path and to push others to try new ways of delivering what they have to deliver. I welcome any development that challenges conventional thinking. But I also worry that we live in a culture in which change is supported for the sake of change itself. For example, while the Coca Cola Company has a lot of products to keep itself growing in the twenty-first century, my suspicion is that Classic Coke is still one of its more successful products.

*. . . what we have been able to do here is to take a model that was working and refine it into one that works better. . . .*

**FC:** You're getting ready to step down as president and CEO of the foundation after almost fifteen years as CEO and twenty years as the foundation's president. As you look back on your tenure, what are you most proud of?

**JM:** Actually, it's twelve as CEO and not quite twenty as president. But looking back, I would say that what we have been able to do here is to take a model that was working and refine it into one that works better with respect to building capacity within the nonprofits we support. There have been many occasions when an organization told us that whether or not their application resulted in a grant, our process was not only helpful but in some cases encouraged people to step forward with an extraordinary act of leadership; that's what the process is designed to do — to turn a capital campaign into a truly transformational experience. The sessions that work best here are those that involve the director or president of an organization, a board or campaign chair, and the director of development. Those three positions are critical to the kind of creative planning that results in growth, and coming out here to talk to us oftentimes creates an atmosphere in which a lot of important issues end up on the table. In fact, I sometimes think that a good deal of the hard work is done on the plane ride out to see us and the return trip back home.

> . . . that's what the process is designed to do — to turn a capital campaign into a truly transformational experience. . . .

**FC:** Rip Rapson, former president of the McKnight Foundation in Minneapolis, was named to succeed you last December. Was your board as careful in choosing your successor as it is in awarding grants, and were you involved in that process? And what makes Mr. Rapson well suited to be the next president of the Kresge Foundation?

**JM:** I'm sure that the search committee, and then the full board, was careful in the search; it took a great deal of their time and effort! I was not part of the process except for briefing the board on what I felt were appropriate skills and experiences and to meet with the three finalists as a resource to their own inquiries. I have met Rip at a few conferences and have found him to be an intelligent, concerned grantmaker, and I wish him all success in his new role.

**FC:** A final question: What is your greatest hope for the colleagues you'll be leaving behind, as well as the field as a whole?

**JM:** My greatest hope for my colleagues is that they truly understand the privilege of the professional positions they occupy, that they take advantage of them to learn from their applicants, that they continue to appreciate that there are limits to their respective roles and responsibilities, but that they also appreciate the collective accomplishment of the nonprofit organizations that approach them for support. Foundations provide about 5 percent of all the funding contributed to nonprofits every year, while individuals contribute something on the order of 80 percent to 85 percent. With that in mind, we have long felt here that the real value of our programs lies not so much in the collaborative programs we develop with other foundations or corporations or government — although those are extremely valuable. Instead, the greatest potential for leadership in the nonprofit sector lies with individuals. As Tocqueville first observed back in the 1830s, when Americans see a need they form a committee and address it. And because that impulse continues to drive many of our most established nonprofits, not to mention the countless number of new ones formed every year, we believe that the way foundations can be most effective is to empower creative individuals by building the capacity of nonprofit organizations.

**FC:** Well, thank you for your time this morning, Mr. Marshall.

**JM:** Thank you.

*Mitch Nauffts, editorial director of* Philanthropy News Digest, *spoke with John Marshall in May 2006.*

# Expanding Opportunity for All Californians

James E. Canales
President and CEO
James Irvine Foundation

*California is a state of superlatives. The most populous state in the Union (home to one of every eight Americans), it boasts an economy that produces $1.4 trillion annually in gross product and ranks as the fifth-largest in the world. Long an agricultural powerhouse, the state also has world-class aerospace, entertainment, technology, and tourism industries; processes (through the ports of Long Beach and Los Angeles) a quarter of all the container cargo shipped to the U.S.; and offers its residents the largest (and one of the best) public university systems in the country.*

*For all its wealth, however, it's also a state of contrasts. Only the third state (after New Mexico and Hawaii) without a majority ethnic group, it contains within its borders some of the most affluent — and poorest — communities in the country. For every Belvedere, Beverly Hills, or Newport, there's a Tobin, Cutler, or Cantua Creek — communities whose lack of infrastructure, services, and opportunities qualify them as among the most disadvantaged in the U.S. And nowhere is that poverty more stark, or those contrasts more pronounced, than in the state's Central and San Joaquin valleys.*

*The Foundation Center's* Philanthropy News Digest *spoke with Jim Canales, president and chief executive officer of the James Irvine Foundation (www.irvine.org), a San Francisco-based foundation dedicated to expanding opportunity for all Californians, about the demographic and economic challenges confronting the state, the foundation's work in the Central Valley and Inland Empire, and the importance of leadership as a driver of change.*

*Canales was named president of the foundation in 2003, and prior to that served as its vice president and corporate secretary for four years, providing oversight for Irvine's grantmaking programs and communications and evaluation functions. His service at the foundation began in 1993 and has included roles as special assistant to the president, program officer, and chief administrative officer/corporate secretary.*

*A graduate of Stanford University and a co-founder and past board chair of Grantmakers for Effective Organizations, he is active on the boards of various nonprofit organizations and currently serves on the board of trustees of Stanford University, the Monterey Bay Aquarium, and the Education Financing Foundation of California, a newly created private foundation dedicated to helping California students attend college.*

―――――――――――――――――――

**Foundation Center (FC):** Tell us how you got into nonprofit work, and how you wound up at the James Irvine Foundation?

**Jim Canales (JC):** My initial thought when I was an undergrad was to go into education, so I stayed on at Stanford to get a master's in education as well as a single-subject teaching credential in English, which in turn led to a teaching job at San Francisco University High School. I really enjoyed my time there. I taught English, coached cross-country, was a class dean, and eventually became director of admissions and financial aid. Then, in 1993, I was offered a job at Irvine as Dennis Collins's special assistant. Dennis, of course, was the longtime president of the foundation and had been the founding headmaster at University High. In part because the offer allowed me to stay in a nonprofit educational environment, it just seemed like the right job at the right time.

So I took it and have had wonderful opportunities in the twelve years I've been here. I was special assistant to the president for a few years; I then became a program officer and, eventually, the foundation's chief administrative officer. In 1999, I was named a vice president, with responsibility for communications, evaluation, programs, and grantmaking. Finally, in 2003, I was given the terrific opportunity to lead the foundation — which, as you can imagine, has been an enormous privilege.

**FC:** The James Irvine Foundation was established in 1937 by James Irvine, one of California's agricultural pioneers, and was guided for years by close associates of his. Sixty-eight years after its establishment, is the foundation still a family foundation?

> . . . many of the values that led Mr. Irvine to create the foundation still inform its work today. . . .

**JC:** If you define a family foundation in the traditional sense — as one whose founding family is still involved in its operations — then the answer is no. We do not have any family members on the board, and indeed Mr. Irvine, when he created the foundation, did not give the family the controlling vote on the board of directors. There certainly were family members on the board in those early years, but even in the '70s, '80s, and '90s, we had only one family member on the board, and that was Katie Wheeler, Mr. Irvine's granddaughter, who served on the board for forty-seven years, until her retirement in 1997. So, in one sense, the foundation has never been a "traditional" family foundation.

At the same time, many of the values that led Mr. Irvine to create the foundation still inform its work today. For example, one thing Mr. Irvine speaks of in the indenture of trust, which guides the foundation's work, is the concept of the foundation working to provide Californians with an opportunity "to gain a leg up" — he even used that expression in some of the founding documents. And, indeed, that charge has remained a critical component of the way we think about the role of the James Irvine Foundation, except that we express it slightly differently today in our mission statement, which says that the foundation works to expand opportunity for all Californians. In fact, today we are the largest multipurpose private foundation in the state established to benefit Californians only. There are other foundations in California that are larger, but they work, at least in part, nationally and even internationally, or focus on a particular program area, such as health and health care. That puts us in a unique and wonderful position to help the people of this state — something James Irvine would have understood and been proud of.

**FC:** The historian Kevin Starr, who also happens to be California's librarian emeritus, has written that the state's most salient demographic feature is its diversity, as illustrated by the fact that one out of every four Californians was born outside the United States. To what extent does the state's demographic diversity inform your programs and approach to grantmaking?

**The diversity of California is one of the key issues informing the work of the foundation today. . . .**

**JC:** The diversity of the state is one of the key issues informing the work of the foundation today, and we tend to think about that diversity in three ways: ethnic diversity, economic diversity, and the diversity of the state's many different geographic regions.

In terms of ethnic diversity, you're right: One in four Californians today was born outside the United States. As you also probably know, California is one of the few states in the union where a majority of the state's residents are non-white. And those demographic trends are going to result in an even more diverse population over the next twenty to thirty years. So we think a lot about the ways in which we can work, through our grantmaking programs, to make the state a more livable and harmonious place for all its residents, regardless of race or ethnicity.

Socioeconomic diversity is another big issue for us. For all the talk about California having the fifth-largest economy in the world, parts of this state are really poor. It's important to us to change that reality and support opportunities for people from low-income environments.

In terms of geographic diversity, we are very focused on the fact that the state's major population centers, as well as its media and political power, are concentrated in the state's coastal regions. But as we look to the future — and this is already starting to play out — the inland portions of the state are going to become more and more important. The state's population today is roughly thirty-six million, and it's projected that within the next twenty years the population will grow to between forty-five million and forty-six million people — an almost 50 percent increase. But here's the interesting thing: The inland portions of the state — the Central Valley and the Inland Empire, which consists of Riverside and San Bernardino counties — are going to grow by more than 50 percent over the next twenty years, while the coastal regions will grow by only 15 percent. Because we're very concerned about whether these inland counties are prepared to deal with that kind of growth, we have identified both the Central Valley and the Inland Empire as regions of priority interest and are working to engage more deeply in these regions to help build their nonprofit and philanthropic infrastructure and the leadership we think they will need in the social and civic arenas to be able to handle that growth.

**FC:** Both regions are substantially agricultural in nature and have large minority populations, correct?

**JC:** Certainly that's true of the Central Valley, where agriculture continues to be the dominant economic force. In contrast, the Inland Empire, which had been largely rural for much of the twentieth century, has been changing as land pressure and rising real estate prices force more and more people from the greater Los Angeles-Orange County area to relocate to less expensive communities and regions of the state. As a result, we now have many people who commute significant distances from Riverside and San Bernardino counties, where they can afford to buy homes and provide opportunities and a good quality of life for their families, to their jobs in Los Angeles or Orange County. And that's creating significant pressures — in terms of sprawl, traffic, water, and other infrastructure issues — as well as opportunity for the region.

**FC:** You mentioned some of the economic pressures on Californians. Increasingly, agriculture is a global business, as is technology, another of the economic pillars of your state. In terms of grantmaking, are you doing anything to mitigate the adverse consequences of globalization on the state's economy?

> **We're a young state — and getting younger — and one of our concerns is whether young Californians are prepared and equipped to participate in the global economy of the twenty-first century. . . .**

**JC:** As we look at the population in the state today, we realize that we're a young state — and getting younger — and so one of our great concerns is whether young Californians are prepared and equipped to participate, in a meaningful way, in the global economy of the twenty-first century. Unfortunately, we see some significant disconnects between the reality around us and the opportunity, particularly the disproportionate number of low-income and minority students who are dropping out of high school. As we look to the future, we are focusing on how we can increase the number of low-income Californians who graduate from high school on time and who go on to receive some kind of postsecondary credential by their mid-twenties. In our view, the solution must involve the development of multiple pathways to meaningful adulthood for these youth. It's not just about graduating from high school and going straight to a four-year college or university; it's about ensuring that there is a range of options for low-income and minority students that makes it possible for them to find a path leading to economic success and engagement with the civic life of their communities. That's something we're very much focused on.

**FC:** If one defines "strategic philanthropy" as using outcomes and measurement to define and shape an effective giving strategy, does the James Irvine Foundation take a strategic approach to its grantmaking?

**JC:** I certainly want to believe we do. But these are the questions we ask: Are we being clear about what it is we seek to achieve? Are we holding ourselves accountable to our objectives and assessing our progress toward those objectives, and refining our approach as necessary? And are we finding ways to share the lessons we have learned with colleagues in the philanthropic arena?

In addition to those questions, we've spent considerable time thinking about how we should characterize Irvine's approach to its philanthropic work, and have identified four principles that are salient to the way we approach our grantmaking. Let me say that I don't think they make us unique — there are many foundations doing the same kind of thing — but what's important, from our perspective, is that we've articulated these principles and are holding ourselves accountable to them in our day-to-day work.

The first of these principles is a focus on place — understanding that as a regional grantmaker we have an obligation to think about California and about the different regions within California. Many of our approaches are very attuned to the particular environment or region in which we are working and must often be customized to the specific needs of that region or environment. The second principle is about building effective organizations. As we make grants to individual organizations and institutions, we're focused on ensuring that we find ways to build elements into those grants which strengthen our grantees' infrastructure and overall effectiveness. The third is to build leadership through our grantmaking, and to think about ways we can develop the leaders of tomorrow — that's a vital component of our approach. And the fourth involves thinking about ways we can go beyond grants and use our intellectual capital to connect — whether through convening, networking, or brokering relationships — the efforts we support with similar efforts in order to maximize the impact of our grant dollars and enhance the effectiveness of our grantees.

**FC:** Obviously, you and your colleagues place a great deal of importance on leadership. Can you tell us a bit more about what the James Irvine Foundation is doing to foster effective leadership in California nonprofits?

**JC:** We're convinced that one of the keys to achieving the mission we've articulated for our foundation is to ensure that we are fostering the new leadership this state will need and, at the same time, nurturing those who are in leadership roles today so that they can continue to be effective. Let me give you an example. We recently made a series of grants as part of a new initiative we call the Fund for Leadership Advancement, which will focus, at least initially, on Irvine grantees. Through a competitive application process, we've identified eight leaders at Irvine grantee organizations to receive grants of up to $75,000. These resources will support customized professional development activities that are designed to enhance the ability of these leaders to direct their organizations and which, at the same time, are linked to what their organizations are trying to achieve. That's important. We don't want this to be seen as a professional-development opportunity that's disconnected from the day-to-day work of the organization; we want it to be integrated with that work and the organization's challenges and opportunities.

> . . . one of the keys to achieving the mission we've articulated for our foundation is to ensure that we are fostering the new leadership and nurturing those who are in leadership roles today. . . .

**FC:** Does the program target a certain demographic?

**JC:** We made a conscious effort to ensure that the first eight recipients were representative of the diversity of our state.

**FC:** I know the fund is new, but in the short time it's been up and running have you noticed any commonalities in the kinds of challenges faced by nonprofit leaders in California?

**JC:** It's well documented that one of the great challenges for many talented executive directors of nonprofits today is the fact that so many of them feel, or are on their way to feeling, burned-out. You've probably seen the studies produced by groups like CompassPoint, here in the Bay Area, which point to the fact that many current executive directors would not seek another ED position because of the burnout factor. Many of them feel immense pressures to raise funds and will tell you they spend more time on fundraising activities than on the core work of their organization. And that's one of the objectives of the Fund for Leadership Advancement initiative — to provide talented, capable nonprofit leaders with tools that will help them stretch and expand their skills and, at the same time, provide them with resources that will help them to address some of the institutional challenges they might be facing.

> **I think one of the key challenges facing the sector is whether we are doing enough to foster the next generation of nonprofit leaders. . . .**

But it goes beyond that. I think one of the key challenges facing the sector is whether we are doing enough to foster the next generation of nonprofit leaders. You often hear people bemoan the fact that there are no John Gardners around today, that the sector lacks powerful and effective spokespeople, and I think that "leadership gap," if you will, is something we all need to think about. How do we equip people to play that role on behalf of the sector, and what kind of conscious strategies are we putting in place to ensure that the sector will be ably led tomorrow? It's a challenge we're very much focused on here, and as we do more work in this area I hope we'll be able to share lots of information and valuable lessons about ways not only to support nonprofit leaders, but ways to surface new leaders.

**FC:** As much as we've all heard that philanthropy is about relationships — between organizations, between people — one also hears grumbling from time to time about the uneven power dynamic that exists between funders and grantees. Have you and your colleagues done anything to change or mitigate that dynamic?

**JC:** In my opinion, this is a critical issue for the field, and at Irvine we are working very hard to remain attuned to the dynamic you've described. The most important way we do that is to ensure that the people who represent the foundation are always aware of their privileged position and good fortune. As long as my colleagues, our board, and yours truly approach our work with humility and a desire to meet the great obligation conferred on us by the tax-exempt resources at our disposal, I think we'll be able to keep this power imbalance from undermining our work. As I say, it's something we're very much attuned to and think about, even when we're hiring. We put a premium on hiring people who can bring to their work here a sense of what it's like to be on the other side of the table. In fact, we have a number of people on staff who either have run nonprofit organizations or have been on staff at a nonprofit organization and understand how difficult it can be to come to a foundation office and ask for support.

**FC:** The private foundation structure is a legacy of the great fortunes created during the Industrial Revolution. Is that structure suited to the unique challenges we face today? In other words, are private foundations flexible enough, and do they take enough risks, to tackle the challenges — global warming, the spread of WMDs, the need to reform public education — we face in the twenty-first century?

> **We put a premium on hiring people who can bring to their work here a sense of what it's like to be on the other side of the table. . . .**

**JC:** I would like to believe it is, but I think in order for private foundations to address those challenges it is critical they remain attuned to the environment in which they are working and remain focused on refining their strategies based on what they learn from that environment. Let me give you an example.

One out of every ten Californians lives in the Inland Empire, and the region's population is projected to grow from approximately 3.8 million people today to just over five million people in the year 2020. This is a region that today has more residents than half the states in the U.S., and yet a significant number of Californians don't know what or where it is. It's also one of the poorest and least-educated regions in the state. Obviously, the region presents huge challenges, and the only way we have any chance of creating opportunity and a better future for the people who live there is by truly understanding the forces and trends that are shaping the region today and how those forces and trends will shape its future.

So, yes, I think that our commitment to the people of California — and to the people of the Inland Empire, in particular — is something that not only informs our strategy but will enable us to make a difference in the region and the state as a whole. And I think the same thing can be said of private foundations in general: If they stick to what they know and feed the lessons they learn back into their work, they can be very effective in addressing some of these big challenges.

**FC:** As you and your staff consider whether to devote resources to a specific problem, what kind of time frame do you think in terms of? And has that calculation changed as the foundation's assets and the scope of its work have grown?

**JC:** The question of time frames is an interesting one. Generally speaking, I think grantmakers need to foster a certain amount of creative tension between having a sense of urgency, on the one hand, and being deliberate and thoughtful on the other. Certainly, we need to have a sense of urgency about some of the challenges we've been talking about. But at the same time we have this wonderful luxury — and, indeed, obligation — of being able to take the long view and, with an eye on the future, say, "How can we begin to put in place a set of strategies and interventions that will address, or even forestall, challenges and problems that are likely to surface ten or fifteen years down the road?" Maintaining that sense of balance between the short and long term is one of the great challenges of foundation work. But, frankly, it's also one of the things that makes it exciting.

> . . . grantmakers need to foster a certain amount of creative tension between having a sense of urgency, on the one hand, and being deliberate and thoughtful on the other. . . .

**FC:** Given the nature and scope of the challenges we've been talking about, do you think American philanthropy is as generous as it could be?

**JC:** Philanthropy is fundamentally about personal choice, and what's wonderful about American philanthropy is that it accommodates all sorts of choices. After twelve years in the field, it's clear to me that the richness and diversity of the sector is only enhanced by people who bring different ideas and approaches to the work of making a difference. It's one of the exciting things about being in this field, collaborating with and learning from colleagues. It's what's exciting about the engagement of a new generation of donors with some of these problems. And it's what's exciting about the experiments that do succeed. So, speaking for myself, I hope this will always be a field that permits and encourages a range of approaches to the challenges we face as a society.

**FC:** You've been president of the Irvine Foundation for almost three years now. While it's a little early to ask you to talk about your legacy, I wonder if you could share with us some of the metrics you use to measure your own effectiveness?

> . . . Alan Pifer used to say that the human qualities of foundation staff may in the end be the most important determinate for what a foundation can achieve. . . .

**JC:** For much of the time I've been president, I've been focused on building a team here that can achieve the things we hope to achieve. Former Carnegie Corporation president Alan Pifer, who passed away last year, used to say that the human qualities of foundation staff may in the end be the most important determinate for what a foundation can achieve. I think he's absolutely right about that. He also talked about people needing to bring a sense of humility to the work, needing to be conscious of their shortcomings, and needing to have a sense of curiosity, and he was absolutely right about that, too. Having the right people on the team is critically important, and I think we're there now. We have a strong sense of purpose in terms of what we're trying to achieve in each of the program areas, and as long as we remain clear about what it is we're trying to achieve and stay focused, I think we can say, in good conscience, that we fulfilled our obligation.

**FC:** A decade from now, what do you hope to be able to say about the James Irvine Foundation and the work it has done in California?

**JC:** I would hope to be able to say that this foundation is viewed as a leadership institution in California — and I don't say that with any sense of ego. Rather, to the extent the foundation can help to frame and draw attention to some of the significant issues confronting this state and help others understand those issues and engage with them, I think we will have made an important difference. I would also hope that we'll be able to say we approached our grantmaking intelligently and thoughtfully. And I hope that along the way we will have made some good choices about who to invest in and which issues to address, so that, at the end of the day, people will view Irvine as an institution that has used its resources and standing to serve those Californians in greatest need.

**FC:** Well, thanks, Jim, for taking the time to speak with us today.

**JC:** Happy to do it. Thank you.

*Mitch Nauffts, editorial director of* Philanthropy News Digest, *spoke with Jim Canales in January 2006.*

# 8

# Building the Field of Social Entrepreneurship

Sally Osberg
President and CEO
Skoll Foundation

*As international labor expert Susan Davis notes, we live in an age of entrepreneurship. From Palo Alto to Austin, Bangalore to Boston, the rapidly changing, technology-intensive economy of the twenty-first century is generating innovation — and wealth — at a breathtaking pace. Unfortunately, far too many people have yet to enjoy the benefits of this entrepreneurial revolution. Mired in poverty, hampered by outmoded gender and generational attitudes, lacking access to meaningful work, tens of millions struggle to survive on the equivalent of a dollar or two a day.*

*In response to that grim reality, we are seeing a "revolution in the organization of human society," argues Bill Drayton, president and founder of the social change organization Ashoka. Characterized by the emergence, in country after country, of "the same sort of open, competitive-yet-collaborative relationships that marked the birth of the modern competitive business sector three centuries ago," this social entrepreneurial revolution has gone little noticed by politicians or the press. Nevertheless, says Drayton, "when the history of these times is written, no other change will compete with it in terms of importance."*

*The Foundation Center's* Philanthropy News Digest *spoke with Sally Osberg, president and CEO of the Palo Alto-based Skoll Foundation (www.skollfoundation.org), about the emerging field of social entrepreneurship and the foundation's efforts to advance systemic change by investing in, connecting, and celebrating innovative nonprofit organizations and social entrepreneurs around the globe.*

*Osberg, who joined the foundation as its first president and CEO in 2001, has more than twenty years of social sector leadership experience, with special expertise in organizational development, strategic positioning, and innovative public programming. Prior to joining the foundation, she was executive director of the Children's Discovery Museum of San Jose, which she guided from its inception to national recognition as a leader in the museum field and the broader arena of informal learning. The museum received the National Award for Museum Service from the White House in 2001. In addition, she has held adjunct faculty positions at Hamilton College and Utica College, where she was co-director of the Writing Center.*

*Ms. Osberg has served as a member of the board and president of the Association of Youth Museums, as well as on the board of the American Association of Museums and on both the Silicon Valley chapter and national boards of the American Leadership Forum. Currently, she sits on the boards of the Oracle Education Foundation and the Children's Discovery Museum, and on the advisory board of the John Gardner Center for Youth and Their Communities.*

*Osberg earned her M.A. in literature from the Claremont Graduate School and her B.A. in English from Scripps College, where she was elected to Phi Beta Kappa. In 1998, she received the John Gardner Leadership Award from the American Leadership Forum, and in 1999 the* San Jose Mercury News *named her to its "Millennium 100," recognizing her as one of the key individuals who have shaped and led Silicon Valley. Earlier this year, she was inducted into the Junior Achievement Business Hall of Fame.*

---

**Foundation Center (FC):** What is a social entrepreneur? And why has the Skoll Foundation decided to invest its resources in building the field of social entrepreneurship?

**Sally Osberg:** For us and for our founder, Jeff Skoll — a true social entrepreneur himself — social entrepreneurs are the frontline drivers of positive social change globally. We see them as pioneers, as the folks out there on the forefront who are innovating and providing the models to bring about the kind of change needed in the twenty-first century. They're like business entrepreneurs, in that they have the ability to identify an equilibrium that is unsatisfactory. But true social entrepreneurs don't stop there. They take the next step by putting in motion a strategy or creating a better model to achieve a new, more satisfying equilibrium — one that benefits those whose opportunities are limited by existing systems or whose needs are neglected by market gaps or failures.

**FC:** What do you mean by "equilibrium"?

**SO:** At the Skoll Foundation, we're systems thinkers: for us, equilibrium describes a stable state, generally economic or social, controlled by and benefiting established entities. It's a neutral term in itself, but for the social entrepreneur it represents both challenge and opportunity. The social entrepreneur sees the limitations of an existing equilibrium — the pharmaceutical industry's focus on drugs for developed country markets would be a good example — and offers a new solution with the potential to benefit those not served by the existing model.

**The social entrepreneur sees the limitations of an existing equilibrium and offers a new solution with the potential to benefit those not served by the existing model. . . .**

Most people think of Muhammad Yunus, the founder of Grameen Bank, as the quintessential social entreprencur — and he is, having demonstrated, almost single-handedly at the outset, the credit-worthiness of poor people in the developing world, which then drove him to launch the microcredit revolution. I'd like to suggest, however, that someone like Robert Redford — whose name doesn't usually surface in conversations about this field — is also a great example of a social entrepreneur. It was Redford, back in the 1970s, who identified Hollywood's limitations, seeing it as an equilibrium controlled by the studios and not at all suited to finance or nurture the emergent independent filmmaker. That realization, in turn, led him to a series of innovations that ushered in and helped build the independent film industry. It's thanks to his vision and creativity in establishing the Sundance Institute and Festival that today documentaries like *Bowling for Columbine* or *An Inconvenient Truth* — produced, proud disclaimer here!, by Jeff's media company, Participant Productions — can be successful at the box office and also have an extraordinary impact in terms of the public debate.

Let me give you another example, this one from our portfolio. Andrea and Barry Coleman were traveling in Africa in the 1990s when they were suddenly struck by the number of rusting trucks and vehicles on the side of almost every road they traveled. Well, it didn't take long for them to realize that, given the state of Africa's roads, motorcycles were a far more practical and efficient means of delivering services, especially healthcare services, in rural areas. So they set up an organization called Riders for Health to do just that. But they didn't stop there. They also understood that teaching local people how to sell and repair motorcycles, establishing the equivalent of micro-businesses, needed to be part of their strategy. It's that kind of systemic approach, that desire to establish a new equilibrium, a more efficient way of getting benefits to populations that traditionally have been marginalized, that we look for in the social entrepreneurs we support.

**FC:** Do you and your colleagues consider social entrepreneurship to be a field unto itself, or is it just one tool in the larger philanthropic toolbox?

**SO:** We view it as a field of practice that is still young but on its way to becoming a field of knowledge. In the same way that entrepreneurs tend to be the drivers of innovation in business, creating new business models that can turn into successful industries, social entrepreneurs are the frontline innovators who create new, more successful ways of bringing about positive social change. At the same time, we think it's important to develop knowledge around the innovations and successful paradigms that social entrepreneurs create, so that the media and researchers and policy makers have access to the data needed to convince people that these new models are primed for the level of investment required to bring about large-scale social change. Remember, a century ago there was no field of business per se, while today there are business schools at universities around the world, as well as recognized sub-fields in areas such as accounting and finance and strategy and entrepreneurship. We think social entrepreneurship is at a similar stage. That's why we created the Skoll Center for Social Entrepreneurship at Oxford University, to bring together knowledge and best practices in the field of social entrepreneurship and provide resources for those interested in and committed to bringing about positive social change.

That's also why we "connect" and "celebrate" social entrepreneurs in addition to investing in them and their organizations. Jeff's core belief is that the widening gap between the "haves" and "have-nots" in the world is the root cause of most of the world's big problems — environmental degradation, disease, conflict — and that it's in the enlightened self-interest of those "haves" to become engaged, lots more engaged, in making a positive difference. So for us, the "celebrate" piece of our work is key, with media the tool we use to activate their interest. *The New Heroes*, a four-hour series profiling thirteen social entrepreneurs that we underwrote and that was broadcast last summer on PBS, was our first big initiative in this area.

**FC:** The world is a big place, with lots of problems and lots of people working to solve those problems. How does the Skoll Foundation identify social entrepreneurs in which to invest? And have you found that there are commonalities among your grantees, irrespective of nationality or the particular focus of their work?

**SO:** We try to operate as efficiently as possible, which means we take a networked approach to identifying social entrepreneurs. Consequently, we work with partners all over the world — the AVINA Foundation in Latin America and the Asia Foundation for the Far East, as well as with Ashoka, the Schwab Foundation, and others — to identify folks who fit the profile we're looking for. We're also in touch with issue-area experts. Just this morning, in fact, Ruth Norris, who oversees our Skoll Award for Social Entrepreneurship, Lance Henderson, our VP of Program and Impact, and I were on the phone with folks at the Carter Center discussing innovators in the peace and human rights fields.

> **We try to operate as efficiently as possible, which means we take a networked approach to identifying social entrepreneurs. . . .**

Second, we have an annual competition, the Skoll Awards, that is open to all comers — although we do apply rigorous criteria in selecting the winners. For starters, we're looking for people with a demonstrated track record who have developed or identified an innovative solution to an important social problem and are poised to expand their impact significantly with the kind of investment and services the Skoll Foundation can provide. We also consider issue areas — in fact, we've identified six that are spawning tremendous social innovation: human rights, health, environmental sustainability, peace and security, institutional responsibility, and economic and social equity. More than the right issue, however, we want to see the right issue in the right place. Ann Cotton, the founder of the Campaign for Female Education (CAMFED), has worked brilliantly and with great passion and impact for more than a decade to bring education to young girls in Africa. That's the right issue in the right place.

Our third criterion has to do with finding social entrepreneurs at an inflection point. We're looking for people who have a compelling proof of concept and who are poised to move up the "S" curve and take their idea to scale, whether that means scaling deep within a particular region, moving from one region into multiple regions, expanding from one country into multiple countries, or influencing significant change within a system. We're looking for that inflection point and that readiness to move up the "S" curve in a significant way.

FC: What's an "S" curve?

SO: An "S" curve graphs the arc of an innovation's diffusion, from its modest acceleration at the outset as the model is proven and taken up by early adopters, through the more dramatic rise described by the neck of the "S" when the innovation is appropriated by whole markets, constituencies, communities, and then its tapering off — what we'd see as evidence of a new equilibrium — once peak adoption is achieved. In the social realm, of course, real systems change of the kind driven by innovators like Muhammad Yunus can take decades. It's because of the longer time horizon over which real social change takes place that I prefer the term "S" curve over the more common, and to my mind profligate, use of the phrase "going to scale."

**We're looking for people who have a compelling proof of concept and who are poised to move up the "S" curve and take their idea to scale. . . .**

FC: Sorry, I interrupted you. You were saying?

SO: That's okay. Anyway, as the applications come in, they're reviewed by two staff members and are scored against a rubric we've developed. Out of the initial group of applicants we come up with a semi-finalist pool and make a point of meeting all the semi-finalists personally — if not in the field, then in a location that's convenient for them. It's vital, we feel, to get to know the people behind the ideas and to establish a basis for trust from the outset. Jeff and the board are involved throughout the process — not in the heavy lifting of due diligence, of course, but in developing the criteria and staying abreast as the pool takes shape. But it's the board that makes the final decision on the finalists. While the process is not without its flaws, it's rigorous, it's thorough, and we feel as if we improve it every year.

**FC:** Have you learned anything about the personality of social entrepreneurs over the four or five years you've handed out Skoll Awards?

**SO:** Well, we've learned that social entrepreneurs are almost always what we call, in John Gardner's wonderful phrase, "tough-minded optimists." These aren't folks who believe they can parachute into a situation and bring about instant change. They understand that making change takes time and is complicated, and they respond to that reality with a tenacity and level of commitment that is impressive. They also recognize the extraordinary potential in the billions of poor people who inhabit the planet and are absolutely committed to unlocking that potential and helping people realize their gifts. Lastly, they almost always possess extraordinary integrity. In terms of their honesty, personal ethics, and willingness to be transparent, these are people who are leaders in the truest sense of the word, and it's inspiring to be around them.

> We've learned that social entrepreneurs are almost always what we call, in John Gardner's wonderful phrase, "tough-minded optimists". . . .

**FC:** Do social entrepreneurs have a responsibility, in your view, to be innovative? Or is it enough if they take a tried-and-true idea and tweak it to achieve better results?

**SO:** That's a good question. Innovation is identified with entrepreneurship, even if it means taking a proven idea and applying it in a new way or in a different context. Again, Ann Cotton's CAMFED is a perfect example. Ann realized that the primary barrier to female education in sub-Saharan Africa wasn't cultural, it was economic; it was the endemic poverty of the people in those countries. So she developed a scholarship program for girls, and in the dozen or so years since it was founded, CAMFED has provided scholarship support to more than eighty thousand young women in Zimbabwe, Zambia, Ghana, and Tanzania. Now, scholarships are not a new idea, but the way Ann re-imagined the process was — empowering committees at the district level to identify young women, girls really, who, but for this support, most likely would drop out of school and marry and whose talents and potential would be lost to their communities and countries as a result.

**FC:** Are your grantees expected to develop a plan to achieve sustainability?

**SO:** In the same way that there's no holy grail out there in terms of the sustainability of innovative business models, there's also no guarantee that a social entrepreneur working in the gray area between the marketplace and civil society will be able to develop a self-sustaining revenue model for his or her idea. On the other hand, for many startup organizations there is such a thing as a healthier revenue mix, a mix that is more aligned with the mission of the organization as it matures and/or paradigms change. That's where we try to fit in. At the outset of our engagement with an entrepreneur, we'll analyze the financial model he or she has developed and will work with them to refine the model so that it's more sustainable. For one organization that might mean more public-sector support, while for another it might mean a more robust earned-income stream or greater volunteer participation. Again, for us the question is not, "Is this model self-sustaining?" but rather, "How can this model be aligned with the mission of the organization to help ensure its sustainability over the time needed to make meaningful change?"

> **. . . there's no guarantee that a social entrepreneur working in the gray area between the marketplace and civil society will be able to develop a self-sustaining revenue model. . . .**

**FC:** What is your time horizon for investing in a venture? And how do you address the exit-strategy question?

**SO:** With the Skoll Awards, our initial commitment is for three years. From that portfolio, we will then identify social entrepreneurs who are really delivering outstanding results and whose innovations show systemic impact, and they become eligible for another three years of follow-on funding. Our assumption is that, at the end of that period, they will be on track with a more sustainable model than they had at the outset of their engagement with us. That doesn't preclude the possibility of additional or continued support from us — that depends on the performance of the organization in question and whether there really is an opportunity there to bring about equilibrium-shifting change.

**FC:** The vocabulary you and your colleagues use in talking about social entrepreneurs and social entrepreneurship borrows heavily from the venture capital world. What are the advantages of looking at social change through a business/venture capital lens?

> **In the same way that a public company has shareholders, social entrepreneurs have stakeholders. . . .**

**SO:** It's really less about business and more about discipline and results. As Jim Collins has pointed out — and here at Skoll we agree with him completely — greatness is not a function of whether you're a successful business or a successful nonprofit; it's defined by your discipline, your focus, and your results. We look for that kind of discipline, that kind of strategic perspective, and the efficiencies, commitment, and accountability that, in our view, are indicators of whether a social entrepreneur is likely to be successful or not.

Look at it this way. In the same way that a public company has shareholders, social entrepreneurs have stakeholders. In fact, in some ways social entrepreneurs work in a more complex milieu than your typical shareholder-owned public company. They don't have the benefit of a single criterion, the bottom line, against which they can measure their performance. The bottom line for a social entrepreneur is social benefit, which is much harder to quantify and measure. At the same time, social entrepreneurs have to be concerned about revenues and financial performance. They have to be concerned about accountability and transparency and governance. They need a solid organizational structure and have to worry, just like for-profits, about recruiting and retaining top-notch employees. At the end of the day, they have to worry about everything that a public company has to worry about — as well as social return.

**FC:** So, to the extent that a social entrepreneur is able to demonstrate results, that's a good thing, right?

**SO:** Yes. But it's important for people to understand that real social change — the kind of equilibrium shift I've been talking about — and measuring that change is not easy. Yes, it's easy for an organization like CAMFED to measure the number of girls who have received scholarships, but then tracking those girls beyond their graduation, evaluating their productivity as citizens, their contributions to their communities and families and societies — that requires longitudinal measurement which, while tougher and more expensive to carry out, ultimately is more important. I like to cite the example of Andrew Carnegie's libraries in this context. You can count the number of libraries that were built with Carnegie money, you can count the number of bricks needed to build them, you can probably even track the circulation rates in those libraries. But it's much harder to measure the value of those libraries as an educational resource for a young democracy at a pivotal point in its social and economic development.

> There's a growing awareness in corporate America that companies need to have a triple bottom line — that they should be accountable for the social and environmental impacts of their activities, as well as their profits. . . .

**FC:** Do you believe the traditional distinctions between the for-profit and nonprofit sectors are blurring? And if so, is that a good thing?

**SO:** Yes and yes. And I'll tell you why. In some cases, the single bottom line is no longer a sufficient measure of whether a public company is doing well or not. Take the reality of climate change and the environmental and economic risks inherent in continuing our reliance on fossil fuels. We're beginning to see more and more businesses and their management teams come to the realization that our dependency on oil comes with costs that eventually will impact their businesses, if not their bottom lines, and they're beginning to appreciate the importance of factoring those costs into their business models. In fact, there's a growing awareness in corporate America that companies need to have a triple bottom line — that they should be accountable for the social and environmental impacts of their activities, as well as their profits.

**FC:** What about the other side of the equation? Is there a danger that, as nonprofits and social entrepreneurs become more focused on results and demonstrating those results, they'll become more risk averse and less willing to innovate?

**SO:** That's where the entrepreneur will prevail. Whether they happen to be social entrepreneurs or business entrepreneurs, that desire to innovate, to take risks, is just too deeply embedded in the typical entrepreneur's DNA to be compromised by measurement for the sake of accountability. In fact, it's usually just the opposite. Entrepreneurs are driven to demonstrate results, they're driven to prove that their innovation is worthy of investment and can achieve the kind of impact they think it can. So, yes, maybe for a more traditional organization the increased emphasis on demonstrating results could dampen its desire to innovate. But not for the entrepreneur, and certainly not for the social entrepreneur.

**FC:** Earlier this summer, the world was taken aback — astonished might be a better word — when Warren Buffett announced that he had decided to give the lion's share of his fortune, about $37 billion, to the Bill and Melinda Gates Foundation and three smaller foundations run by his children. Are there implications in Buffett's decision for the field of social entrepreneurship?

**SO:** Well, I think there's a pretty big challenge for social entrepreneurs in that most of them aren't operating at a scale that can attract significant investment. Which doesn't mean that they can't begin to prepare for that kind of investment. For example, Victoria Hale, the founder, chief executive officer, and chairwoman of the Institute for OneWorld Health, the world's only nonprofit pharmaceutical company, is a grantee of the Gates Foundation and a social entrepreneur with whom we work. In fact, we're her second largest investor after Gates. Now, the Gates Foundation's investment in OneWorld has been in a specific drug that OneWorld is developing to combat visceral leishmaniasis, also known as black fever, which kills two hundred thousand people a year, primarily in India, and for which a readily available treatment, paromomycin, exists. The drug has made it through

> . . . there's a big challenge for social entrepreneurs in that most of them aren't operating at a scale that can attract significant investment. . . .

phase III clinical trials, and OneWorld has submitted an application for its approval to the Drug Controller General of India. While the Gates Foundation has been very focused on providing OneWorld with the resources to carry out the clinical trials, to negotiate with the Indian government, and to meet the regulatory hurdles — all requiring very-large scale investments — we've been providing additional support so that it can build its capacity to develop a pipeline of drugs targeting other neglected diseases in the developing world.

So again, to answer your question, there's an opportunity for organizations like the Skoll and Gates foundations to work together, on the impact side as well as in helping to ensure that organizations with effective programs and a proven model are able to scale those programs up to deliver maximum social benefit.

**FC:** In a recent thread on Social Edge, the online community created by the Skoll Foundation for social entrepreneurs, one participant suggested that the next ten years will prove to be the tipping-point decade — in a Gladwell-ian sense — for many of the urgent challenges confronting humanity. Do you agree?

**In order to make an appreciable difference, NGOs and nonprofit organizations are going to have to be better networked and do a much better job of coordinating their efforts. . . .**

**SO:** I'm glad you mentioned Social Edge since I haven't really spoken to the "connect" piece of our strategy! As a small shop, we're not able to support all the great folks out there who see themselves as social entrepreneurs, but through Social Edge we provide a platform that makes it possible for thousands and thousands of those change-makers to learn from one another, anytime, anywhere.

But to your specific question. I think we're seeing an enormous ground swell of civil society actors who believe that grassroots initiatives can help bring about positive social change in communities around the world. Literally millions and millions of nonprofit and nongovernmental organizations have been formed around the world in the last two decades. So in that sense, yes, the next ten years could be a tipping point for global civil society. But the sobering fact for all of those organizations is the scope of the problems — from economic inequality, to gender disparities, to global climate change — that need to be tackled. And in order to do that successfully, in order to really make an appreciable difference, NGOs and nonprofit organizations are going to have to be better networked, among themselves and with the public and private sector, and do a much better job of coordinating their efforts.

At the root of all this, and maybe it's the challenge of challenges, is leadership. But social entrepreneurs really do offer a paradigm for a new kind of leader, one who melds the discipline of business with the perspective of those less fortunate, less advantaged, and brings that tough-minded optimism I described earlier to bear on the challenges confronting our communities, our countries, and the planet.

**What terms like "social entrepreneur" or "S-curve" or "equilibrium" can't describe is what hope looks like. . . .**

**FC:** And, of course, technology makes all of that much easier to accomplish.

**SO:** Absolutely. One of the social entrepreneurs with whom we've been working, Jim Fruchterman, the CEO of Benetech, argues that while it's possible to create technology solutions that serve humanity and empower ordinary people, the markets won't encourage or support those applications because they don't produce the desired level of profit. It's folks like Jim who are bringing these technologies to bear on problems such as land mine detection and human rights violations and, in the process, are changing the world for the better.

**FC:** Your boss, Jeff Skoll, quoting the journalist David Bornstein, likes to point out that, over the last twenty years, the world has produced many more social entrepreneurs than terrorists. That's not only validation of the work you and your colleagues do, it's a source of hope for the rest of us. Does one have to be an optimist to engage in this kind of work?

**SO:** Yes, but again, a tough-minded optimist, which is how I'd describe Jeff, too! It's okay to think you can change the world, but you won't unless you also combine that ambition with the rigor of business thinking and the discipline of being focused on the results you want to achieve. Optimism alone is not sufficient, but it's yin to the yang of our work — that focus and discipline — at the Skoll Foundation; it's what inspires and drives us.

Earlier this summer, I traveled to Africa, to Zambia and South Africa, where I had an extraordinary time in the field with Ann Cotton and Taddy Blecher, another of our Skoll Awardees, experiencing first-hand the impact of their work through CAMFED and CIDA City Campus. And, you know, what terms like "social entrepreneur" or "S-curve" or "equilibrium" can't describe is what hope looks like. Hope is what I saw, what I felt, what I realized was very much alive in those countries — hope in the faces and voices of thousands of young people, as well as in their teachers, their parents, their siblings, and their communities. Hope that their lives mattered, that they had the power to create better futures for themselves and their villages and their countries. That's the promise of social entrepreneurship. And that's what the Skoll Foundation will continue to invest in and celebrate.

**FC:** Well, thanks very much for your time this afternoon, Sally.

**SO:** You're welcome. Thanks for your interest.

*Mitch Nauffts, editorial director of* Philanthropy News Digest, *spoke with Sally Osberg in July 2006.*

# 9

# Working to Catalyze Social Change

Emmett Carson
Former President and CEO
Minneapolis Foundation

*Over the last forty years, it has become an article of faith in the philanthropic community that foundations play an important role in creating and promoting social change. Moreover, as Helmut Anheier and Diana Leat write in* Creative Philanthropy *(Routledge, 2006), foundations perform that role, at least in theory, in a variety of ways: by fostering recognition and exploration of new needs, ideas, and cultural forms; by changing the way people think about social issues and their solutions; by increasing the empowerment of those traditionally excluded from policy considerations and practice; and by demonstrating the feasibility of new ways of working.*

*But that view, as Anheier and Leat note, has always had its critics. No one was more articulate in this regard, Anheier and Leat suggest, than former Carnegie Corporation president Alan Pifer, who, writing in the 1980s in response to a congressional inquiry into the practices of U.S. foundations, argued that the "great myth" about foundations "is that they are firmly ensconced on the leading edge of social change, managed by far-sighted trustees and staff who make brilliantly daring decisions about the disposition of funds over which they have stewardship. In this myth," Pifer added, "the funds are known as seed corn and venture capital, thereby associating the foundation vicariously with two of the noblest traditions in American life, the agrarian and the entrepreneurial. But foundations in fact have a highly restricted capacity to influence social change...."*

*The Foundation Center's* Philanthropy News Digest *spoke with Emmett Carson, then president and CEO of the Minneapolis Foundation (www.minneapolisfoundation.org), one of the oldest and largest community foundations in the nation, about foundations and social change, the barriers that keep foundations from devoting more of their resources to a social change agenda, and the future of the community foundation field.*

*Carson is well known as a writer and speaker on persistent and emerging social issues and as an advocate for progressive social change. During his tenure at the Minneapolis Foundation, the foundation received national recognition for its grantmaking and communications efforts, while more than tripling its assets from $186 million to $650 million. Prior to joining the foundation, he was the first manager of the Ford Foundation's worldwide grantmaking program on philanthropy and the nonprofit sector and also worked for the Joint Center for Political and Economic Studies and the Congressional Research Service.*

*In addition to serving on a number of nonprofit boards, he also has been named on several occasions to the* Non-Profit Times' *annual list of the fifty most influential nonprofit leaders in the United States.*

*In the summer of 2006, Dr. Carson, who received his Ph.D. and M.P.A. degrees in public and international affairs from Princeton and his bachelor's degree in economics from Morehouse College, was named president and CEO of the Silicon Valley Community Foundation, which was created by the merger of two of the Bay Area's largest foundations, the Peninsula Community Foundation and the Community Foundation Silicon Valley.*

---

**Foundation Center (FC):** You've written and stated in various forums over the past few years that community foundations are at a crossroads. Is that the same as a crisis? And what, in your view, has brought the community foundation field to that pass?

**Emmett Carson (EC):** A crossroads is not the same as a crisis, unless you're talking about a crisis of identity. For people who are content to focus on asset accumulation — the donor focus, as I call it — there's no crisis at all. That's how they interpret their mission: to accumulate assets. On the other hand, for those who say the issue is not just how much you raise, but what you do with that money, then yes, you're talking about something altogether different. That's why I've talked about a crossroads in the past, and by that I mean, where does the community foundation field want to go from here? Do we want to look like Fidelity and Vanguard, which are transactional institutions that do little to inform their donors about the value of doing good in their communities? Or do we want to be something more? I think we want to be something more. I think we *should* be something more.

**FC:** Does the entry of Vanguard, Fidelity, and other financial services firms into the philanthropic arena represent an opportunity for the community foundation field or a threat?

**EC:** It's both. It's an opportunity in that those firms have spent enormous sums of money — money that community foundations, as a rule, don't have — to market and explain the concept and value of donor-advised funds to literally hundreds of thousands of people. They've done a great deal to explain, to market, to make information about donor-advised funds available to people who may not know such a thing exists.

> . . . the Fidelities and Vanguards of the world are a threat to community foundations in the sense that they dumb us down. . . .

On the other hand, the Fidelities and Vanguards of the world are a threat to community foundations in the sense that they dumb us down. They aren't interested in improving a particular community or in addressing issues from a values perspective or a social equity perspective. Their interest is in charging a fee and completing transactions with charities specified by their customers. I believe community foundations stand for more than that. I believe community foundations stand for collective action and people learning from each other to address problems within their community with shared resources. That's a different kind of institution. And yet the threat represented by some of the financial giants has led some community foundations to think — wrongly, I believe — that they ought to look and act more like a commercial fund than a traditional community foundation.

**FC:** As president and CEO of the Minneapolis Foundation, you've been an outspoken advocate for what you call social change grantmaking.

How do you define that term? And how does social change grantmaking differ from more traditional philanthropic strategies and approaches?

**EC:** I use the terms "social change" and "social justice" grantmaking interchangeably. Let me explain.

First, I have never come across a foundation with a mission statement that says its job is to promote the status quo. I have heard foundations talk about wanting "to advance," "to improve," "to enhance," "to do better." By definition, those kinds of phrases evoke change. Part of the challenge for foundations is to live up to the dreams of their founders. Now, many people — too many people — interpret that as advocating a progressive agenda or a conservative agenda; in other words, they put a political lens on it. But if you're Melinda Gates and you say you want to eradicate disease in the Third World, that's not a progressive or conservative agenda. That's a social justice agenda, in that disease typically prevents people from fully participating in society. It's not making a value judgment about a particular political or economic system.

> **I have never come across a foundation with a mission statement that says its job is to promote the status quo. . . .**

**FC:** Do you believe social change should be a component of every foundation's grantmaking?

**EC:** I think every foundation has the obligation to review their mission statement and ask whether they are being called to engage in promoting social change. It may be a change that you and I don't agree with, but that's the beauty of the American system of philanthropy. When you have competing ideas vying for legitimacy in the court of public opinion, everyone benefits; we all learn more, foundations tend to invest more, and, at the end of the day, we end up with an improved understanding of what kind of society we would like to become.

**FC:** Are there barriers or structural impediments that discourage foundations from directing more of their resources to a social change agenda?

**EC:** I think so. First, foundations are exceedingly sensitive to bad press or people disagreeing with them. It's curious, because you would think that institutions largely insulated from public opinion by virtue of their endowments would be willing to take more risks. Secondly, it's often the case that the boards and staff of foundations who take over after a founder is no longer on the scene are far more conservative and worried about the image and reputation of the founding family's name than the founder himself. I suspect that's because the typical founder tends to be entrepreneurial and more interested in making a difference than the professional managerial types who usually succeed him or her. Again, I would point to Bill and Melinda Gates, who have been very willing to take risks and challenge conventional wisdom.

**FC:** Do foundations need to have an explicit theory of change in order to be effective change agents?

**EC:** No. I don't think that level of detail and meticulousness is necessary, or even useful. I do think foundations need to have a clear idea of where they're trying to go and why they think that's a good thing. A foundation can believe, for example, that full-day kindergarten is good for a community. It can believe that immigrants in a community, however they got there, probably ought to have access to basic health care. And it should be able to articulate why it believes those things. That's all it needs to get started.

**FC:** Is it important for foundations to be able to communicate their change agenda to stakeholders, both internal and external?

**EC:** I believe foundations are responsible for articulating and promoting their missions. And as I said, most mission statements articulate a vision of a better society, regardless of whether the particular focus of the mission statement is the arts, the environment, education, or health care. That's a change agenda. So the real question is not whether foundations are able to articulate a change agenda; it's whether they actually act on that agenda.

**FC:** How does the Minneapolis Foundation measure success in a social change context? Do you look at concrete outcomes, or are you more interested in seeing movement toward solving the particular problem you're trying to address? Or is it a little of both?

**EC:** It's both. If you can get the public to think about an issue differently, that can create enormous change. Similarly, investing in a new idea that works, or doesn't work, can encourage others to adopt a particular approach, or to avoid it.

**FC:** To what extent, in your view, is foundation impact a function of grant size or the dollar amount of a foundation's grantmaking program?

**EC:** Not much. Impact is a function of vision, of taking risks, and of understanding how to use money to leverage the change or changes you're trying to bring about. I've seen community foundations initiate meaningful community dialogues with a relatively modest investment of funds. In fact, some would argue that the more money you have for grants, and the larger your grantmaking program, the more problems you're bound to have. But while I don't think grant size or asset total is a determinant of impact, I do think they are a determinant of the kinds of strategies you can use to create impact.

> While I don't think grant size or asset total is a determinant of impact, I do think they are a determinant of the kinds of strategies you can use to create impact. . . .

**FC:** Can you give us an example?

**EC:** Sure. Every year, we convene a series of public meetings called "Minnesota Meeting" that focus on a particular topic of interest to the community. In the past we've held meetings on education, on immigration, and we're currently holding meetings around the topic of racial disparities. Funding for Minnesota Meeting represents a modest cost relative to other grants we've made, and yet we draw upwards of eight hundred people to each meeting. The meetings are also broadcast on Minnesota Public Radio, are taped and re-broadcast on local public television stations, and are broadcast live by satellite to several out-of-state locations. And I can tell you, you can literally see how those meetings transform people's thinking about an issue.

I'll give you another example. From time to time, we publish reports on an issue we care about. One such report looked at the criminal justice system in Minnesota with regard to people who had been convicted of a felony. In Minnesota a felon is entitled to restoration of the full rights of citizenship after they have served their sentence; that's been the case since 1857. Well, we made a grant — I think it was for $15,000 — to retain a blue-chip law firm, which confirmed that, notwithstanding existing law, there was no process in Minnesota whereby a felon who had served his time could have his voting rights reinstated. There's a process to take you off the voting rolls, but no process to get you back on. Well, our report was introduced into the Hennepin County Commissioners' public record, and the commissioners subsequently established a process through which convicted felons who had served their time could have their voting rights reinstated. Why is that important? Well, in Minnesota stealing anything valued at more than $500 is considered a felony, which means an eighteen-year-old kid could be caught and convicted for joy-riding and wouldn't be able to vote in the state for the rest of his or her life. That's not right. For a small investment of $15,000, however, we were able to document that the existing law was being ignored, and a process was put in place that returned that right to felons who had paid their debt to society. It didn't take a lot to leverage that modest investment into big change once we understood what it was we were trying to achieve.

**FC:** Is collaboration part of your leveraging strategy?

**EC:** Collaboration is wonderful when partners share a vision. But you know what they say: Too much water in the brandy ruins the drink. The question you have to ask is, Are the partners in a collaboration adding brandy to the mix or are they adding water? Too often, I think, we substitute a desire to be seen as team players for actually wanting to get things done. I would much prefer to collaborate with one or two partners who really believe passionately in what it is we're trying to achieve than be involved in a multi-party collaboration where the partners agree on very little — and I think a lot of people in the field share that view.

> **Collaboration is wonderful when partners share a vision. . . .**

On the other hand, if you're a foundation with modest resources and you're interested in taking something to scale, how do you do that without collaborating? It's a dilemma we all face. If you're trying to get to the top of the mountain and the people you're collaborating with are only willing to go as far as the first ridge, it doesn't necessarily help your agenda to partner with them. I'm aware of collaborations that have spent all their time and resources trying to get people to go beyond the first ridge, whereas if the respective parties to the collaboration had struck out on their own, one of them, at a minimum, would have made it up the mountain and back again by the time the other partners made it to the first ridge. Those are the decisions one has to weigh. So I'm not against collaboration, but I'm not automatically for it. If it can be helpful in achieving the goals an organization has set for itself, well, it's worth a try. If, from the outset, on the other hand, the goal of the collaboration is that first ridge rather than the mountaintop, then I think you have to ask whether it's the best use of your resources.

**FC:** A lot of people in nonprofit organizations seem to be intimidated by the foundations they approach for funding. Do you think the lopsided power dynamic between funders and their grantees hampers foundation effectiveness?

> . . . the real question for me, as a funder, is whether nonprofits are my vendors or my customers. And the short answer is, they can be both. . . .

**EC:** It certainly makes it more complicated. As you say, funders and grantees are locked in a power relationship, and it doesn't benefit anyone to ignore power relationships in society. But the real question for me, as a funder, is whether nonprofits are my vendors or my customers. And the short answer is, they can be both. Unfortunately, too many nonprofits think of themselves as customers exclusively, when they ought to be thinking of themselves as vendors.

**FC:** Interesting. Can you give us an example?

**EC:** As a foundation president, I'm interested in what a nonprofit organization can do to advance the mission of my foundation in the community or communities we serve. Take education. If I want to improve test scores for the 40 percent of African-American kids who are dropping out of high school, my "customer" is the kid whose test scores I'm trying to improve. The "vendor" in this scenario is the nonprofit which says, "I can help you do that." If a nonprofit can indeed help me improve that kid's test score, then you bet I'm going to be concerned about its organizational health and capacity — at least until another "vendor" comes along and says, "I can help you improve the test scores of African-American kids, and I can do it better, faster, cheaper, and for more kids than your current vendor." Well, as they say in the movies, that's an offer I can't refuse. It's not that I don't like the first vendor. It's not that I'm being unfair to the first vendor. It's about me trying to create the best outcomes for my customers. That's what my mission statement says. The mission statement of the Minneapolis Foundation states that we work "to improve the health of the community." It doesn't say we work to improve the health of nonprofits.

I'm not saying that to be provocative. What I'm saying is that it changes your mind-set when you start to think of nonprofits as vendors rather than as customers. It doesn't mean nonprofits aren't our partners, or that they don't deserve to be treated with respect and courtesy. Unfortunately, too many nonprofit organizations see themselves as a customer of rather than as a vendor to foundations. If, instead, they viewed themselves as vendors and said, "Hey, you have an interest in health care, or an interest in education, or an interest in job training, and we do that better than anybody else; we can help you meet the needs of your customers in that area better than anybody else," it would lead to different kinds of conversations, instead of the one that goes, "If I don't get this grant, I'll have to lay off staff" or "I won't be able to pay my benefits." Sorry. That's not my problem. My customers are my problem, and you're of interest to me only insofar as you can help me serve those customers.

**FC:** Let's stick with that metaphor a minute. Is it sometimes difficult to find vendors with the capacity and skill sets required to help you maximize your investments in the community?

**EC:** Yes.

**FC:** What do you do in a situation like that?

**EC:** It depends. The issue becomes, do you try to grow a nonprofit from scratch, or is there another organization out there that could do the job if we made a strategic investment in its capacity? As always, the devil's in the details. But I will tell you that there is work that doesn't get done at community foundations because they aren't always able to find organizations that have the capacity to spend a million-dollar or half-million-dollar grant effectively.

> . . . community foundations aren't always able to find organizations that have the capacity to spend a million-dollar or half-million-dollar grant effectively. . . .

**FC:** How common a problem is that?

**EC:** It's a problem most funders face at some point or another. That is, they'll have a specific problem in mind and a concrete idea about what kind of organization or organizations they want to work with to address that problem, and they'll look across the nonprofit landscape and won't see any organizations prepared to step into that role. I mean, I've been in meetings with organizations and have said, "Hey, we liked what you did in this area or with this program, would you ever be interested in doing X, Y or Z?" And they'll say, "No, that's outside the scope of our mission. That's not our role." I'm sitting there thinking, "Boy, I'd like to give them a grant," and they're sticking to the letter of the mission statement. Don't get me wrong — I applaud them for that. But it's not always the foundation that says, "Nope, we don't do that."

Look, to a certain extent, foundations sail along with a fixed view of the world and then something exogenous happens that changes the whole picture. Now, many foundations will see that as an opportunity but won't be able to find a nonprofit that's equipped or ready to take advantage of that opportunity, and so the opportunity is lost. And sometimes a nonprofit will recognize an opportunity before a foundation does because the foundation isn't down in the trenches working to address the problem, whatever it may be, and again, the opportunity is lost. It's one of the great frustrations of foundation work.

**FC:** One of the exogenous factors likely to reshape the nonprofit sector over the next decade is the retirement of the baby boomers, particularly at the organizational leadership level. Is that a problem in your community?

**EC:** Yes.

**FC:** What, if anything, are you doing about it?

**EC:** The short answer is, not much. And I'll tell you why. It goes back to what we were talking about a minute ago, and it's something I feel strongly about: It's not our job. If my mission statement stated that our job was to advance the health and well-being of the nonprofit sector, then I'd be very worried about the looming leadership deficit; it would be one of my highest priorities. Don't get me wrong: I do worry about it, as it relates to issues and areas we care about. When I see turnover in the institutions that are doing the best job for me in those areas, it's an issue for me. But if you say to me, "Well, you know, it's happening in a whole lot of areas," helping the sector deal with that transition just isn't my number-one priority.

**FC:** You've suggested that a key justification for the existence of foundations is that they, uniquely, are positioned to provide the risk capital to test innovative solutions to systemic problems. Do foundations take as many risks as they should?

**EC:** Well, I think the glass is half full and half empty on that score. I look at Bill and Melinda Gates and the monies they're expending in the fields of education reform and global public health and I say, "Yes, that's risk. That's innovation. That's trying some new and different things." But overall, I believe the field shies away from risk, and it does so for a number of reasons. We're afraid of criticism. We're afraid of failure. We are afraid of talking about values that may make somebody else uncomfortable.

> **I believe the field shies away from risk, and it does so for a number of reasons. . . .**

**FC:** And wary of political retaliation?

**EC:** Absolutely. We find ourselves in an environment in which people are quick to attach labels to ideas and opinions. We find ourselves in an environment in which certain kinds of free speech are questioned. We find ourselves in an environment in which the right to assemble around certain issues is being questioned. That can be chilling. Those of us who work in the field ought to feel we are the most empowered to speak out, but in fact we feel the most vulnerable because we are regulated by Congress. As a result, we're reluctant to do anything that would lead to additional regulation that might compromise the unique role we play in our democratic society.

**FC:** As the head of one of the largest community foundations in the country, what do you see as the greatest challenge for Minneapolis and Minnesota over the next decade or so?

**EC:** The challenge and opportunity in Minnesota over the next decade is one and the same — immigrants. Immigrants have brought a wonderful diversity and vibrancy to Minnesota. Southeast Asian Hmong, Somalis, Russian Jews, and Hispanics, among others, have strengthened our labor market, added to our cultural richness, and helped to connect us to an ever-smaller global village. Unfortunately, many people see immigrants as a threat, do not appreciate their wealth of talents, and conveniently forget their own family's origins and background, while blaming immigrants for the community's social ills.

**FC:** As your community grows more diverse — racially, ethnically, and socioeconomically — what are you doing to make sure the programs and grantmaking of the Minneapolis Foundation reach the groups and people most in need?

**EC:** We try to do that in several ways. First, we make every effort to have our twenty-five-member board and our staff reflect the diversity of the community we serve as well as bring the skills and talents we require. Second, we encourage staff to attend meetings of various community groups and to develop relationships with various community leaders so that diverse communities feel they have a channel through which they can share their ideas with us. And lastly, we have provided endowment funds to another foundation, the Headwaters Foundation for Social Justice, to work with nonprofit organizations, especially from communities of color, that require technical assistance and organizational development before they seek more traditional funding.

> . . . we make every effort to have our twenty-five-member board and our staff reflect the diversity of the community we serve. . . .

**FC:** What do you think the community foundation field will look like in ten or fifteen years? Will community foundations continue to flourish in the face of competitive threats from major financial services firms and other new giving vehicles? Will they still be relevant in a world in which the problems confronting society are increasingly global in nature? Will the continued spread and power of information technologies render their traditional role as gatekeepers obsolete?

**EC:** I think community foundations ten or fifteen years from now will comprise a network of institutions focused less on the transactional aspects of the work — finance, gift planning, administrative cost structures, and so on — and more on what is in the best interests of individual communities. So, you might see campaigns, projects, programs that community foundations across the country are doing simultaneously while, at the same time, sharing knowledge more freely and regularly around specific topics and best practices. I think you'll see networks within those networks using the Web and other online tools to showcase how they have improved conditions for members of their community. You might even see community foundations step up and present a specific change agenda and policy recommendations to different levels of government based on their unique understanding of rural communities, or urban communities, or low-income communities. I firmly believe community foundations are capable of achieving all that and more with the support of their donors, nonprofits, and, most importantly, their customers — the people in the communities they were established to serve. I believe that is our destiny, and it only remains for community foundations to believe it, embrace it, and actively work to make it happen.

**FC:** Well, thank you, Emmett, for speaking with us this afternoon.

**EC:** Thank you.

*Mitch Nauffts, editorial director of* Philanthropy News Digest, *spoke with Emmett Carson in July 2006.*

# 10

# Nonprofits, Philanthropy, and the Democratic Process

Rick Cohen
Former Executive Director
National Committee for Responsive Philanthropy

*The role and activities of private foundations have been debated since the days of Andrew Carnegie and John D. Rockefeller. Alternately viewed as bulwarks of a class-based status quo or as parties to the inexorable growth of the welfare state (depending on the orientation and depth of one's political beliefs), foundations have had to explain themselves to politicians and a sometimes skeptical public at various points over the past half century.*

*One such effort to do that, the Commission on Private Philanthropy and Public Needs, better known as the Filer Commission, issued its final report,* Giving in America: Toward a Stronger Voluntary Sector, *in 1975, complete with recommendations designed to improve and strengthen the practice of private giving and the nonprofit sector. A year later, the Donee Group, a coalition of nonprofit leaders and activists who believed that nonprofits, especially those serving the disadvantaged and disenfranchised, had been underrepresented in both the composition and deliberations of the commission, issued a dissenting report which called attention, in the words of philanthropy expert Robert L. Payton, to the "neglected voices of minorities and others, as well as the need for greater openness and accountability."*

*In the more than thirty years since the publication of* Giving in America, *the National Committee for Responsive Philanthropy (www.ncrp.org), the successor organization to the Donee Group, has advocated for foundations and the philanthropic community to provide nonprofit organizations with more resources and opportunities to work toward social and economic justice.*

*The Foundation Center's* Philanthropy News Digest *spoke with Rick Cohen, the longtime executive director of NCRP, about his definition of responsive philanthropy, the relationship between accountability and foundation effectiveness, the relevance of ideological labels in a philanthropic context, and philanthropy's role in strengthening democracy and the democratic process.*

*Prior to joining NCRP in 1999, Cohen was vice president of the Local Initiatives Support Corporation in charge of strategic planning, and also served as vice president at the Enterprise Foundation, where he directed the organization's field programs. Both LISC and Enterprise work to support the work of nonprofit community-based developers.*

*Cohen has served in the public sector as Director of Jersey City's Department of Housing and Economic Development and in the private sector as a consultant to nonprofits, foundations, and government agencies. He began his professional career as a planner with Action for Boston Community Development, one of the nation's original anti-poverty agencies, and has worked for the Trust for Public Land in New York City.*

*He has also authored or co-authored three books and numerous articles and op-eds for professional journals and newspapers. In 2002, 2003, 2004, and 2005 he was named to the NPT Power & Influence Top 50 by the* NonProfit Times, *and in October of 2003 was one of twelve people from nonprofits across the nation selected to be in the first class inducted into the Public Interest Hall of Fame.*

*After more than seven years as the executive director of NCRP, Cohen announced in mid-September 2006 that he was stepping down from his post in order to write on larger issues of public policy affecting lower-income communities and the nonprofits that advocate for social justice causes, and to devote more time to family and health issues.*

**Foundation Center (FC):** In advocating for a more responsive philanthropy, what do you and your colleagues think philanthropy should be responsive to?

**Rick Cohen (RC):** That's the hardest question you could ask. Actually, thirty years after its founding, I'm not sure the word *responsive* really captures what NCRP stands for. Rather than trying to induce a meaning from the word itself, however, a better way of figuring it out might be to add up the key components of NCRP's philosophy.

Fundamentally, NCRP believes in making philanthropy more democratic. Philanthropy in the United States is still structured around a highly undemocratic dynamic, with few opportunities for the voices of communities, nonprofits, and their constituents to be heard. By that I mean, most foundations are relatively immune to or removed from input, criticism, dialogue, and debate. Second, the structure of philanthropy reinforces that lack of democratic give-and-take, in that foundation boards of trustees are still pretty narrowly comprised in terms of race, ethnicity, and, particularly, social class. Third, although the Filer Commission back in the 1970s urged philanthropy to measure itself against public needs and priorities, much of philanthropy does relatively little to address critical issues in our society, much less put money into the hands of groups that are on the frontlines working to address society's most pressing problems and concerns. And fourth, while the foundation field pays lip service to the legality and legitimacy of funding groups that do advocacy work, most foundations still seem reluctant to engage in that kind of work themselves, at least with any passion or vigor. That's particularly evident in foundations' support, or lack thereof, for grassroots, community-based organizations, which most authentically represent the concerns of constituencies that don't get a fair shake in our society.

> **Philanthropy in the United States is still structured around a highly undemocratic dynamic. . . .**

**FC:** When you talk about the foundation field, are you talking about the relatively small handful of professionally staffed foundations? Or do your concerns extend to the tens of thousands of unstaffed foundations that most people never hear about?

**RC:** Actually, we're concerned about both. Our primary focus is on the role of philanthropy as a sector in service to society, and that includes the activities of small as well as large foundations. Fundamentally, we're concerned about supporting a democratic dynamic within philanthropy that, when unleashed, will lead to social change and progress. So we're concerned about both ends of the spectrum. Unfortunately, in our view, many people focus so much on the large foundations that they fail to see that there are needs out there that can and should be met by smaller foundations.

**FC:** Many people believe the primary concern of any private foundation should be to honor donor intent. Are you suggesting that private foundations should also be viewed as mechanisms to redistribute wealth?

> The best we can hope for is that an increasing portion of foundation activity can and should support organizations and constituencies advocating for social change. . . .

**RC:** I don't think either charity or philanthropy in this country operate as mechanisms of wealth redistribution. On the contrary, the bulk of charitable and philanthropic giving goes to organizations that serve the needs and interests of the classes that are the sources of that giving. To imagine that philanthropy, which is generated mostly by people of wealth and administered by boards of trustees populated largely by people of wealth, could ever function as a wealth-redistribution mechanism is something of a daydream. The best we can hope for, I think, is that an increasing portion of foundation activity can and should support organizations and constituencies advocating for social change — in other words, that philanthropic grantmaking to nonprofits will lead to an increase not for X cause or Y cause specifically, but for the nation's democratic discourse. That doesn't mean that the half a trillion dollars currently sitting in foundation endowments should be viewed as a substitute for government. Those assets should not be viewed, as many people view them, as a ready source of funding for social causes that government can no longer afford to support. Instead, they should be seen as a resource for promoting the causes and interests of people who are not well served in our society and for engaging people in a revitalized democratic process.

**FC:** Is that what people mean when they say that, when it comes to poverty and social justice issues, foundations talk left and act right?

**RC:** Here's what I would say: Philanthropy in general doesn't do that much to advance social justice, and by that I mean the serious imbalances in our society that have led to and perpetuated poverty and racism and other maladies in our society. Do you know the work of Joan Roelofs? Roelofs suggests that the real purpose of philanthropy in a society is to defuse and channel discontent into acceptable places and to protect and undergird the existing socioeconomic system, which is the same system that gave rise to philanthropy in the first place. So, although NCRP has a long history of talking about left- and right-leaning foundations, I'm not convinced there are that many left-leaning foundations out there, in the sense that they're trying to subvert the fundamental market mechanism that helped create them.

Let me give you an example. How many foundations can you think of that have devoted significant resources to seriously monitoring the corporate sector? Not many, right? And even when foundations do work to promote social change, they don't do much to challenge corporations or corporate influence in American society. So I'm not sure the real issue is whether we should be trying to encourage more foundations to think and act "left" rather than "right"; the real issue is how we get foundations to direct their resources to the nation's critical social problems and to constituencies with the least wealth and least opportunity in our economy and society.

**FC:** Using political or ideological labels in a philanthropic context makes a lot of people nervous. Do you think those kinds of conversations should be avoided, or is there a way to use ideological labels to unite rather than divide people?

**RC:** I think the sector would be better off having serious discussions not about labels but about how philanthropy, of all stripes, measures up to the critical problems confronting our society. Sometimes ideological labels just muddle the picture, especially when you consider how many organizations deemed to be progressive fund large nonprofits while ignoring grassroots groups

> **If we believe in democracy and the democratic process, we should be encouraging foundations of all stripes to do more to mobilize constituencies at the grassroots. . . .**

that operate on shoestring budgets. Which is why I always come back to my concern about democracy. If we had more foundations thinking about how they can contribute to a vigorous democratic process in our society, that would be a phenomenal change. I don't think that's a particularly ideological position. If we really believe in democracy and the democratic process, then we should be encouraging foundations of all stripes to do more to mobilize constituencies at the grassroots, to support the airing of authentic community voices, to support the empowerment of organizations that truly listen to what communities have to say — as opposed to those that purport to speak for communities but don't show much interest in what those communities actually have to say. That's how you get past ideological labels that divide, by focusing on philanthropy's role in promoting a more vigorous, more dynamic democratic process.

**FC:** How do you convince foundations that they can fund those kinds of activities without running afoul of regulatory agencies or politicians?

**RC:** Foundations know the law by now. They know what they can do to promote citizen action and more advocacy by nonprofits without running afoul of the IRS or SEC, no matter how vague some of the guidelines may be. Most of the time, what deters foundations is not the law but the tendency of many of them to avoid risk, to want to steer clear of issues and constituencies that might generate controversy. And that's something the nonprofit sector has to push foundations to start addressing. These kinds of changes won't come about because foundations come to recognize them as important; they'll come about as a result of nonprofits saying to the philanthropic sector, "We need your resources at the table to help promote our sector's involvement in the democratic process."

> *. . . what deters foundations is not the law but the tendency of many of them to avoid risk, to want to steer clear of issues and constituencies that might generate controversy. . . .*

**FC:** Moving from the theoretical to the practical, do you think the mandatory payout rate for foundations should be raised? And do you believe the additional dollars generated by such an increase would make a real difference in solving some of the problems we're talking about?

**RC:** Some people argue that since foundations represent only a small percentage of overall charitable giving, why bother increasing the payout rate when the impact of such a move would likely be marginal. My position is that charitable donations are not fungible. Foundation dollars, foundation resources, are different in how they can and should be used than individual charitable donations or public-sector funding. When she was president of the Council on Foundations, Dot Ridings was fond of saying — and I always quoted her — that foundation grants are, or should be, the risk capital for social change. Well, the more risk capital you have, the better your chances of making something good happen. Which is why I think nonprofits should be advocating not only for an increase in the payout rate — which, by the way, is entirely achievable — but should also be advocating for changes in the way foundations spend their grant dollars.

**FC:** Do you believe there's a correlation between foundation giving in the aggregate and philanthropy's ability to solve social problems? And to whom or what, in your view, should foundations be accountable when it comes to their effectiveness?

**RC:** Let me first say that the conversation about foundation effectiveness inevitably involves the issue of accountability, and when I think about foundation accountability I imagine a three-legged stool. One leg has to do with improved and toughened foundation self-regulation. The second leg has to do with improved and toughened government regulation. And the third leg involves more resources for oversight and enforcement of existing foundation regulations.

> **Self-regulation on its own has been demonstrated to be pretty much inadequate to the task, notwithstanding the PR to the contrary from the sector itself. . . .**

Now, self-regulation on its own has been demonstrated to be pretty much inadequate to the task, notwithstanding the PR to the contrary from the sector itself. In terms of the bigger picture, however, foundation accountability and effectiveness aren't really issues of self-regulation at all. If I believe that foundations should be doing more to promote and support democracy and democratic dialogue, as I do, that is not going to happen as a result of improved and toughened government regulation. It's going to happen because the nonprofit sector wakes up and begins to constructively criticize and make demands of philanthropy. It is not going to happen because a foundation commissions a study that measures how happy or unhappy their grantees are with the way are treated by their program officer. It's going to happen when grantees and nonprofit organizations and communities themselves weigh in on whether foundations are living up to the trust the public has placed in them.

This is where I'll probably get myself into trouble, but foundations have been entrusted by the public to use their resources for the public good. And the public has a right and an opportunity to weigh just how much good they're getting from those dollars. Harvard professor Michael Porter did a study several years ago in which he argued that, based on foundation spending rates, the federal treasury loses more than a dollar in forgone revenue for every grant dollar awarded. If that's the price of philanthropy, then we ought to demand that foundations deliver big time on the social benefit part of the bargain. That said, the sector would benefit from increased levels of grantmaking, based on percentage of foundation assets and the establishment of foundation-like payout minimums for donor-advised funds and supporting organizations.

**FC:** As I recall, Porter's study was challenged by foundations and other experts, including former Senator Bill Bradley, who rebutted Porter's arguments in a lengthy article published by the *Harvard Business Review.*

**RC:** The one thing Bradley and Porter both agreed on was that foundations ought to spend more money and that foundation assets were not being adequately mobilized to achieve all the good they possibly could. And if I recall correctly, Bradley got into some hot water himself with foundations over that. As I said earlier, if you look at the large number of grassroots organizations around the country that get by on shoestring budgets and are barely holding on, and you look at the steady increase in foundation assets, adjusted for inflation, over the last twenty years or so, I think it's hard to argue that foundations can't do more to support nonprofits and the nonprofit sector.

**FC:** The difficulty inherent in measuring social benefit is one reason many of the tech entrepreneurs who have become philanthropists have opted to apply a business lens, with its emphasis on quantifiable outcomes, to their philanthropy. Does the increased emphasis within the sector on outcome measurement bother you?

**RC:** I think nonprofits' operating more efficiently and accountably is fine. Too bad so many for-profit corporations have yet to learn the same thing. But if we insist on turning all our philanthropic activity into programs that only address things that can be quantitatively measured, I think we run the risk of turning philanthropy away from the intractable social problems where foundation resources are so crucial. I think it's important for philanthropy to be able to address larger, more complex, system-change issues that don't lend themselves easily and neatly to simple outcome measurement, much less a profit-oriented income-generating model. On the other hand, what some people may be advocating for isn't just more of a business orientation. Some people have the belief, unjustified in my view, that business and the market combined with science and technology are able to solve complex social problems such as poverty and inequality. I think foundations need to keep in mind that it's not only outcome measurement that might be suspect; their reliance on science and technology to solve problems that are actually political and economic and cultural is also an issue.

> . . . it's important for philanthropy to be able to address larger, system-change issues that don't lend themselves easily and neatly to simple outcome measurement. . . .

Let me give you another example. NCRP's Spring 2006 issue of *Responsive Philanthropy*, our quarterly newsletter, featured a really stimulating debate between the CEO of the Northwest Area Foundation in Minnesota and critics of the foundation regarding Northwest Area's core commitment to anti-poverty work. What was especially interesting to me was how the foundation defined and addressed issues of poverty, and how critics of the foundation reacted to that approach. I mean, here you had a foundation sincerely trying to do the right thing but thinking about it from one theoretical construct, running up against the problem of matching its strategy with the concerns and interests of real people and communities — in this case, several urban Indian communities. This is even more relevant when you consider the Gates Foundation's otherwise laudable commitments to addressing health and poverty in Africa. Social issues and processes don't lend themselves to algorithms and technical fixes; they're about real people and communities. And that's the level at which philanthropy needs to be more engaged.

**FC:** Do you subscribe to the notion, recently promoted by Warren Buffett, among others, that it's harder to give money away than it is to make it?

**RC:** No. The most generous people in this nation aren't the Warren Buffetts of the world. They're working people who, statistically, give a higher proportion of their incomes to charity than the wealthy. The problem with the "harder to give than make" formulation is that it reduces our image of philanthropy to a small group of plutocrats who, because they have bottomless wallets, somehow know more about life than the rest of us. Somebody in the *Boston Globe* actually said that. I would just add that if we're willing to rely on plutocrats to determine what "good" philanthropy is, rather than relying on the judgment of our nonprofits and the communities they serve, well, I don't hold out much hope for our democracy.

> **I have trouble with the idea that, in terms of social and societal responsibility, you can set your judgment aside when making money so long as you're able to entrust some of that money at a later date to wise and thoughtful philanthropic professionals. . . .**

**FC:** I actually interpret that formulation differently. When used by someone like Warren Buffett, I see it as a ready admission of ignorance, for lack of a better word, of how to tackle the pressing social problems of the day.

**RC:** Sure, there's an element of that. But Buffett's own behavior as an investor was partly responsible for some of problems we are now trying to address through philanthropy. Remember, at a time when American society was coming to grips with the problem of tobacco addiction, Warren Buffett's Berkshire Hathaway made major investments in tobacco companies, and Buffett himself went out of his way to promote those companies as attractive investment opportunities. I have trouble with the idea that, in terms of social and societal responsibility, you can set your judgment aside when making money — and get a pass for doing so — so long as you're able to entrust some of that money at a later date to wise and thoughtful philanthropic professionals. In my view, one's role in addressing social problems should be an element of every aspect of your life, in business as well as in philanthropy. That's why the socially responsible business movement is so important.

**FC:** Speaking of Warren Buffett, what do you make of his decision to donate the bulk of his fortune to the Bill and Melinda Gates Foundation? And why do you think it got such play in the national media?

**RC:** I think the size of the gift and its potential impact on philanthropy had a lot to do with the media coverage — although I believe that when John D. Rockefeller, Sr., at the end of his life, donated the bulk of his estate to philanthropy, it actually represented a larger percentage of the country's gross domestic product than the combined assets of the Gates-Buffett foundation. Nevertheless, Buffett's decision to team up with Bill and Melinda Gates is a remarkable development — and one that raises some very large questions. On one hand, you have the Gates Foundation, which really has been one of the very best foundations when it comes to most measures of foundation accountability and effectiveness, tackling major problems and investing significant risk capital in addressing those problems, and doing so with a relatively low overhead compared to other giant foundations. Nevertheless, I think we should be concerned when a single foundation becomes so large that its assets exceed the assets of the next nine or ten largest foundations combined — or, more accurately, since Buffett's gift will take the form of annual capital infusions into the Gates Foundation rather than one lump sum, whose eventual grantmaking may comprise roughly 10 percent of all foundation grantmaking in this country.

> **What really concerns me is the notion expressed by many commentators that size alone translates into greater effectiveness and efficiency, that bigger is better. . . .**

But what really concerns me is the notion expressed by many commentators in the nonprofit as well as the mainstream press that size alone translates into greater effectiveness and efficiency, in the sense that bigger is better. I'm also concerned by the fact that the major decisions made by this giant entity are in the hands of three or four trustees whose business investments overlap — remember, Bill Gates is a major investor in and board member of Berkshire Hathaway. Those are the issues that the Gates-Buffett philanthropic merger challenges us to think about. Clearly, Bill and Melinda Gates and Warren Buffett have demonstrated an altruism that surpasses pretty much anything our society has seen in recent decades. But that doesn't mean we shouldn't be willing to think about the implications of that merger for a society which has witnessed a startling concentration of wealth over recent decades — a concentration of wealth, in my opinion, that doesn't bode well for our democracy or the democratic process in this country.

**FC:** Will the altruism you just alluded to inspire others with enormous wealth to follow the lead of Buffett and the Gateses?

**RC:** Yes. And I would also point out that Warren Buffett has been a major supporter of the estate tax, which, as is well recognized by most people, plays a significant incentivizing role for people of great wealth to set aside portions of their estates for charitable and philanthropic purposes. So Buffett deserves credit for being both a role model and for being wise enough to register the importance of public policies that support this kind of activity.

**FC:** With the first anniversary of Hurricane Katrina still on everyone's mind, can you talk about what the public-sector and philanthropic responses to Katrina say about American society?

**RC:** How much time do you have? I mean, it's such a complex issue, and it's still unfolding. For me, after you get past all the critiques of FEMA and the Red Cross and others, the striking thing in both the philanthropic and government response to Katrina is the lack of any impetus at the government level for an inspector general or watchdog agency to monitor how funds earmarked for relief and recovery have been used and to what benefit and impact.

**FC:** You're talking about the tens of millions in federal funds that have been earmarked for Gulf Coast recovery?

**RC:** Yep. I mean, the Justice Department has a task force dedicated to ferreting out Katrina-related abuses, but what are they looking at? Mostly at cases of individuals fraudulently applying for FEMA assistance and other government benefits. No one has done real-time inspector general-style digging into government contracting, and no one has pushed for the same kind of thing on the philanthropic side. For all the concern about accountability in the charitable and philanthropic sectors, for all that happened in the aftermath of 9/11 and the Indian Ocean tsunami, you would think that someone on Capitol Hill would have had the courage and vision to insist on that. And in fact, there was such a provision in the Katrina charity relief act that was eventually passed, but it was dropped before the bill went to conference.

What's more, as far as I know, we still have the process of expedited IRS approvals for Katrina-related funds and nonprofits, as we did after 9/11, even though most experts will tell you that the process was indirectly responsible for some of the fraud and abuse we saw after 9/11. I think we'll see some of the same thing when we look back on the response to Katrina. You would think our sector would say, "We're concerned about accountability, so let's make it real time, let's do it now, and let's put some meat on it." But that didn't happen. Some parts of the nonprofit sector still seem to think that if you don't look, you won't see it, and if you don't see it, you don't have to deal with it. But, of course, if we're really serious about keeping the public's trust, the misuse and misdirection of philanthropic resources has to be addressed. And that means in the context of Katrina, as well as everywhere else.

**Some parts of the nonprofit sector still seem to think that if you don't look, you won't see it, and if you don't see it, you don't have to deal with it. . . .**

**FC:** Do you think philanthropy and the nonprofit sector have a vision of what needs to be done in New Orleans and along the Gulf Coast to address the racial and economic disparities that were exposed by Katrina?

**RC:** Well, philanthropy isn't a monolith; it's pretty diverse, so it's hard to say what "it" envisions. But if it were up to me, the vision would look something like this. First, nonprofits and foundations need to view this as nothing less than a long-term reconstruction effort. As part of that effort, they should focus on rebuilding the community base and nonprofit ecosystem in the region. That's critical. While they're at it, they should also make sure that government and major national organizations aren't simply experimenting with people's lives. There are dozens of proposals at the national level for rebuilding the region, but none of them has been adequately vetted by the people in the region. You can't play with people's lives that way.

Philanthropy should also focus its resources on examining why this happened, on doing something about the appalling performance of incompetently managed agencies such as FEMA, and on prodding legislators and government officials who basically sat on their hands as FEMA fell into disarray and pork was handed out like ice cream at a Fourth of July picnic to make sure it doesn't happen again.

Finally, we need to recognize, particularly in the aftermath of Katrina, that there were some significant examples of corporate profiteering under the guise of relief and recovery. It's up to philanthropy, in my view, to play the watchdog role, not just for what government does, but on the corporate side as well.

> . . . there are points in the history of every society where underlying issues surface in a very visible way. And in those moments, I think the response of philanthropy is actually in some ways more measurable than it is on a day-to-day basis. . . .

**FC:** At the same time, more than a few people have pointed to Katrina as a test of the sector's ability to respond effectively to a major national disaster. Looking back a decade from now, how will we know whether philanthropy met and passed that test?

**RC:** Again, I think it's less a question of whether philanthropy responds effectively to this kind of national disaster and more about the role philanthropy should play at pivotal moments in our history. Whether it's Katrina or 9/11 or the South Central riots in Los Angeles, there are points in the history of every society where underlying issues surface in a very visible way. And in those moments, I think the response of philanthropy is actually in some ways more measurable than it is on a day-to-day basis. You can see which foundations showed up at the table and which didn't. You can see what they delivered and what they didn't. You can see which foundations talked but didn't back the talk up with money, and which foundations decided talk was cheap and instead brought their resources and talents and skills to bear on the situation. It really comes down to looking at philanthropy at pivotal moments in our history and asking, Who was there and what did they contribute?

**FC:** Well, thanks so much for your time this afternoon, Rick.

**RC:** My pleasure.

*Mitch Nauffts, editorial director of* Philanthropy News Digest, *spoke with Rick Cohen in July 2006.*

# 11

# Philanthropy and the Next-Generation Web

Daniel Ben-Horin
Founder and President
CompuMentor

*Today, five million years after humans emerged as a distinct species on the plains of East Africa, we are generating information at ever-faster speeds and in unprecedented amounts. As Alvin Toffler points out in* Revolutionary Wealth, *researchers have estimated that the amount of data, information, and knowledge produced and stored in 2002 alone was equivalent to that "contained in half a million new libraries the size of the Library of Congress," or roughly equal "to every word uttered by a human being since the dawn of time."*

*While still in its infancy, this global "megabrain," as Toffler calls it, is expanding at an unbelievable rate — and has spawned a new generation of Web-based tools designed to harness the collective intelligence of a billion human beings working feverishly to connect with each other and to be connected.*

*The Foundation Center's* Philanthropy News Digest *spoke with Daniel Ben-Horin, founder and president of CompuMentor (www.compumentor.org), one of the largest nonprofit technology assistance organizations in the world, about the emergence of this so-called "social Web" and what nonprofits can and should do to tap its revolutionary potential.*

*In addition to its technology assistance work, CompuMentor is the operator of TechSoup (www.techsoup.org), a nonprofit technology Web site, and TechSoup Stock, a distribution service for technology product donations. The San Francisco-based organization's newest initiative, NetSquared (www.netsquared.org), is designed to help nonprofits use new Internet-based tools such as blogging and podcasting to extend their reach and impact.*

*Ben-Horin serves on the board of the Nonprofit Finance Fund and speaks and writes frequently on issues related to the underserved's access to technology. In 2004 and 2005, the* Nonprofit Times *included him on its "Power and Influence Top 50" list. A former journalist, he lives in San Francisco with his wife, Jamie, and their two teenage sons.*

---

**Foundation Center (FC):** You created CompuMentor in 1987. What need were you trying to address?

**Daniel Ben-Horin (DBH):** I was trying to address two needs simultaneously. Because I'd had exposure to them, I was very interested in the people who were characterized, at the time, as "tech nerds." Far from being nerdy, I had found most of them to be articulate and interested in the world around them. They certainly weren't the reclusive pocket-protector types popularized by the mass media, and I wondered what they could offer to society, given the opportunity. And, having worked extensively in the nonprofit world, the second need had to do with the fact that nonprofits were always the last to the table when it came to anything related to technology. The more I thought about the situation, the more it seemed to me that, with a little creative deployment of the "nerds," there might be an opportunity to move nonprofits a little closer to the meal, so to speak.

**FC:** What was the original CompuMentor service model? And how, if at all, has that model changed in the almost two decades since you started the organization?

**DBH:** The original model was quite simple. It basically involved reaching out to technology experts on The Well, one of the early pioneering online services here in the Bay Area, and asking them if they would volunteer to work with nonprofits that needed help with technology.

Our role was to make sure that there was a match between the volunteer expert's skill set and the nonprofit's technology — to make sure that Mac guys weren't being sent to DOS sites, and so forth. That was the basic idea. So I went to an Oakland foundation, the L.J. and Mary C. Skaggs Foundation — which, by the way, no longer exists — and my contact there was willing to take a chance on this unproven notion and gave me a $2,500 grant. And with that, I was able to go on The Well, round up some volunteers, do a mailing to the foundation's grantees, make some matches, monitor the results, and declare victory.

**FC:** And today CompuMentor has a staff of 110 and a $15 million annual budget. . . .

**DBH:** Not quite — more like $13.5 million. But, you know, our vision from the beginning was not that we were going to do this one thing, mentoring, and just grow it and grow it. The vision I was interested in, the vision the people who were part of the initial team were interested in, was to be nimble and flexible in response to what the "haves" — those with knowledge and resources — could offer to "have-nots," the technology-challenged nonprofits. For example, in the late 1980s, early '90s, nonprofits were just getting into online communication. Well, in the Bay Area, there were all sorts of tech startups looking to build customer bases that we could bring to the table as funders. So we began to develop programs that were specifically about helping nonprofits build networks to foster online communication.

> **The vision was to be nimble and flexible in response to what the "haves" — those with knowledge and resources — could offer to "have-nots," the technology-challenged nonprofits. . . .**

At the same time, we began to move to more of a staff-based model, having learned that we could do a better, more reliable job of providing that kind of help if there was a staff component working with the mentors. From there, with support from the California Wellness Foundation, we moved into working with community technology centers. And then, serendipitously — though some might call it rank opportunism — I noticed that my friends at computer magazines in the Bay Area, all of whom were being inundated by review copies of shrink-wrapped software, were tossing boxes of the stuff into the garbage. They only needed one copy for review purposes, and the rest, from their point of view, was excess. But for us, it seemed like a way to make new software available to nonprofits so they could have some fun with the stuff. That's sort of been our credo from the beginning: technology doesn't have to be grim, you can have fun with it, and the more fun you have, the more you're likely to do with it.

So, we started making this grab bag of extra review copies available for very little, $5 or something, to nonprofits in the Bay Area. We started out with one or two copies of roughly two hundred titles, and over time that has morphed into what this year is going be about $200 million worth of products, retail value, entering the nonprofit sector — mostly domestically, but increasingly on a global basis. We apply an administration fee to each transaction, which covers all handling and mailing and supports TechSoup, the program we consider our value-add to the software program. The TechSoup site provides the knowledge nonprofits need to effectively use the products they acquire through TechSoup Stock, our software distribution arm. That's the value proposition we take to our vendors, that if they work with us they'll not only get efficient distribution for their products, their products will be distributed in an environment of knowledge and support. And the evolution of that model, over time, has been the key to our sustainability.

**Our credo from the beginning has been that technology doesn't have to be grim. . . .**

**FC:** Was it difficult, in the pre-Web years, to convince funders to support you?

**DBH:** Initially, like a lot of startups, we were viewed as a novelty and managed to secure our share of "neat idea" funding, which allowed us to make it to the next stage of organizational development — call it adolescence. But the stage after that, going from organizational adolescence to maturity, is the tough one, and in that sense we were fortunate in our timing. For us, that stage coincided with the economic boom of the 1990s and the general perception in the world of philanthropy that something important, if not well understood, was happening in the world of technology. As a result, organizations that had a track record and some credibility and a certain amount of chutzpah about technology could get a hearing.

In retrospect, those years were . . . I'm not going to say easy — I'll never say that. What I will say is that it was easier in the boom years of the '90s to initiate a conversation with a funder. And that lasted right up until April of 2000, when the Nasdaq cratered. After that, a lot of foundations began to look at things differently, and to say things like, "To keep going as we have been with incremental technology support is incredibly expensive and the benefits of it are not immediately apparent." I guess what you see depends on where you sit, but there was a tremendous sense that the technology boom had been chimerical, that in lots of ways foundations had been led astray by predictions of a "long boom" and so forth. It was almost with satisfaction, I think, that many foundations began to say things like, "You know, we went this far, but we're not going any further. This stuff is not as good or as important as it was cracked up to be." There was a retrenchment, in other words. And the upshot was that from 2000 to pretty much the present, it has been much more difficult to get funding, although I think things are changing.

> [With the new generation of Web-based tools], funders can make small investments that have big impact, which is much more pleasant than huge investments with incremental impact. . . .

I will say that I'm really glad we have a healthy earned-income stream. This is a hell of a time, in a lot of ways, to expect foundations to support what's needed, both in terms of nonprofit technology broadly, as well as in terms of support for nonprofit technology assistance providers. It's so expensive to do anything significant with tech, and there are so many competing needs, that it has been almost psychologically necessary for foundations to do a kind of triage and declare a truce, if not victory. That's one of the things that makes the new generation of Web-based tools so interesting. They're not nearly as expensive, and they facilitate community engagement, so funders can make small investments that have big impact, which is much more pleasant than huge investments with incremental impact.

**FC:** Do foundations "get" technology? Do they see technology as a critical component of nonprofit organizational capacity, and are they willing to fund it at levels that truly make a difference for their grantees?

**DBH:** I think I need to back up a little bit to answer that. Does "getting" technology mean being able to do a lot of cool things with these things we call computers? That's one form of getting technology. From the point of view of someone who works in philanthropy, though, I think a much more important way of "getting" technology would be to understand how technology is shaping specific organizations and institutions, the sector as a whole, and, when you come down to it, the times we live in. And my lens on all that is that we're dealing with two major disruptions.

The first happened with the advent of the personal computer. Regardless of when you date that, by the 1990s and right up through the present we witnessed this incredible proliferation of technology on people's desks, at work and at home, and, increasingly, in their pockets. This has all cost an immense amount of money, but unlike, say, the early and even the late '90s, when the productivity benefits of technology were claimed but not so apparent, we've passed to the stage where they are manifestly apparent. So philanthropies, which are full of intelligent people, have, over time, come to terms with how essential this back-office or behind-the-firewall infrastructure is for nonprofits. It's like electric lighting. If keeping the lights on is a given in our society, increasingly so are these techno-lights; it's the cost of doing business. And philanthropy has done a pretty good job of adjusting to that disruption, even though, as I just mentioned, it's expensive and competes with myriad other needs.

**What you do with the Web is not question number fifty, which is how it was viewed until very recently. It's question number one, or very close to that. . . .**

The second disruption is the one that, in our opinion at CompuMentor and TechSoup, is happening now and started about a year or two ago. And that disruption has to do with the other side of the firewall — namely, what happens out in the world with technology that no single organization controls, can't control, or should want to control. What happens on the Web, to put it in the simplest possible terms, is now an absolutely pressing organizational question. What you do with the Web is not question number fifty, which is how it was viewed until very recently. It's question number one, or very close to that. It will impact how organizations get their work done, whether they survive, how they survive. It will influence who the new players are in any kind of socially engaged activity. I don't think philanthropy really gets that. I don't think anyone does, yet. I think a bunch of people are fumbling with it. It's all very new, very disruptive, and its permutations are far more social than they are technological. But it's where the excitement and challenge is, and it's still early days.

**FC:** Does it have a name?

**DBH:** The phrase I use is "social Web," which is less catchy than Web 2.0 but much more accurately suggests what this is all about, which is the empowerment of individuals to create, to connect with each other, to share tools and to experience themselves in society in a way that is fundamentally different than what was possible previously.

**FC:** What are you and your colleagues doing to tap into the energy and creativity coalescing around the social Web?

**DBH:** Well, we're fortunate we've been able to develop the business that is TechSoup Stock and the revenue stream that comes with that, because in addition to giving us a certain amount of organizational stability, it also gives us the ability to look at something like the social Web and take the longer-term view. As an organization, we believe the thing which sets us apart is the set of cross-sectoral partnerships we've developed over the last twenty years. We also figure that because of these partnerships, we're especially well positioned to initiate a dialog about the implications of the social Web for social change. Our goal at this point is to create that dialog as quickly and effectively and in as action-oriented a way as we can — which is what the NetSquared project is designed to do — and then hang on. It's going to be a wild ride.

> . . . a key part of the disruption we're talking about is the empowerment of all the spokes in the wheel at the expense of the center of the wheel. . . .

You know, a key part of the disruption we're talking about is the empowerment of the edges of the network, the empowerment of all the spokes in the wheel at the expense of the center of the wheel. You can't launch projects on the social Web and expect to direct them in a tightly controlled way. That's not to say you can't articulate your vision and influence what happens. Wikipedia is a great example of everything I'm talking about. It's the product of legions of essentially anonymous individuals contributing their knowledge and time to this thing they don't own or control but which, in an odd way, is theirs.

Sure, in the background is something called the Wikimedia Foundation, which tries to impose broad standards on the collective effort and keep the vision focused. But in terms of NetSquared, I think we're going to see an incredible catalyzing of energy, lots of projects, some of which will fail and some of which will succeed in ways we can't even imagine, and we hope to be part of that.

**FC:** Terms like "social Web," "social software," "participatory media" — all of which have been used to describe aspects of the disruption we're talking about — are pretty new to most of our readers. Could you give us a couple of examples of nonprofits that are using some of the tools associated with the social Web to mobilize their constituencies?

**DBH:** Sure. But first, I think it's really important to say that if nonprofits or foundations are looking, right now, to other nonprofits and foundations as their sole source of ideas and inspiration for social Web applications, they're missing a big part of the picture. To my mind, the Dean campaign in 2004, Craigslist, and eBay are all great examples of what's at stake here and what is possible. What they all have in common is that they utilize Web-based services and technologies, as distinct from shrink-wrapped software you buy and load onto your desktop or laptop, to excite and empower a user community that they probably wouldn't have reached with more traditional means. They also allow the user community to establish and enforce many of the rules of engagement for that community, while consciously trying not to "own" what the communities do. I don't think too many people think of eBay as the cutting edge of social change, but it's really important to the discussion we're having. It's a new way of organizing huge amounts of commercial information and allowing users, in a personalized way, to set their terms of engagement with that information, and, obviously, it's a huge success.

> **If nonprofits are looking to other nonprofits as their sole source of ideas and inspiration for social Web applications, they're missing a big part of the picture. . . .**

At the other extreme, you have small projects like Freechild that are using these tools. Freechild has intersected with MySpace, the huge social networking site, as well as Frappr, the community mapping service, and a collaboration tool called Writeboard, to engage youth in social change activities. Rather than sort of telling kids what they ought to do, Freechild gives them a set of tools to explore solutions to problems themselves.

Here's another example. We just had an event here in the Bay Area called Net Tuesday — we have them once a month, and they're one of the building blocks of our NetSquared effort. The point of them is to bring in someone from the technology industry to talk about a new tool and match them with a nonprofit that is using that tool. At the last one, we were fortunate to get Mena Trott, the president of Six Apart, which makes TypePad, the wildly popular blogging tool. On that particular night, Mena was followed by Seth Mazow, the techie by default at Interplast, which has been around since the late '60s and sends doctors around the world to perform reconstructive surgery for children in developing countries. I'm talking about surgery that's the difference between someone being permanently and horribly disfigured or living a more or less normal life.

> . . . it's important, when we're talking about virtual versus face-to-face, not to think in terms of either–or. . . .

Anyway, Interplast has a staff of about twenty, and for a long time it had a brochure kind of Web site and was really dependent on the media to tell its story. Then young Seth took it upon himself to get doctors affiliated with the organization to blog, and eventually they ended up with Six Apart's tool. Well, the Six Apart people were blown away when they saw how their tool was making a difference in the lives of disadvantaged people around the world, and, after hearing Seth's presentation, they went to work to make it possible for volunteer surgeons, using their cell phones, to post before-and-after pictures to the Interplast site. That, as you might imagine, has increased the immediacy and impact of the site enormously.

**FC:** Are virtual communities like those created on the eBay and MySpace platforms a substitute for off-line communities? And if they aren't, what are virtual communities especially well suited to, and what are some of the things you can't do in a virtual community that you can do in an off-line community?

**DBH:** Well, the first thing I would say is that it's important, when we're talking about virtual versus face-to-face, not to think in terms of either–or. It's important when we ask these kinds of questions to examine what the word "community" means. You know, it's not as if people wake up in the morning and say, "I will go on to this community today and not that community." Our lives are the intersections of our work community, our neighborhood, our kids' school community, our family, our hometown, and so forth. In other words, we all belong to many communities at once. So, I think the way to approach this question is to ask, "What is going to be the impact of having virtual access to so many people?" — and not just virtual access in the sense that I can send somebody in Cleveland an e-mail. I mean, today, I can learn enough about that person — and he or she can learn enough about me — to know that we like the same bands, we like or dislike the same movies, we read the same books. So our online connection, if we both wanted it to, could be very rich. It might take time to get there — we can't just lean over the back fence and talk to each other — but the possibilities are fascinating.

There are implications to all this, of course, but — I know this will sound like I'm begging the question — I think the jury is still out. In fact, the jury hasn't even been impaneled. What we're seeing, I think, is that people aspire to a higher level of community, regardless of the form it takes. If you look back a bit, it's obvious that most people grew up in communities that revolved around their hometowns and families, and the erosion of those communities and community norms is a widely remarked phenomenon of American life. Hometown, family, workplace, bowling club — those kind of lifetime affiliations are under tremendous pressure. At the other end of the scale are the very ephemeral connections that come when you share your music with someone you've never met. Obviously, it doesn't replace your family, but what I think people are discovering is that some of these online interactions have the kind of value that makes you want to travel and meet that person, makes you want to stay in touch and not just have an ephemeral, online sort of connection. And what happens next will sort itself out in ways that are both predictable and unpredictable.

**FC:** As the social Web insinuates itself into every aspect of our lives, and as more power is pushed to the edges of the network, will the traditional role of the gatekeeper be weakened? And if so, is that something we should worry about?

**DBH:** Yes, the gatekeeper role will be weakened. And we can worry about it all we want, but we might want to put our time to more productive use. We all have our perspective on the value of the gatekeeper. And what's going on now around the veracity or trustworthiness of the information in Wikipedia is an interesting lens through which to look at the question. I think it's fair to say that at any juncture and, really, in any field you can think of, there are people who have more property, if you will, and there are people who have less property — and I include intellectual property in that definition. Now, there's a natural bias on the side of the people who have property to want to keep it, just as there's a bias on the other side, among people with little or no property, to want to get some. I don't think anyone can predict the consequences of this trend toward less power and control for the gatekeeper and more power and control at the individual consumer/creator end. But I think one's sense of whether it's a good or bad thing has a lot to do with whether you think there's a correlation between positive evolution of the species and constructive, creative engagement between as many members of the species as possible.

> **We all have our perspective on the value of the gatekeeper....**

I know that's very abstract, so maybe it would be better to talk about it in the context of something like Wikipedia. I don't think the change in how information is organized and accredited is a bad thing. We're seeing abuses of something that is still pretty new, and I think the system has the means within itself to correct those abuses. For example, I recently saw a story about Senate aides accessing their boss's Wikipedia entries and "correcting" information to make it more laudatory. But what's worse for a politician: A less-than-flattering remark in a Wikipedia entry or a news story about how his aide tried to rewrite the entry to make him look good? I keep saying that we're in the early stages of all this, and as such it's hard to predict how it's going to shake out. But I truly believe that this is a fundamental disruption whose implications should not be compared to, say, another doubling of processor speed. This is a different creature entirely, and it's still way too early in its evolution to really see its true dimensions, except to say that they are large.

**FC:** CompuMentor, through its TechSoup subsidiary, is a publisher of technology assistance information and therefore a gatekeeper of sorts. I couldn't help noticing that you've recently invited — indeed, are encouraging — people to republish TechSoup content protected under the Creative Commons license. How did you arrive at that decision?

**DBH:** Well, I've enjoyed the interview up to now. [Laughter.]

Obviously, it's far easier to tell other people to not worry so much about having control of their content than it is to give up control of your own content. In fact, it has been a bear for us, at every stage. But we've decided to make that commitment, to embrace Creative Commons, to embrace transparency, to embrace the idea of sharing our information as freely and widely as possible. And I think it's the right thing to do, even if it's hard. It was easy to come up with reasons for why we couldn't, or shouldn't, do it. The most compelling one had to do with whether we had the capacity to deal with other organizations and constituents if they took our offer seriously. I mean, it's not like you push the content out and never see it again. Invariably, people who start to use that content will want other things from you; there's a feedback loop there. And dealing with that loop is time-consuming, especially if you're a nonprofit organization that is already stretched in terms of its staffing and resources. I mean, suddenly, you have all these new constituencies engaging with you and editing your stuff and adding to it and improving it, or maybe not improving it. It can be crazy-making. It really can be.

**FC:** Are you committed to seeing it through?

**DBH:** Absolutely. There's no going back for us. I don't mean to sound Pollyanna-ish about this, in terms of how we as an organization feel about it. At any given moment, someone on staff is having their ox gored as a result of that decision. But I think if you polled staff and asked them, "Are you in favor of CompuMentor and TechSoup opening up their processes and essentially walking the talk of being an open-source organization and a social Web-oriented organization?" I think 90 percent to 95 percent of them would say "yes." And if you asked them, "Would you continue to work here if CompuMentor/TechSoup didn't do that?" I think you'd get 30 percent to 40 percent — a lot of them our best people — saying they would leave. It's that important to people here. As for where it all leads, well, have I mentioned that I think we're all at a very early stage of a long process?

**FC:** As an organization determined to walk the open-source talk, what do you think nonprofits should be doing, right now, with respect to the social Web? Should they be committing resources to it? Should they be developing Web-based applications using some of the software tools we've been talking about? Or is it too early in the game for that?

**DBH:** I think one of the wonderful things about the social Web is that it has a built-in mentoring capacity. I mean, what I was trying to do with CompuMentor in 1987 happens almost automatically on the Web today; it's self-organized, and the enthusiasm level of the people who want to help is unbelievable. So, in terms of nonprofits adding Web 2.0 application developers to staff, that's not something they have to worry about. Instead, they should be looking for partners and allies who will be more than happy to contribute on that level.

As to the larger question of what nonprofits should be doing in general, I would say this. We've always been an organization that has warned nonprofits against impaling themselves on the bleeding edge of technology. Our message has been, Let someone else make the first mistakes. Match technology to the capacity of your staff. If you're excited about new technology and want to push the envelope, fine, but don't get caught up in technology for technology's sake. It's not about having the coolest Web site. It's about having the right Web site. So, it would be a contradiction for us to say, "You must be on the cutting edge of Web 2.0." We're not going to say that. Our problems, society's problems, intersect with a host of realities, not all of which can be influenced, in 2006, by what the social Web has to offer.

> **We've always been an organization that has warned nonprofits against impaling themselves on the bleeding edge of technology. . . .**

What we would say instead is, "Be open." One of the great changes in the nonprofit world has been the infusion of technical talent. I'm referring to the "accidental techie" phenomenon you see in the new generation of nonprofit employees, young people in their twenties and thirties who not only are idealistic and smart, but who also happen to be absolutely fluent with technology. And that's an opportunity for the 58-year-old white men and women, speaking as one of them, who run a lot of nonprofits. You want a sense of what's possible? A sense of which social Web tool is right for your organization? Talk to the young people on your staff; bring them into the process. Remember the Interplast example I gave earlier? Seth Mazow was empowered by his superiors. They gave him a platform and encouragement, and he delivered for them. He brought his director of communications and public education — a wonderful, seasoned veteran of the sector — to the Net Tuesday event, and she was absolutely thrilled by the fact that he had, in effect, created this low-hanging fruit for her to grab.

**FC:** As these social Web tools become more powerful, do you expect them to change the way nonprofits do their work and, more broadly, the way Americans do philanthropy?

**DBH:** Well, yes. By definition, disruptions change things, usually dramatically, and I think nonprofits and philanthropy will both change. I was talking to someone the other day about homelessness in San Francisco, and it was one of those conversations in which we both expressed our frustration with how difficult it is to deal with the problem on an individual level, and how frustrating it was to come up with institutional solutions. Then somehow we started talking about the social Web and NetSquared, and the person I was talking to said, "Do you think we might ever see a movement whereby individuals on a one-to-one basis would relate to a homeless person?" And the more we talked about it, the more it seemed possible that people would be able to do something like that because it would be so easy for them to form a community and communicate with other people who were doing it, in ways that simply weren't possible before. I know that seems like quite a stretch from giving someone a dollar. But if you think about broad social disruptions, and you think about the way we've related to communities in the past and the way we might relate to them in the future, you have to believe that the world could change dramatically.

What does that say about philanthropy? Well, maybe philanthropy is looking at a future in which an incredible surge of super-empowered individuals assumes much of what has been the burden of organizations and institutions. I don't know. I'm not suggesting that institutions will go away. There's a big role for institutions in any scenario I can imagine. But they might be changed versions of the institutions we know today. Or they might be different institutions altogether. There might also be a lot more emphasis on what individuals are doing, and that, of course, would have important consequences for the way we do philanthropy. Philanthropy and nonprofits tend to operate with such a zero-sum-game mentality, but what we're starting to see now has the potential to explode that, which would be amazing.

**FC:** Well, thanks, Daniel, for speaking with us today. And best of luck with NetSquared.

**DBH:** Thank you. It's been a pleasure.

*Mitch Nauffts, editorial director of* Philanthropy News Digest, *spoke with Daniel Ben-Horin in March 2006.*

# 12

# Governance, Accountability, and the Charitable Sector

Diana Aviv
President and CEO
Independent Sector

*Fueled, in part, by demographics, the devolution of federal programs to the states and private sector, a prolonged bull market in stocks and other assets, and the persistence of longstanding social problems, the charitable sector in the United States has experienced unprecedented growth over the last thirty years. That growth has come at a cost, however, as state governments and legislators on Capitol Hill failed to adequately fund the oversight activities of the IRS and other entities charged with monitoring the sector. The predictable result has been a spate of media reports about alleged wrongdoing and self-dealing at foundations and nonprofits and a corresponding drop in the public's confidence in the sector.*

*To ensure that America's charities and foundations uphold the highest possible ethical standards and remain a vibrant and healthy part of American society, Independent Sector (www.independentsector.org), with the encouragement of leaders of the Senate Finance Committee, convened a group of nonprofit leaders in 2004 to recommend actions designed to strengthen the governance, transparency, and accountability of charitable organizations. After eighteen months of listening and discussion, the Panel on the Nonprofit Sector (www.nonprofitpanel.org) issued its final report to Congress in June 2005 and, like almost everyone else in the sector, watched as congressional conferees negotiated whether to include a package of charitable reforms and giving incentives in pending legislation.*

*The Foundation Center's* Philanthropy News Digest *spoke with Diana Aviv, president and CEO of Independent Sector (IS), about the work of the panel, the current status of suggested charitable reforms, Warren Buffett's historic gift to the Bill and Melinda Gates Foundation, and the ability of the charitable sector to re-invent itself to meet the challenges of the twenty-first century.*

*Aviv joined IS in April 2003 after nine years at United Jewish Communities, where she worked closely with federations and national agencies concerned with the domestic health and welfare needs of vulnerable people. Prior to that, she was associate executive vice chair at the Jewish Council of Public Affairs, director of programs for the National Council of Jewish Women, and director of a comprehensive program to serve battered women and their families.*

*A noted expert on major issues affecting the nonprofit and philanthropic communities, Aviv is a frequent speaker on the accountability and transparency of nonprofit organizations, the financial state of the nonprofit sector, the role of civil society in democracy, and civic engagement. She has testified before Congress and has been quoted in numerous print, broadcast, and online media outlets, including the* New York Times, *the* Washington Post, *the* Wall Street Journal, *and* National Public Radio.

*Ms. Aviv is, in addition, a past chair of the National Immigration Forum, an advisory board member of the Stanford Social Innovation Review and the Center for Effective Philanthropy, a member of the board of governors of the Partnership for Public Service, and a member of the board of directors of GuideStar. A native of South Africa, she graduated with a B.S.W. from the University of Witwatersrand in Johannesburg and received a Master of Social Work degree at Columbia University.*

---

**Foundation Center (FC):** The charitable sector has been hurt in recent years by stories in the press detailing instances of alleged fraud and self-dealing, excessive compensation of executives and trustees, and other abuses of the public trust. How would you characterize the health of the sector?

**Diana Aviv (DA):** If an indication of health is how much money is available to the sector to do its work, I would say the sector is in relatively good shape. Look at giving for disaster relief. The most recent studies show giving for disaster relief up a significant amount — I think the overall figure was $7.37 billion in 2005. I also think the public views the sector's response to Hurricane Katrina in a favorable light; the public saw faith-based organizations and local charities responding immediately to the disaster, even as FEMA and state and local government stumbled in their response.

Another indication of the health of the sector is the growing number of nonprofit organizations in this country. Something on the order of 70,000 new nonprofit organizations are being formed every year, and the sector itself has more than doubled in size over the last twenty years.

> **[The media] can bring to light situations that need to be fixed and can help keep organizations vigilant in examining their own actions and policies. . . .**

On the other hand, it's also true, as you say, that there have been stories in the press over the last few years about alleged wrongdoing at nonprofits, examples of excessive compensation of executives and board members, self-dealing, and improper if not unethical fundraising practices. I think it's worth remembering, however, that to the extent those stories are true, the number of organizations involved comprises a very small percentage of the overall sector. Unfortunately, because those are the kinds of stories the press tends to focus on, the public might believe that wrongdoing in the sector is more pervasive than is actually the case. So, again, it depends on what your criteria are for assessing the health of the sector.

**FC:** Given the reluctance of government, especially at the federal level, to fund enforcement of existing regulations, isn't it a good thing the press has assumed a sort of watchdog role with respect to the sector?

**DA:** It's the media's responsibility to investigate and report. They can bring to light situations that need to be fixed and can help keep organizations vigilant in examining their own actions and policies. We often say that leaders and staff at nonprofit organizations should ask themselves, Am I comfortable with our activities and policies being reported by the local newspaper? If the answer is no, they need to think about whether they are comfortable with what they are doing. It would be great, as well, to hear more about the hundreds of thousands of nonprofits doing good work.

**FC:** In addition to your day job as president and CEO of Independent Sector, you've been executive director, for almost two years, of something called the Panel on the Nonprofit Sector. The panel recently submitted a final report to the Senate Finance Committee that included a comprehensive series of giving incentives and reforms designed to strengthen the transparency, governance, and accountability of charitable organizations. For the moment, at any rate, that package seems to have stalled in Congress. Why did Congress decide to table the panel's recommendations?

**DA:** I'm not sure that's the case. If you look at any major initiative in Washington — and this is true for any field of endeavor — unless there's a crisis that galvanizes legislators into action, it typically takes years for Congress to agree on the specifics of legislation and to pass a bill. Look at how long it took for Congress to pass a major highway bill. Look at the pension bill currently under consideration; everybody said it was a must-pass, but it's in trouble. Even must-pass legislation takes longer to pass — sometimes much longer — than its supporters would like. The fact that Senator Grassley (R-IA), chairman of the Senate Finance Committee and the main leader of the reform effort, dropped some legislation into the hopper at the end of last year doesn't mean that that legislation will automatically be converted into a bill that can be signed by the president a few months down the road.

*. . . it would not be accurate to say that everybody in Congress agrees with Senator Grassley that what the sector needs right now are reforms or changes to existing tax law. . . .*

Secondly, it would not be accurate to say that everybody in Congress agrees with Senator Grassley that what the sector needs right now are reforms or changes to existing tax law to encourage more charitable giving. There are folks like Senator Santorum (R-PA) who have argued that the sector is doing fine as is and doesn't need more regulation or more tax incentives for giving. You have differences of opinion on that score. It's Senator Grassley's job to persuade his colleagues on the Senate Finance Committee of the value of the legislation and, just as importantly, to persuade Bill Thomas (R-CA), chairman of the House Ways and Means Committee, which has jurisdiction over tax-related issues in the House, to support the reforms and see that they are passed into law.

As you might imagine, that's no easy task — especially when some groups believe their ox is about to be gored, which is the case whenever you are trying to close loopholes in the tax code or trying to increase penalties with respect to certain kinds of abuses of the code. Inevitably, somebody is going to be unhappy at the prospect of changes. Frequently their response will be to hire a lobbyist to persuade other lawmakers that the proposed changes are bad policy. Those lawmakers, in turn, may try to persuade Senator Grassley, for reasons unrelated to the specifics of the charity bill, to change or even eliminate something in the bill. It's a form of horse-trading, and it goes on all the time in Washington. Even when legislators are clearly for or against something, they'll weigh their vote on a bill against what else they might want or be able to get for their constituents. As a result, in the grand congressional scheme of things, legislation seldom moves forward quickly or easily unless there is a major crisis.

> **What I do know about Senator Grassley is that he is actively committed to this issue and these reforms. . . .**

What I do know about Senator Grassley, however, is that he is actively committed to this issue and these reforms. In fact, it is my understanding that recently he indicated that charitable sector reform is among his top three or four priorities. And don't forget, he is the chair of an extremely powerful committee. So I would say that it's too early to say what will happen with the legislation.

**FC:** Is it your sense that Senator Grassley believes charitable organizations routinely betray the public trust?

**DA:** I think Senator Grassley's perception of charitable organizations and the charitable sector have evolved over time. There was a point, a couple of years ago, when he described the sector as a "cesspool" — he actually used that word — and said that, in too many instances, it was a place where people viewed their tax exemption as an opportunity to pay for their country clubs and European vacations, rather than as an incentive to do the good work the sector was created to do. More recently, however, both Senator Grassley and Senator Baucus (D-MT), the ranking minority member on the Senate Finance Committee, have been very careful in their statements to differentiate between the vast majority of charitable organizations doing good work and the unscrupulous individuals who have exploited loopholes in the tax code for their own purposes and financial benefit.

**FC:** At a time when public-sector institutions increasingly seem unresponsive and ineffective, do you personally believe that more government regulation of the sector is the answer to its problems, perceived or otherwise?

**DA:** If you look at the recommendations made by the Panel on the Nonprofit Sector, you'll see that we said that there were three sets of actions that needed to be taken, and that all three needed to happen simultaneously. That is, if you pursued one set of actions in isolation — say, the recommendations designed for charitable organizations to improve their own governance — you would partially solve the problem, but you wouldn't really solve the whole problem. Another set of recommendations has to do with looking at existing regulations and making them work better — for example, providing more funding to the IRS for oversight, electronic filing of tax returns, and so on. And the third set of recommendations has to do with beefing up government's oversight role of the sector. I would suggest to you that if someone deliberately uses a charitable organization or engages in fraudulent practice to enrich him- or herself, only a government oversight body can stop that, because those kinds of individuals don't join organizations like Independent Sector, they don't join associations of grantmakers or nonprofit organizations, and they're not subject to group pressure because they are not there to serve the public in the first place. So we need to make sure that government is seen as the primary enforcer of existing regulations and has the authority and wherewithal to do its job effectively.

**The recommendations of the panel's final report are focused on three different areas of action: actions to be taken by charitable organizations, by the IRS, and by Congress. . . .**

**FC:** And yet some critics of the panel have suggested that its recommendations put too much emphasis on self-regulation as the solution to the sector's problems. Is that a valid criticism?

**DA:** The recommendations of the panel's final report are focused on three different areas of action: actions to be taken by charitable organizations, by the IRS, and by Congress. Over 80 percent of the recommendations focused on specific changes for Congress and the IRS to make to existing laws and regulations to prevent unscrupulous individuals from taking advantage of tax loopholes. Self-regulation is very important, but it must be coupled with legislative changes and effective oversight.

**FC:** To a large degree, effective self-regulation hinges on questions of organizational and financial capacity. Did the panel consider those kinds of issues in making its recommendations?

**DA:** We were so concerned about that issue that we actually created a working group whose sole charge was to focus on the special considerations of small nonprofit organizations. When I appeared before Congress twice to testify on these issues, I told members of the committee that it was vitally important they take into account questions of capacity, especially as it relates to smaller organizations. We know that 73 percent of the organizations in the sector have budgets of less than $500,000; we know that a large percentage of foundations — I believe the figure is 83 percent — have no paid staff at all. That's also true for about 40 percent of public charities. Congress needs to take all that into consideration as it thinks about how to regulate the sector.

> **Self-regulation is important, but it must be coupled with legislative changes and effective oversight. . . .**

Let me give you an example of how we made adjustments for small organizations. With respect to audit committees, we recommended that smaller organizations be allowed to choose whether they have a separate audit committee, rather than be required to have one. We also suggested that only organizations with annual revenues of more than $1 million be required to audit their books, and that organizations with revenues between $250,000 and $1 million should only be required to have their financial statements reviewed by an independent public accountant. That particular recommendation was based on what we heard from people in listening sessions we conducted around the country; in all of those sessions, an overwhelming majority of people welcomed the idea of having an independent accountant review their financial statements.

**FC:** Will that group continue its work even though the panel has submitted a final report to Congress?

**DA:** Yes. The panel submitted two reports to Congress: the final report last June and the supplemental report in March. The former included nine areas of recommendations, and within those nine there were a whole bunch of sub-recommendations. We also noted in the supplemental report that there were two areas where we hadn't finished our work. One is self-regulation, and the other concerns Forms 990 and 990-PF — the tax forms that public charities and private foundations are required to file with the IRS. We believe those forms could be made much clearer and more consistent, in terms of the information they seek to obtain. The focus of the self-regulation advisory committee, which has thirty-three members and has met three times, is on additional actions the sector might consider adopting to improve its own standards and practices.

*The focus of the self-regulation advisory committee is on additional actions the sector might consider adopting to improve its own standards and practices. . . .*

**FC:** As the CEO of an organization whose membership comprises both large private foundations and small grassroots nonprofits, you're more familiar than most with the unequal power dynamic that exists between funders and their grantees. From your perspective, has that dynamic become more lopsided over the last twenty years?

**DA:** Before I answer that question, let me share a fact with you. Of the combined revenues of the 1.4 million charitable organizations on file with the IRS, only about 3 percent come from foundations and corporate giving programs — a very small percentage. So, if you want to talk about the power dynamic between foundations and nonprofits, you really have to talk about the power dynamic between foundations and their grantees. The American Heart Association and the American Cancer Society and United Way of America and AARP and hundreds of other major national nonprofit organizations get little or no money from the foundation world, and organizations like those, in many instances, are much larger than the majority of private foundations.

The second myth about foundations worth noting is that the vast majority of them — about 83 percent, according to the National Center of Charitable Statistics — have no paid staff. In these instances, a wealthy individual has decided he wants to give some or all of his money to a charitable cause or causes and has created a foundation as a vehicle to do that. These small foundations bear no resemblance to the Bill and Melinda Gates Foundation.

**FC:** Which, with almost $30 billion in assets, is the largest foundation in the world. Recently, Warren Buffett stunned the philanthropic community and much of the rest of the world by announcing that he planned to give the bulk of his fortune — something on the order of $31 billion — to the Gates Foundation. The gift, which is structured in such a way that the foundation will receive annual payments of approximately $1.5 billion as long as either Bill or Melinda are alive, will effectively double the amount of the Gates Foundation's annual grantmaking. Do you expect Mr. Buffett's announcement to lead to similarly structured gifts down the road? And are you concerned about the concentration of so much wealth in a single institution?

**DA:** While it is the largest philanthropic gift in history, it's worth noting that, according to the Foundation Center, foundations gave away $33.6 billion in 2005, and that the combined assets of foundations were roughly $510.5 billion in 2004. So Mr. Buffett's gift would add another $2 billion a year to what foundations give.

That said, it is still a huge amount of money to be going to one organization, and some people will express concern whenever so much money is concentrated in the hands of so few. Only time will tell if the money is used effectively, but Bill and Melinda Gates have assembled a magnificent staff, and it should not be assumed that larger organizations cannot be as accountable or transparent as smaller organizations. Don't forget it was smaller charities that were involved in the Abramoff scandal, which demonstrates that the size of a nonprofit organization has little or no correlation with its accountability.

You know, I think Mr. Buffett's gift sends a lot of messages. It sends a message to wealthy people that it is good to give back to society. It also shows that a large donation does not have to be about name recognition. Warren Buffett could have created his own foundation, but instead he decided to give the money to people he trusts and a foundation he believes in. And, maybe most importantly, his gift may inspire and create new philanthropists, especially among the ranks of wealthy business leaders.

**FC:** Buffett's gift was nothing if not creative. In their new book, *Creative Philanthropy*, Helmut Anheier and Diana Leat suggest that the foundation field is suffering from a sort of low-key malaise related to what they describe as "a lack of awareness of the possible." Have foundations lost their nerve?

**Nobody says you have to be a genius or even be generous to establish a foundation. . . .**

**DA:** Good question. All it takes to establish a foundation is a lawyer and a certain amount of money. Nobody says you have to be a genius or even be generous to establish a foundation. The question really is, are all wealthy people brilliant and creative, and I would say to you the answer is no. That said, it's also true that large foundations that can afford to hire staff are in a position to hire some of the best minds in the business. So, if you're asking whether very large staffed foundations have lost their nerve and some of their creativity, I would say that the answer really depends on whom you're talking about. When I think about what the Gates Foundation has done over its short lifespan to organize a vaccine distribution system for the developing world before the vaccines have even been created, I will tell you that that's creative philanthropy in action.

Another foundation that comes to mind in this context is the Edna McConnell Clark Foundation, which has been making large investments in a limited number of organizations working in the youth development field. One of those is an organization called Harlem Children's Zone, which works to improve the quality of life for children and families in Harlem. McConnell Clark gave HCZ a grant of $250,000 in 1999 and followed that up with a grant of $1 million a few years later to help HCZ develop and implement a business plan and scalable management structures. That, in turn, has enabled HCZ to do some extraordinary work and to leverage McConnell Clark's initial investment many times over.

On the other hand, it's no secret that there are foundations out there that don't do a lot of due diligence and are not particularly effective. On that score, one of the interesting new tools on the market for foundations was created by an organization called the Center for Effective Philanthropy, which has designed an instrument for foundations that informs them in some detail about grantee perceptions of various aspects of their operation. What I'm saying is that when you look at the field as a whole, you see a mixed picture: There are some great things happening, some okay things happening, and some things that should be fixed.

**FC:** In *their* new book, the futurists Alvin and Heidi Toffler suggest that most of the philanthropic organizational structures with which we're familiar — private foundations, community foundations, the United Way, et cetera — are products of a 19th-century form of wealth creation that is rapidly giving away to new, knowledge-based forms of wealth creation. In the new world the Tofflers describe, only institutions that are capable of reinventing themselves rapidly and repeatedly are likely to survive. Do you agree?

**DA:** Well, I think the Tofflers have the right idea, though I'm not sure current reality comports with their predictions. The fact of the matter is that there are some organizations and businesses in our society that have survived the period of disruptive change we are living though only because someone bailed them out. Take the savings and loan industry, or the airline industry. These are not profitable industries in any recognizable definition of that word, and yet the government bailed them out because those kinds of industries and institutions need to exist in order for society to function smoothly.

I would suggest to you that the same is true of the charitable sector. In most cases, people give their time or money to a nonprofit organization because they believe passionately in the mission of the organization, not on the basis of a rigorous assessment of that organization's effectiveness. Which is not to suggest that organizations in the sector are incapable of making serious changes and re-inventing themselves. Two that come to mind are the United Way of America, which, under the leadership of Brian Gallagher, has done a terrific job of looking at different ways of relating to its local chapters; and the other is the March of Dimes, which has completely re-invented itself from an organization that was created to serve people suffering from polio into an organization that works to prevent premature baby births. Then you have an organization like the Nature Conservancy, which has been taking a close look at its practices to make sure they are relevant and align with current best practices and heightened scrutiny of the sector. The American Red Cross is an organization that needs — and is trying — to make those kinds of changes.

**FC:** Are you optimistic about the prospects of the charitable sector emerging from this period of heightened scrutiny and disruptive change strengthened and with its values intact?

**DA:** Absolutely. This is the first time in over thirty years that there has been a major examination of the rules governing the sector. The charitable sector has grown tremendously during that period and the tax laws have not kept up. The IRS's audit rate has been falling for some time and today less than one percent of nonprofit organizations are audited.

> **This is the first time in over thirty years that there has been a major examination of the rules governing the sector. . . .**

But while only a small number of organizations operate illegally or unethically, that is still not acceptable, particularly since we depend on the public's trust to do our work. New legislation needs to be passed, the IRS and state oversight bodies must be able to effectively monitor and enforce existing tax laws and regulations, and many charitable organizations may require help with governance and good practice.

We've already seen, through the work of the Panel on the Nonprofit Sector, that staff at nonprofit organizations are taking a look at their own practices and policies and thinking about what they can do better and what needs to be changed. And for me, that's a clear indication that the charitable sector will emerge from this period with its values, its capacity, and its reputation not only intact but strengthened.

**FC:** Well, thank you, Diana, for speaking with us today.

**DA:** Thank you.

*Mitch Nauffts, editorial director of* Philanthropy News Digest, *spoke with Diana Aviv in June 2006.*

# 13

# Philanthropic Leadership in a Changing World

Steve Gunderson
President and CEO
Council on Foundations

*Organized philanthropy in the United States finds itself at a pivotal moment. Driven, in part, by new money, new ideas, and increased scrutiny, foundations around the country have been engaged in a re-examination of their core values and practices, even as the introduction of new philanthropic vehicles has broadened the definition of philanthropy and thoroughly democratized the business of giving.*

*Around the world, in fact, interest in — and expectations surrounding — American philanthropy as a contributor to the common good and a catalyst for social change have never been greater. But whether philanthropy, at the start of a new century, is able to reinvent itself and play a larger role in addressing the unique challenges of our time, while maintaining the flexibility and independence that have been among its defining characteristics, remains an open question.*

*The Foundation Center's* Philanthropy News Digest *spoke with Steve Gunderson, president and CEO of the Council on Foundations (www.cof.org), a membership organization of more than two thousand grantmaking foundations and giving programs worldwide, about public perceptions of foundations and their work, the globalization of philanthropy, and leadership in a time of change.*

*Gunderson, a native of Wisconsin, served three terms in the Wisconsin State Legislature and sixteen years in the U.S. Congress, where his focus was on preparing America's citizens for the twenty-first-century economy. After voluntarily retiring from Congress in 1996, he served as a senior consultant and managing director of the Washington office of the Greystone Group, a Michigan-based strategic management and communications consulting firm.*

*A member of the advisory board of Partners in Surgery, a philanthropic effort to bring surgery to the rural poor of Guatemala, Gunderson has served on the boards of Gallaudet University, the Mary Fisher Family AIDS Network, and the Human Rights Campaign.*

*A graduate of the University of Wisconsin-Madison, he lives in Arlington, Virginia, with his partner Jonathan Stevens.*

---

**Foundation Center (FC):** HR-4, also known as the Pension Protection Act of 2006, was passed by Congress in August and signed into law by President Bush shortly thereafter. The bill includes a package of charitable incentives and reforms that some have characterized as the most sweeping legislation to affect charities since the Tax Reform Act of 1969. In a statement released the day the bill was passed, you and your colleagues spoke out against the bill. What are your objections to HR-4 as it relates to foundations and the charitable sector?

**Steve Gunderson (SG):** The position we've taken on HR-4 is the most important position the council has taken since I became president of the organization in the fall of 2005. We are strong advocates for reforms in the philanthropic sector, but we believe those reforms have to treat everyone the same way and apply a common set of standards, rules, and regulations to the charitable sector. If you look at the details of HR-4, you'll see that donor-advised funds at community foundations and certain kinds of supporting organizations are being singled out for special treatment, and it's that unfair treatment that the council opposes.

Moreover, even though the bill includes some of what we assume Senate Finance Committee chairman Charles Grassley (R-IA) believed were important reforms that needed to be made at this point in time, the legislation fails to consider the impact of many of those reforms. You especially see that in the denial of IRA rollover eligibility to donor-advised funds, supporting organizations, and private foundations. Last year's Katrina legislation, for example, made it possible for people to claim 100 percent deductibility for their charitable contributions but failed to give that same tool to supporting organizations and donor-advised funds at community foundations. Now, in HR-4, Congress has decided to deny IRA rollover eligibility to community foundations and supporting organizations, and — adding insult to injury — has also denied it to private foundations. And they didn't even warn us. As I said, that sends the signal that all philanthropy is not created equal, and that's an inappropriate signal, in my view, for government to be sending.

> [HR-4] sends the signal that all philanthropy is not created equal. . . .

**FC:** As you know, donor-advised funds and Type 3 supporting organizations have received considerable scrutiny from both Congress and the media after reports of alleged self-dealing at many such organizations began to surface. Is there a way, in your view, to extend IRA rollover eligibility to donor-advised funds and supporting organizations that does not reward people for using those vehicles solely or primarily as estate-planning devices?

**SG:** The new donor-advised fund and Type III supporting organization reforms enacted as part of HR-4 address the concerns that donors are using these charitable giving vehicles improperly. With the new rules in place, there is no reason why Congress should not extend IRA rollover eligibility to donor-advised funds, supporting organizations, and private foundations.

**FC:** The bill did not address the question of foundation payout. You're on record as saying it's only a matter of time before members of Congress — and you were an eight-term member of Congress — introduce a bill calling for an increase in the payout rate for private foundations. What are the forces driving the call for a higher payout rate?

**SG:** There are a couple, and, frankly, they're connected to legitimate concerns. If you followed my speaking and writing over the last decade, you know I'm one of those people who believe we are in a period in which government is in full retreat on the domestic front, with dramatic consequences. I mean, we're seeing needs on the domestic front that are as great as I have seen in my lifetime. And it's absolutely appropriate that many people are concerned that those needs are not being met. If you're the executive of a nonprofit organization trying to deliver services to a population in need and have to confront the fact that the government programs you rely on are being reduced or zeroed out, you're naturally going to look for resources elsewhere — not because you're conditioned to always want more, but simply because there's a legitimate and real public need out there that you're not able to meet.

The second thing that is happening has to do with the perception — and it's fueled, in part, by high-profile media stories like Warren Buffett's donation to the Bill and Melinda Gates Foundation — that there is all sorts of new money pouring into philanthropy. Now, when you combine that perception with the needs that clearly exist in our society, an obvious technical response, in the minds of many people, is to increase the minimum payout rate for foundations. It doesn't cost the government a cent, and it will generate additional resources to meet needs that are not being met. Given that calculus, I think it's very likely to happen in the near future. But the council needs to get involved in those conversations now, because it's going to be a difficult conversation for our members.

**FC:** You've been candid about this being a difficult and potentially divisive issue for the foundation and nonprofit communities. How would you recommend foundations get ahead of the issue?

**SG:** We need to explain to foundations that the worst possible scenario for the philanthropic community is to adapt a live-for-today-ignore-tomorrow mentality, especially with respect to the federal deficit. We also need to recognize that one of the strengths of philanthropy is its diversity. We should celebrate those foundations that choose to spend down their endowments during the life of their donors. There's absolutely nothing wrong with that. At the same time, we should celebrate the decision by other foundations to operate in a way that preserves their ability to serve the common good over an extended period of time. That's not a decision government should make. That's a decision for the individual donor to make, and we need to protect that freedom. I don't think anyone can look down the road and say with certainty that the needs and problems of society in the future are going to be any less serious than they are today, so we ought to be moving in a direction that will protect and preserve the ability of foundations to play a role in solving those problems down the road. Given the disappointing stock-market returns of the last few years, however, if you were to increase the minimum payout to 7 percent or 8 percent you'd probably force most foundations into a spend-out scenario.

**FC:** What about increasing it to 6 percent? Returns haven't been that bad.

**SG:** If you can tell me what the average market return for a foundation endowment will be over the next ten to twenty years, I could answer that question. But we just don't know.

**FC:** With government in retreat on the domestic front and increasingly perceived to be dysfunctional, should organized philanthropy try to step in and pick up some of the slack? And, if not, what is the proper role for philanthropy in American society?

**SG:** That's an important question. Whether you're a liberal or a conservative, I don't know of anybody who believes that philanthropy should aspire to be "government lite." First of all, it's just not possible. Foundations awarded about $30 billion in grants in 2005; the federal budget was about $2.4 trillion. There's just no way philanthropy could or should do what government is supposed to do.

> **Government is characterized by a one-size-fits-all mentality. That's exactly the opposite of what philanthropy is all about. . . .**

The second thing that's important to understand is that philanthropy, by its very nature, is different than government. Government is characterized by a one-size-fits-all mentality. That's exactly the opposite of what philanthropy is all about. Philanthropy is about innovation. It's about creativity. It's about taking risks. We try things and sometimes we fail, but we admit those failures and then we try something new. You can't do that in the public sector with public tax dollars. Part of the benefit philanthropy delivers to society is its willingness to fund pilot projects, to fund creative solutions that prove out and then to offer those to government, at all levels, as models to replicate at an appropriate size and scale.

**FC:** Do you think foundations and the role they play in society are misunderstood by the public? And, if so, to what do you attribute that disconnect?

**SG:** I absolutely think that foundations and foundation work are misunderstood, and that was brought home to me most dramatically after Hurricane Katrina, when it became clear that reporters and the media did not understand the difference between charity and philanthropy. Sadly, I don't think we've done much over the last year or so to highlight or explain that difference. I support and am as engaged in charity as any other American. But charity is not philanthropy. Philanthropy is what a friend of mine calls "problem-solving charity." It's more than just the immediate emotional response to a need; it's about taking a strategic approach to long-term problem solving, with strategic being the operative word.

The other thing we need to recognize is that while there's great potential for philanthropy to grow over the next few years, most Americans who have the wherewithal to participate in society in a philanthropic way don't fully understand what philanthropy is or does.

**FC:** And yet, as one editorial writer recently put it, "giving has become the new earning." To what do you attribute the upsurge of interest in philanthropic solutions to the global challenges we face?

**SG:** I think it's a part of our changing world. We live in a global economy. We have instant global communications. One of the results of these changes is a recognition that our world is much more connected than ever before. And because of that, the younger generation is very engaged in global economic and justice issues. We see this even in our small family foundations, many of which want to participate in global philanthropy. At the same time, one of our most important constituencies is corporate giving programs. I can name a corporation that just joined the council because they have a presence in no less than forty-six nations. Another has a presence in almost eighty different nations. Both of them, like most corporations, want to be engaged in the communities in which they do business. But today they're faced with different rules, regulations, and tax laws in many of those nations. And it's our view at the council that we need to respond to this challenge in much the same way we pursued trade standards and agreements in the past.

**FC:** Just before you came aboard as president, the council's board was putting the finishing touches on a new strategic plan for the organization. What is the strategic vision for the council as outlined in that plan? And what do you and your colleagues need to do to turn that vision into reality?

**SG:** That's a good question, and it has something to do with why I was hired. As most people know, I don't have a lot of professional philanthropic experience. But it was clear to me from my discussions with the search committee that the board wasn't looking for that kind of expertise. In part, that's because they were getting ready to recast the council's mission and, with it, some of the organization's programming. As you know, the Council on Foundations has always been engaged in grantmaker education, with a focus on effective grantmaking. That's been a wonderful building block for the organization and a great contribution to the foundation field. But it's very clear the board wants to move the council beyond that role to a place where it is helping to create a vision and voice for philanthropy at the national level and is a significant player in creating a similar vision and voice on a global level. The reality is that we need to see philanthropy more and more as the engine of social change and embrace the concept of philanthropic leadership. That means more than just making sure your grant application and administration processes, your RFP process, your evaluation and reporting mechanisms are transparent and efficient. Obviously, we all want those things. But we need to do more than that. Those of us who work in philanthropy need to see ourselves as leaders of change within our communities. And how foundations go about doing that is part of the council's new mission.

If you look at the strategic framework laid out by our board, it articulates three specific outcomes that are intended to guide our work. The first is to create an environment in which philanthropy can continue to grow. That includes the legislative side you and I talked about, as well as the educational outreach to the American public we've always done.

The second is to increase the role of philanthropy in serving the common good — that's really the leadership aspect I was just talking about.

And the third is emphasizing accountability and diversity in all we do. Foundations have to understand that they simply can't afford to betray the public trust, and when there is misconduct in the field, every one of us has to be willing to stand up and address it. The second aspect of this is how we respond to the changing composition of American society. It's imperative that we reflect the face of those we seek to serve. And the third piece of the puzzle is accountability, which we think is more accurately described as effectiveness. Regardless of what you call it, the field has not done a good job of looking at what the public has received in return for its investment in philanthropy, and it needs to do a better job of demonstrating that the tax-exempt assets held by foundations are generating a positive benefit to society. Unfortunately, we don't have a matrix today we can use to do that, although it's something we at the council hope to be able to develop and eventually share and communicate to the public and policy makers.

> **Foundations have to understand that they simply can't afford to betray the public trust. . . .**

**FC:** Is it something you might develop in partnership with other organizations?

**SG:** That has yet to be determined. We've been talking with a number of people, both in and out of philanthropy, but most of them are engaged in the program side of accountability rather than with the public ROI aspect of it. Certainly, it's a new area for us, but that doesn't mean it's a new discipline. We've had discussions, for example, with people at the Government Accountability Office who have figured out how you calculate return on investment for certain public-sector investments, and we're very interested in exploring whether those techniques and methods might be transferable to the philanthropic sector.

At the same time, I think we need to begin the discussion by acknowledging that some of the things funded by foundations — the local theater or library, a museum, a park or recreational facility — may not lend themselves to a clear-cut analysis of return on investment, even though we know they're important to the quality of life in our communities. In other words, there are some investments that just don't fit neatly into any formula designed to measure effectiveness or return on investment.

**FC:** Workforce development is an area of particular interest to you. Not too long ago you wrote: "America has five, maybe seven years in which to radically revamp its fundamental assumptions about workforce development and then to act. Whatever is going to be done to prepare us for the shortages of workers and skills, increased global competition, disparities in achievement between ethnic American communities and technology that changes while we sleep — whatever we are going to do, must be done now." Do you think that sense of urgency — not just about workforce development, but about many of the challenges we face as a nation — is shared by your colleagues in the world of philanthropy?

**SG:** Absolutely. You now, I've been struck since I've been at the council by the passion and the vision that I routinely encounter among people working in our field. At the same time, they recognize that we're in a period of transition. And as we make that transition, one of the things I find myself sharing with my colleagues in the sector is the need to recognize that the philanthropic sector may be the only sector in society that can serve as an impartial convener and arbitrator. As we see every day, government in this country is increasingly polarized, and that makes it harder and harder for the public sector to bring together diverse parties to address issues and problems, of any kind. Whether you're talking about education or workforce development or the environment, philanthropy is the only meeting ground today where people with different opinions can come together and have a civilized conversation about how we can move forward together.

> . . . philanthropy is the only meeting ground where people with different opinions can come together and have a civilized conversation. . . .

**FC:** On the question of leadership, you've written that "times of flux produce a new kind of leader." What kind of leader is our own time likely to produce? And do you see those kinds of leaders emerging in and from the foundation world?

**SG:** I do, and I think it's one of the fascinating trends in the field. Look at people like Bill Clinton or Tim Wirth or Doug Bereuter, president of the Asia Foundation, all of whom have had stellar careers in public life and have moved to the philanthropic sector. Or look at all the successful folks from the business world — people like Bill Gates, Warren Buffett, and Eli Broad — who have said, "You know, I've been successful in business; now it's time for me to commit some of the resources at my disposal to philanthropic causes." I probably meet with two to three successful senior-level people a week from this town, Washington, D.C., who want to talk to me about transitioning from whatever they happen to be doing into philanthropy. As John Nesbitt would say, it's a megatrend. It's happening, it's accelerating, and we need to recognize and celebrate it. At the same time, we need to recognize that part of what is going on is that philanthropy itself is looking at ways in which it can focus its agenda, increase the amount of expert resources available to it, and maximize outcomes in ways it hasn't done in the past.

**FC:** In what ways do you expect organized philanthropy to change over the next twenty years?

**SG:** I've often said that when you think about philanthropy in the twenty-first century, you need to keep in mind the three S's. The first is size, and by that I mean philanthropy is going to grow dramatically in size. You already see evidence of that. There's a World Bank study, for example, that suggests we'll go from $30 billion a year in foundation grants to $300 billion by the year 2050 — and that study was done before Warren Buffett made his announcement. Personally, I think we're going to get to the $300 billion level much sooner than 2050, but that's just my opinion.

The second refers to our service role. By that I mean we're going to see more and more people in philanthropy acting not just as effective stewards of tax-exempt resources but as leaders, as more and more people turn to philanthropy for the kind of visionary leadership needed to address the unique challenges facing our society.

And the third refers to scrutiny. When you grow in size, when you grow in service, you inevitably grow in terms of your visibility, and the higher your profile, the more scrutiny you can expect. Part of my job here is to try to make sure we strike an appropriate, proper balance between federal and state regulation of our sector and the flexibility we need to innovate, which is the hallmark of philanthropy.

**FC:** Philanthropy is also likely to become more global in outlook, isn't it?

**SG:** Absolutely. Take this week. I began the week speaking with the International Committee of the Council on Foundations. By mid-week

I was engaged in what is now a regular set of phone calls between Gerry Salole and myself. Gerry runs the European Foundation Centre, and he and I are beginning direct and regular cooperation on a number of items. Then I was in discussions with the leadership of both our 2007 annual conference in Seattle and "Philanthropy 2008," an initiative of the council to have everyone engaged in philanthropy convene at the same time here in Washington in 2008. I also communicated with the leadership of WINGS, a global network of membership associations and support organizations serving grantmakers, about their fall conference in Bangkok. And just today I visited with the ambassador from Norway regarding philanthropy in his nation. Finally, when I got back to my office, there was a box of books and a very kind letter from Tadashi Yamamoto, the president of the Japan Center for International Exchange, who recently wrote an amazing book called *Philanthropy and Reconciliation*. These days, it seems every day is global philanthropy day!

**FC:** As information technologies continue to flatten organizational hierarchies and empower individuals, do you think institutional philanthropy will become less institutional? And is that a good thing?

**SG:** That's a good question. My guess is that we'll see new forms of philanthropy built around technology that are perhaps less hierarchical and bureaucratic than a traditional foundation. But I don't think foundations will be transformed into technology-driven giving centers. Instead, my expectation is that philanthropy will become as diverse in structure as it will be in mission and ideology. And as I'm fond of saying, let's celebrate that diversity.

**FC:** Indeed. Well, Steve, thanks for your time this morning.

**SG:** Thank you.

*Mitch Nauffts, editorial director of* Philanthropy News Digest, *spoke with Steve Gunderson in August, and again in September, 2006.*

# 14

# Fifty Years of Promoting Foundation Openness and Transparency

Sara L. Engelhardt
President
The Foundation Center

*As foundation historian James Allen Smith has noted elsewhere, when the Foundation Center was first conceived in 1954 the approximately 5,000 philanthropic foundations in the United States had roughly $4.9 billion in assets and made grants totaling $300 million annually — 4.5 percent of the $6.65 billion in total income received by America's charitable organizations that year. Despite those relatively modest numbers, Congress had evinced growing interest in what one member of the House had termed "the tragic misuse of foundation money" and had conducted a series of public hearings devoted to foundations and foundation practices.*

*Two years later, in 1956, the Foundation (then Library) Center was launched under the able leadership of F. Emerson Andrews, a longtime executive at the Russell Sage Foundation, with the twin goals of promoting foundation openness and improving foundation accountability. As the American economy mostly boomed in the ensuing decades, the number of foundations in the U.S. and the assets under their control increased by an order of magnitude.*

*Today, the more than 68,000 foundations in the United States hold combined assets of $510 billion and make grants of almost $32 billion annually. More importantly, as Allen notes, foundations have emerged as a* *powerful and very visible force in American society — and, increasingly, on the world stage. At the same time, foundations have rarely if ever been subject to more scrutiny, from the media as well as Congress, or have had to contend with such heightened expectations.*

*The Foundation Center's* Philanthropy News Digest *spoke with Sara Engelhardt, president of the New York City-based center (foundationcenter.org), about increased scrutiny of foundations and the foundation field, public perceptions — and misperceptions — about foundations, the impact of globalization on philanthropy, and the significance of Warren Buffett's historic gift to the Bill and Melinda Gates Foundation.*

*Engelhardt joined the staff of the Foundation Center as executive vice president in 1987, having served on the center's board of trustees since 1984. Prior to that, she was on the staff of the Carnegie Corporation of New York for more than twenty years and, during the final twelve years of her tenure there, served as secretary of the foundation, managed its grants, and was program officer in the areas of philanthropy and nonprofit organizations and women in higher education and public life.*

*Engelhardt serves on the boards of the National Council for Research on Women and the Education & Research Foundation of the Metro New York Better Business Bureau, and chaired the Foundations and Corporations Committee of Wesleyan University's Campaign Council.*

*A 1965 graduate of Wellesley College, she holds a master's degree in administration of higher education from Teachers College, Columbia University.*

---

**Foundation Center (FC):** The Foundation Center was created in response to congressional hearings on private foundations in the early 1950s. Many of the features of the philanthropic landscape then are still visible or are re-emerging: rapid growth in the number of foundations and their assets, foundation worries about public perceptions of their work, public concern about abuses of charitable status and misuse of foundation resources. Are foundations today more transparent and accountable than they were fifty years ago?

**Sara Engelhardt (SE):** Yes, I think they're a lot more transparent. It didn't happen overnight, and it wasn't all because of the Foundation Center. But the center played a very important role in the evolution of foundation transparency. In the center's early days, our *Foundation Directory* systematically profiled foundations, whether they wanted to be profiled or not. And from the very beginning we pushed for foundations to publish annual reports and for the IRS to provide better access to foundations' annual 990 filings. Soon, we began asking foundations to send us updates, particularly of their grants. *Foundation News* was the center's original vehicle for publishing grant information, and because we published it every couple of months, the information was pretty timely. All these things helped create a sense that there was a field that foundations belonged to, and the public responded by asking for even more information.

But the big change for foundations came, I think, not from any legislation or IRS initiative but from the Internet. Before the Internet, getting information from foundations was like pulling teeth — mostly because it wasn't a priority for them. Foundations tend to be busy places, with a lot of urgent priorities and a relentless grantmaking cycle, and most of them were relatively slow to get on the Internet. They eventually realized, however, that if they didn't put something online that accurately represented what they did, someone else would do it for them, and it would often be inaccurate. To help foundations get online, the center created a "foundation folders" program at our Web site, giving funders a relatively easy — and free! — way to have an Internet presence. I think we've created more than a hundred and fifty folders — basically, mini-Web sites — over the past few years, so clearly foundations are seeing transparency about their work as more of a priority.

**FC:** When we talk about the foundation field, what are we talking about? And how has the field changed over the last twenty or thirty years?

**SE:** I would say that when the Foundation Center was founded there wasn't such a thing as a "foundation field." You may not know this, but we were the first national organization for foundations. The precursor to the Council on Foundations was established in 1949, but it wasn't reorganized to include private foundations until 1964. The center's first president, F. Emerson Andrews, actually served as a sort of one-man chronicler, organizer, and leader of the field.

But, you know, it's hard for foundations to be a field, and many of them, even today, see themselves as part of the arts field or the environmental field, not as part of a field of entities that make grants. That simply reflects their mission-driven character. Foundations tend to care most about their missions and the recipients of their funding, rather than field-wide issues. Nevertheless, a focus on the "how" of making grants has been expanding in importance over the past thirty years or so. The Tax Reform Act of 1969 created a lot of new rules of practice for foundations, particularly private foundations, and I think there's still a struggle within what we call the foundation field to figure out what its defining characteristics are, beyond the definitions in the Tax Reform Act. At the Foundation Center, we now use the term "grantmaker," to be more inclusive of the many diverse entities that are now arguably part of the field, and we talk about the field itself as "organized philanthropy." The whole point about the role of organized philanthropy in our society is that grantmakers don't all have to march in the same direction, so perhaps we should call it "disorganized philanthropy" instead!

> **The whole point about the role of organized philanthropy in our society is that grantmakers don't all have to march in the same direction. . . .**

**FC:** Is congressional scrutiny of the foundation field, which we saw in the '50s, the '60s, the '80s, and are seeing again today, a recurring response to changes in the political environment? Or is something fundamentally different happening this time around?

**SE:** Actually, scrutiny of foundations by Congress goes back to the teens — with the Walsh Commission — when the Rockefeller and Carnegie foundations were relatively new. It's interesting to note — this is my observation, at least — that these periods of scrutiny occur when two things have happened: first, there has been major growth in the number and/or assets of foundations and therefore a great deal of money in the field compared to prior years; and second, the country's political mood has turned relatively conservative.

The confluence of these two factors leads to some really interesting tensions, which is why the current scrutiny of the field seems so complicated. There's the tension between the government and its agencies not wanting to kill the goose that lays the golden eggs and their desire to tell the goose where to lay them. Government devolution at all levels, combined with the increasing amount of private wealth going into philanthropy, has led politicians to say, "Let's get government out of this; we'll let the free market of philanthropy identify the needs in society and solve these problems."

You know, philanthropy is inherently a social-change activity. Lots of wealthy people don't give their money away. Those that do are seeking some kind of improvement in their world. That leads to a lot of diversity in the foundation field, in that individual donors and boards get to decide on the changes they want to aim for, and our government has given them great freedom to choose the targets of their philanthropy, rather than forcing them to march to the same drummer.

> **Government devolution . . . has led politicians to say . . . "we'll let the free market of philanthropy identify the needs in society and solve these problems."**

**FC:** What changes, if any, is renewed scrutiny of the field likely to result in? Will we see requirements for foundation accreditation, periodic reviews of tax-exempt status, limits on trustee and staff compensation, and/or an increase in the mandatory payout rate, as some have suggested? Or will Congress, having included a package of charitable reforms in the Pension Reform Act passed earlier this year, move on to other issues and concerns?

**SE:** It's always risky to predict what's going to come out of one of these periods of scrutiny. The one that led to our founding, in the '50s, didn't immediately result in any legislation or changes. In fact, it took more than a decade for enough momentum to build to produce the Tax Reform Act of 1969. Of course, many of the laws that have been passed over the years have been beneficial to the field. They've required some rethinking or restructuring of how these institutions relate to the business sector, to the governmental sector, to the social sector, and by and large they haven't been too burdensome. Still, it's always possible that a law will be passed that will kill the goose by making people not want to start a foundation or, worse, forcing existing foundations to go out of business after a set number of years.

**FC:** By imposing a higher annual mandatory payout rate on them?

**SE:** Yes, that's a possibility, because the public and its representatives in government really don't understand the way the field works or its value to our society. I'm not going to try to predict what's going to happen. I will say, however, that it's hard for Congress, particularly when we're going through a transition in the political balance of power, to focus on this issue. It's such a complex area, and its constituency, though small, requires a lot of handling once it's energized, so it's likely that Congress will move on to more pressing public concerns.

**FC:** Historically, private foundations have preferred to work behind the scenes to advance their missions. Given the higher profile of foundations, increased scrutiny of the field, and the magnitude of the challenges the U.S. faces, domestically as well as internationally, is that paradigm obsolete? In other words, are foundations too cautious about promoting their activities and agendas?

**SE:** Well, I would actually suggest that the opposite is happening. Historically, foundations' reputation for working behind the scenes was driven, I think, by the Protestant ethos that prompted philanthropists to create many of the largest foundations in the first place. You see this early on with Carnegie Corporation and the Rockefeller Foundation, but also later with the Pew Charitable Trusts, which were initially extremely secretive — but from a deeply religious conviction that you don't flaunt your good deeds, not because they felt they had something to hide. You also see a uniquely American brand of individualism in many foundations, with each working to find its own niche where it can make a difference. But after the Tax Reform Act of '69, which foundations viewed as the disastrous result of the lack of field-wide standards, transparency, and public outreach, foundations began to work on these issues individually and through their growing "infrastructure" — at that time, primarily the Council on Foundations and the Foundation Center.

**Foundations are communicating as never before, not only with each other but also with the public. . . .**

By the 1980s, many of the large staffed foundations had highly professional communications offices, and in the new-foundation boom of the '90s, virtually all the "born-large" foundations, as one of the center's trustees used to call them, were on the communications bandwagon from the start. Today, foundations are communicating as never before, not only with each other but also with the public — directly and through intermediary groups like the Foundation Center, as well as through the media. Ultimately, the goal is to strengthen the public mandate for foundations to do their work on a tax-exempt basis and to increase public trust in the field as a whole.

**FC:** Is there a gap between how foundations view themselves and how they're portrayed by the media?

**SE:** The media used to cover foundations only rarely, and some of the increased media coverage in recent years undoubtedly results from the increase in foundation communications efforts. But whether that has strengthened public trust and their public mandate is unclear. I don't recall the media ever being impressed with foundations just doing their work, while the press seems dazzled of late by the "celebrity factor" in philanthropy. I think that's what is driving the more positive media coverage of foundations. A lot of new money is coming from high-profile personalities in the business and entertainment worlds, many of whom are relatively young and glamorous, and that helps sell papers. The media are excited about celebrity and big-money philanthropy, not about foundations per se. It's the American version of royalty, which this country has always been fascinated by.

> **I don't recall the media ever being impressed with foundations just doing their work, while the press seems dazzled of late by the "celebrity factor" in philanthropy. . . .**

How is it different from the way foundations see themselves? Well, the media try to simplify things, but the foundation field is very diverse. The media tend to extrapolate from one instance to the whole, but the old saw that "if you've seen one foundation, you've seen one foundation" more accurately represents the reality of the foundation world. Any way you slice it, the result is a gap between the picture of the field presented by the media and the picture of the field that the Foundation Center, for instance, portrays in its reports. Most people in the field believe our research to be authoritative, but they also read the media coverage. And they sometimes challenge us about the gap between what we say and what they hear from the media: "So if the new entrepreneurs are taking over the field, why don't your data reflect that?" Because the reality is that they're not; they're just getting more coverage because they're new and different.

**FC:** What misperceptions about organized philanthropy undermine its potential to contribute to society?

**SE:** The biggest problem, in my view, is the sense of power that the media — and hence the public — seem to believe foundations have. This leads to the misperception that foundations are failing to achieve the positive impact they should be having on society. That perception stands in stark contrast to most foundations, which understand that they have very little power in the great scheme of things, particularly when they're trying to address root causes — what we call "strategic philanthropy" — as opposed to more direct charity for specific institutions or communities. Yet some of those very foundations feed this misperception by stating their ambitions in such grandiose terms that it sounds as though they expect to be held accountable for achieving sweeping results.

In the early '80s, I developed what I call my surfer theory of philanthropy, which owed its origins to the fact that many leaders in the field at that time spoke of foundations, in the idiom of the day, as "making waves." I remember first articulating it at a Council on Foundations meeting convened by Jim Joseph on the Stanford campus. At some point during the meeting, I pointed out that only God or forces of nature can make waves, and that the most a foundation could do is learn to ride them well. Well, I got a pretty hostile response, from the foundation critics as well as from those with extensive foundation experience. Curiously, both insisted that foundations were one of the most powerful institutions in society and only needed to figure out how to convince the public of that fact to get the respect they deserve.

Actually, surfing is a great metaphor for the problems strategic foundations face when they're trying to "make waves." In surfing, you sit on your board watching dozens of waves roll by while trying to decide which one to catch. Once you've decided, you have to really commit. Sometimes you wipe out, and other times you see the wave isn't all you thought it would be. Even when you catch a good one, you have to decide whether to ride it all the way in or whether, at some point, to bail out and get ready for the next set. Basically, it's the same for strategic foundations, which have to weigh the risks they take in any program and grant against potential outcomes, precisely because they aren't powerful enough to "make waves" or control many of the factors that determine the success of a given strategy.

As someone who spent twenty years of her life working for a foundation, I believe that the decisions foundations face on a daily basis make the work terribly stressful. And the people looking over your shoulder — other staff, your board, the media, and to some extent the government — will ask, "So what have you achieved lately?" No matter how you respond, you can always be second-guessed about the decisions you made. In this respect, at least, grantmaking is a risk-taking business.

**FC:** Part of the problem may be that a billion dollars isn't what it used to be. A billion-dollar foundation in the context of a $2 trillion economy is unlikely to achieve the same kind of impact as it might have in a much smaller economy. And yet the public and the media see the billion-dollar figure and think, "Gee, that's a lot of money."

**SE:** As you note, it's much less money than it used to be — and it's not just that the cost of living has gone up. When Andrew Carnegie founded Carnegie Corporation in 1911, its endowment of $125 million amounted to 18 percent of the federal government's annual expenditures of $690 million. By the time the Bill and Melinda Gates Foundation was created in 1999, its assets of $17 billion equaled only 1 percent of federal domestic spending of $1.5 trillion. Yet the sheer size of its endowment relative to other large foundations made us all compare it to Carnegie and Rockefeller in terms of the impact it could have. Of course, with the addition of Warren Buffett's money, the Gates Foundation really does have a lot of money. But even the combined fortunes of Bill Gates and Warren Buffett do not add up to the kind of clout that Carnegie and Rockefeller had when they started.

> . . . in combining their fortunes to achieve their philanthropic goals, Bill Gates and Warren Buffett have set a new standard for philanthropy that others surely will emulate. . . .

That said, Gates and Buffett are like Carnegie and Rockefeller in that they are the wealthiest individuals of their day, and in combining their fortunes to achieve their philanthropic goals they have set a new standard for philanthropy that others surely will emulate.

**FC:** We've been talking mostly about private foundations, which have dominated organized philanthropy since the early part of the twentieth century. The last fifteen years, in contrast, have seen a rise in alternative grantmaking vehicles. To what degree do these vehicles represent the beginning of a new type of philanthropy that has the potential to achieve better results in the decades to come than private foundations have in the past?

**SE:** Foundations, like anything else, are creatures of their time, but I don't actually believe there's a lot new under today's sun. In fact, in the '90s I chuckled whenever new philanthropists held up their "venture philanthropy" as a daring alternative to conventional foundations, especially when they cited Andrew Carnegie as their role model. Well, it was Carnegie's general-purpose foundation that was the model for the institutional philanthropy they were railing against. What's more, they assumed, falsely, that Carnegie Corporation had become captive of a staff that had turned it into an inflexible bureaucracy. Unfortunately, that assumption gave rise to the notion that philanthropists should "give while they live," rather than let later generations of trustees distort the original donor's "intent." I can tell you that Andrew Carnegie's vision for his foundation was extremely "institutional," as was Rockefeller's. They both built major business organizations that were highly "bureaucratic" — in the best sense of the word. And they both built philanthropic foundations that were organized and staffed following that business model, because they assumed it was the best way to achieve their philanthropic goals.

**FC:** Didn't Carnegie and Rockefeller characterize their own philanthropy as "venture" philanthropy?

**SE:** Yes, and they weren't the only ones. Maria Mottola has noted that the venture capitalists who created the New York Foundation even before Carnegie and Rockefeller created their foundations talked about their philanthropy using the language of venture capitalism. It's not a new term. But the more important point is that it's not entirely clear how today's "venture philanthropy" foundations are distinct from the long-established foundations such as Carnegie, Rockefeller, and Ford — all of which, of course, have changed with the times.

This all leads me to conclude that philanthropy is continually changing and reinventing itself in response to forces around it. A major force for change in our own day is technology, which, among other things, has dramatically changed the way companies and organizations do their work. It's probably not a coincidence that technology companies are the ones generating a lot of the wealth driving the new philanthropy, but of course, even the older foundations have adopted new technologies and are working differently.

> . . . philanthropy is continually changing and reinventing itself in response to forces around it. . . .

However, I think it's easy to confuse the way the wealth is created with the way philanthropy gets done. That's why foundations established "in perpetuity," as we say, sometimes get a bad rap. Critics of foundations established in perpetuity fear that a foundation's giving will become mired in an outmoded vision of what it can or should achieve — or, conversely, that the original donor's vision for the foundation will be subverted by later generations of family members or trustees. Andrew Carnegie's deed of gift for Carnegie Corporation stated, "Conditions upon the earth inevitably change; hence no wise man will bind Trustees forever to certain paths, causes or institutions." In that regard, I believe he was a wise model for the philanthropists of today. He understood that future generations would continue to have great need for philanthropic resources but also believed that they would have the wisdom to use those resources well.

**FC:** To what degree are some of the new philanthropic models — the public charity model, for example — a means for philanthropy to do a better job of aggregating resources and applying those resources to problems? And to what extent are they simply a pragmatic way of circumventing the laws and regulations covering private foundations?

**SE:** Well, the Cleveland Foundation, the first community foundation in the nation, was set up in 1914 as a means of aggregating philanthropic resources then managed by Cleveland's banks and trust companies in a way that would produce significant community benefit, rather than being distributed by the banks in dribs and drabs. And as you know, that foundation was the model for the seven hundred-plus community foundations across the country today. United Ways and other federated giving vehicles have also long provided the means for small amounts of philanthropic money to have a large impact. But you're right in suggesting that many of the newer "foundations" are really means for people with similar philanthropic interests to pool their resources and have greater impact on a cause they care about. Examples of those kinds of vehicles include the women's funds and grantmaking public charities that focus on particular issues, rather than primarily on a geographic area.

In light of the phenomenon we've been talking about — of even very large private foundations no longer having the clout they'd like to have — there's a lot of talk in the private foundation world of needing to collaborate more. I must say I have mixed feelings about this, since too much collaboration is likely to reduce what I consider to be one of the great strengths of the private foundation model — the freedom to pursue innovative solutions to social problems without regard to conventional wisdom. That said, we're definitely seeing new collaborative models, including jointly creating new public charities to accomplish a common program goal. I might even suggest that Warren Buffett's decision to join forces with the Gates Foundation is the ultimate expression of this trend, although I believe his motivation had more to do with not wanting to run such a large foundation than of believing his fortune wasn't big enough to have an impact by itself.

The real surprise, however, is the resurgence of the private foundation model. I've been frankly astounded, given the tax laws and regulations, at how many people are going that route. Philanthropists like Bill Gates who put huge amounts into their foundations probably don't get much of a tax deduction and must use other pockets to fund things forbidden to foundations, such as direct lobbying. But a private foundation gives these philanthropists a community and also a platform for interacting with other institutions in society. The benefits of having a "foundation field" make the private foundation a desirable model even today.

**The real surprise is the resurgence of the private foundation model. . . .**

**FC:** What does the emergence of successful, high-profile businessmen like Gates, Ted Turner, George Soros, and Michael Bloomberg as philanthropists say about philanthropy in the twenty-first century?

**SE:** Those are the same kinds of people who have been philanthropists from the beginning. What's interesting to me is the other kind of people who increasingly are seen as philanthropists, people like Bill Clinton, who's considered a philanthropist not by virtue of his money but by virtue of his connections and power.

> **A private foundation gives philanthropists a community and also a platform for interacting with other institutions in society. . . .**

**FC:** His power to convene?

**SE:** More his power to attract and channel large amounts of private money. Maybe it's a coming together of economically and politically powerful people with a common vision for improving the world. It's very interesting, for instance, that Bloomberg is both a philanthropist and an increasingly prominent political figure. The mixing of political clout with philanthropic impulse, I find that fascinating. To some extent it may be the result of the governmental and political gridlock we've had in this country. Frustrated with politics as usual, those in power are using philanthropy to make headway in improving our society. It's definitely something to watch.

**FC:** If philanthropy is the child of American capitalism, and American capitalism increasingly is driven by globalization, do you expect globalization to have a long-term impact on philanthropy? And what, if any, are the implications for democracy and civil society should that turn out to be the case?

**SE:** Globalization is already having a tremendous impact on philanthropy. Many of the issues confronting our global society — including health and environmental issues, immigration and labor issues — know no borders. And these issues are politically globalized, as well as economically and in other ways. So globalization is going to continue to have an impact on philanthropy — not only on how philanthropy is conducted, but even more profoundly, perhaps, on the kind of impact it is able to achieve.

One theory I have is that the twentieth century epitomized philanthropy's use of social science — and to some extent the health and hard sciences — to get at the root causes of social ills and to develop new methods of studying society that would yield new ways of improving it. But as the twentieth century came to an end, it seemed that philanthropists and foundations began to embrace politics as a more effective way to change the world. Maybe that's partly because in a global society no one can afford the luxury of dealing with just one political system; today, people who want to make a difference must navigate multiple systems and cultures and ethnicities and languages. And in this environment, the practice of politics becomes much more important than social science research in achieving social change. Social science is still important, but philanthropy in the twenty-first century may be defined by the dominance of political strategies as the favored means to achieve philanthropic goals.

> **As the twentieth century came to an end, it seemed that philanthropists and foundations began to embrace politics as a more effective way to change the world. . . .**

**FC:** Interesting. Does that put philanthropy on a collision course with democracy? In other words, who has a vote in how the Gates Foundation spends its money or what any large NGO does in country X or Y?

**SE:** That's the key question. One of the major goals of the '69 Tax Act was to cordon private foundations off from the political arena precisely because, unlike public charities, they didn't have a broad constituency. They were forbidden to lobby, except on their own behalf; they were forbidden from explicitly funding organizations to influence legislation; they were forbidden from supporting voter registration, as opposed to voter education; and so forth. During the '60s, the power of foundations to drive public issues had become apparent, although they were doing it primarily by funding demonstration projects or commissions charged with studying an initiative that the federal government would then pick up. Head Start, public television, and a lot of other Great Society programs came out of those kinds of partnerships. And to some degree the Tax Reform Act of '69 was the backlash against foundations driving the public agenda in this way.

Starting in the '80s, as the federal responsibility for many social programs was devolved to the states, neither government nor foundations had the capacity to take demonstration programs to scale. Foundations switched to a focus on public policy as the means to achieve an impact on major social issues. More and more foundations — which represent no one, or perhaps everyone — are now trying not so much to influence public policy as to help policy makers become informed by the research they fund and the experts they convene. At some point, the public could balk at this strategy, as well as at giving foundations too much influence.

**FC:** A final question: Given foundations' relatively modest resources, where does organized philanthropy have the best chance to achieve breakthroughs over the next ten or fifteen years?

**SE:** It's tempting to say health or public health because of all the breakthroughs achieved in those fields by foundations over the years. As you have reported in PND, a number of major foundations today, including the Gates Foundation, focus on disease, especially in the developing world, as a social ill that can be conquered. One of the problems, though, is that in an age of all-embracing globalization, new diseases and how they travel and mutate — AIDS being a sobering example — will make it much harder to solve health issues. So foundations might not look to the health field for the big breakthroughs in the future.

I guess I go back to my hypothesis that politics is going to be a key to making social advances in the future. In a connected and interdependent world with so many different political structures and systems, how does philanthropy help all people advance without imposing "solutions" developed for one nation with its own values and history and political system on nations with different beliefs and political systems? Left to their own devices, governments are more likely to fight for their own survival and supremacy than to work for the global good. I don't have the answer to that question, but I have a strong feeling that finding that answer is the breakthrough that philanthropy — global philanthropy — might be capable of. And next to that, any other breakthrough pales in its capacity to improve human society.

> **I guess I go back to my hypothesis that politics is going to be a key to making social advances in the future. . . .**

**FC:** Well, thank you, Sara. And congratulations on the Foundation Center's 50th anniversary.

**SE:** Thank you. It has been an honor to lead the Foundation Center these past fifteen years, and I'm delighted to have the chance to share my thoughts with PND's readers.

*Mitch Nauffts, editorial director of* Philanthropy News Digest, *spoke with Sara Engelhardt in November 2006.*

# 15

# Philanthropy as Social Incubator

Vartan Gregorian
President and CEO
Carnegie Corporation of New York

"The problem of our age," argued Andrew Carnegie in his 1889 essay Wealth (republished in England as The Gospel of Wealth, a name Carnegie subsequently adopted as his own), "is the administration of wealth."

For Carnegie, who emigrated to the United States from Scotland as a boy and amassed a fortune while still in his thirties, the problem wasn't the morality of capital accumulation — whether, as he put it, the "contrast between the palace of the millionaire and the cottage of the laborer . . . [is] to be deplored." An ardent proponent of the wide-open capitalism that developed in the United States after the Civil War, Carnegie viewed the concentration of wealth in "the hands of the few" as both temporary and "essential" for "the progress of civilization."

Instead, the crucial question, as he saw it, was how best to dispose of that wealth for the common good. Arguing that there were but three possibilities — passing it on to one's heirs, leaving it for public uses at one's death, or attending "to the administration of wealth during [one's] life" — Carnegie argued that the last was "by far the most fruitful" and, if widely adopted, would lead to "an ideal state, in which the surplus wealth of the few . . . can be made a much more potent force . . . than if it had been distributed in small sums to the people themselves."

*Determined, as always, to prove his point, Carnegie labored diligently over the next thirty years to give away his fortune, endowing and/or supporting a long list of institutions and causes, among them the Carnegie Institute of Technology (now part of Carnegie Mellon University), the Carnegie Institution, the Carnegie Foundation for the Advancement of Teaching, the Carnegie Hero Fund, the Carnegie Endowment for International Peace, and, most famously, the creation of thousands of free public libraries around the country and abroad. As it became apparent, however, that plans to dispose of his fortune while alive were no match, as biographer David Nasaw puts it, for the "inexorable logic of compounding interest," Carnegie, in 1911, set up the Carnegie Corporation of New York to "promote the advancement and diffusion of knowledge and understanding."*

*In the eight-plus decades since, the Carnegie Corporation has distinguished itself as one of the most influential private foundations in the world. Its contributions to American society include efforts to expand higher education and adult education, the advancement of research on learning and cognitive development in early childhood, the promotion of educational and public interest broadcasting, the advancement of minorities and women in pre-college and higher education, the heightening of public understanding of the education and health needs of children and adolescents, and the investigation of risks of superpower confrontation, nuclear war, and ethnic and civil strife.*

*The Foundation Center's* Philanthropy News Digest *spoke with Vartan Gregorian, the Corporation's twelfth president, about the evolution of organized philanthropy in the United States, current perceptions and misperceptions of philanthropy, the emergence and impact of new philanthropic vehicles on the foundation field, and the challenges confronting philanthropy in an increasingly globalized world.*

*Prior to joining Carnegie as president in 1997, Gregorian served for nine years as the sixteenth president of Brown University and, before that, for eight years (1981–1989) as president of the New York Public Library.*

*He has, in addition, taught European and Middle Eastern history at San Francisco State College (now University), the University of California at Los Angeles, and the University of Texas at Austin. In 1972, he joined the University of Pennsylvania faculty and was appointed Tarzian Professor of History and professor of South Asian history. He was also founding dean, in 1974, of the Faculty of Arts and Sciences at the University of Pennsylvania and four years later became its twenty-third provost, a position he held until 1981.*

*Dr. Gregorian is the author of* The Road to Home: My Life and Times, Islam: A Mosaic, Not a Monolith, *and* The Emergence of Modern Afghanistan, 1880–1946. *A Phi Beta Kappa and Ford Foundation Foreign Area Training Fellow, he is the recipient of fellowships from the John Simon Guggenheim Foundation, the American Council of Learned Societies, the Social Science Research Council, and the American Philosophical Society. He is also a Fellow of the American Academy of Arts of Sciences and the American Philosophical Society.*

*Gregorian was born in Tabriz, Iran, of Armenian parents and received his elementary education in Iran and his secondary education in Lebanon. In 1956 he entered Stanford University, where he majored in history and the humanities, graduating with honors in 1958. He was awarded a Ph.D. in history and humanities by Stanford in 1964 and received the Danforth Foundation's E.H. Harbison Distinguished Teaching Award in 1969. In 1998, he was awarded the National Humanities Medal by President Clinton, and in 2004 he was awarded the Presidential Medal of Freedom, the nation's highest civil award, by President Bush.*

---

**Foundation Center (FC):** Private foundations have dominated organized philanthropy for the better part of a century. In contrast, the last fifteen years have seen a rise in alternative grantmaking vehicles, many of them structured as public charities. To what degree are new forms of organized philanthropy simply pragmatic ways of circumventing the laws and regulations covering private foundations? Or do they represent the beginnings of a new type of organized philanthropy that has the potential to achieve better results in the decades to come than private foundations have achieved in the past?

**Vartan Gregorian (VG):** Philanthropy has always been multifaceted; over the years, philanthropists have structured their giving in many different ways. What has changed is that state and federal regulations, along with case law developed over the last century, have provided more flexibility for individuals to give to charity and provide philanthropy in different ways. Since 1917, for example, individual federal taxpayers have been allowed to deduct gifts to charitable and certain other nonprofit organizations — although since 1986, this benefit has only been available to those who itemize their deductions. And the Internet, certainly, has revolutionized charitable giving, as the response to Hurricane Katrina demonstrates: of the $34 million raised by the Humane Society in connection with Katrina, for instance, 53.8 percent was donated online. The American Red Cross received 22.3 percent of its Katrina donations online, which amounted to $479 million. Even smaller groups like Mercy Corps raised significant sums online; of the nearly $10.2 million in Katrina money donated to that group, 45.5 percent came in online.

Foundations, too, are now structured in multiple ways, each following the dictates of the individual or family that created them. For example, operating foundations generally are not grantmaking institutions but rather operate facilities or institutions devoted to a specific charitable activity spelled out in their charters. Some operating foundations may use their endowment to conduct research while others may have been created to provide such direct services as managing museums, historical sites, providing assistance to the handicapped, et cetera. Generally, operating foundations are focused on having a specific, and sometimes immediate, impact. Other foundations, such as the Aaron Diamond Foundation and the Vincent Astor Foundation, were created by their donors with the intent of spending their entire endowment in the service of particular ideas or causes and then to close their doors. Family foundations often have a twofold purpose: to make grants but also to maintain the foundation as a kind of laboratory to train future generations of the family and promote the art of giving as part of the family culture. Private grantmaking foundations, such as Carnegie Corporation of New York, the Rockefeller, Ford, MacArthur, Hewlett, and Mellon foundations, along with others, were created by their donors to carry out philanthropic efforts in perpetuity and focus on accomplishing their goals over the long-term by supporting research and scholarship or by investing in existing organizations rather than by replacing them or attempting to replicate their work.

> . . . that Americans continue to try to help their nation and their fellow citizens through both voluntary efforts and financial support is a lasting cause for pride and hope. . . .

Thank goodness there are so many different ways of being both charitable and philanthropic, because the 1.4 million nonprofit organizations in the United States and the roughly 65,000 grantmaking foundations are addressing problems that, unfortunately, are likely to remain with us in the future. The fact that Americans continue to try to help their nation and their fellow citizens through both voluntary efforts and financial support is a lasting cause for pride and hope.

**FC:** What misperceptions about organized philanthropy — either on the part of the media or among the public at large — persist and undermine its full potential to contribute to society?

**VG:** It has surprised me that philanthropy, which is such a major enterprise and has such a significant impact on American society, did not receive equally significant coverage in the media until the inception of publications like *Philanthropy News Digest*, the *Chronicle of Philanthropy*, and even the *Chronicle of Higher Education*, which often highlights philanthropic support of education. The public needs more information about both philanthropic and charitable activities — in fact, they also need help in understanding the difference between the two. Charity, which is derived from the Latin word *caritas*, meaning "dear" has a long religious history; for Christians, Jews, and Muslims, for example, it has meant giving immediate relief to human suffering without passing judgment on those who suffer. Philanthropy has a more secular history and comes from the Greek word *philanthropos*, meaning "love of mankind." The Greek meaning carried over to English, and, for the longest time, philanthropy referred only to a caring disposition toward one's fellow man. Now the word is used to describe generosity that promotes human progress in any field.

It's important to understand that, generally, philanthropy's role in our society is not to respond to immediate needs or to displace the role of the municipal, state, or federal government in providing the civic supports that impact our lives. But what foundations, in particular, can do is support efforts that offer innovative solutions to civic problems, or even develop model solutions to problems. Foundations can also fund projects that serve as incubators for progressive, even pioneering ideas, providing the public with program and policy alternatives they might otherwise never even know about or have the opportunity to consider. Perhaps one of the most important characteristics of foundations is that they have the capacity to be flexible, which is a valuable attribute in a complex society such as ours, with all its checks and balances. Other institutions and government agencies can be highly bureaucratized — in fact, one of the ways they protect themselves is by armoring themselves with an elaborate bureaucracy and complicated processes for getting things done. Because foundations are able to proceed more quickly, and with wider latitude, they can help put important issues on the nation's agenda; they can invest in innovative, experimental, and demonstration efforts; they can challenge orthodoxies; and they can support basic research that may not produce immediate results but produces knowledge that proves to be of lasting value in the long run.

**FC:** Citing developments such as the disposal of Warren Buffett's fortune, the creation of the loosely for-profit Google.org, and Richard Branson's recent announcement at the Clinton Global Initiative that he planned to "give" $3 billion of his company's profits for alternative fuel research, some observers have described what is happening in the field as the "deconstruction of philanthropy." Is that a useful characterization?

> **The more anybody and everybody gives, the better for all. Large gifts and large-scale philanthropy do not make smaller foundations irrelevant. . . .**

**VG:** This is hardly doomsday for other forms of philanthropy — the more anybody and everybody gives, the better for all. Large gifts and large-scale philanthropy do not make smaller foundations irrelevant. After all, some of the current "small" foundations were once "big," and that includes Carnegie Corporation of New York. In fact, a recent edition of the Foundation Center's *Foundation Yearbook* ranked Carnegie Corporation twenty-fourth by assets among U.S. foundations. It's not the amount of money that's important, it's the ideas and imagination behind it and the responsibility with which it is used and the real-world impact it has. In other words, it is not time to "deconstruct" philanthropy in the way that one might deconstruct literature. Small and medium-size foundations with clearly defined missions have no reason to develop an inferiority complex or lose direction. Indeed, smaller foundations may be able to move more swiftly, more effectively, and in a more focused manner than their larger counterparts, especially those with a cumbersome bureaucracy that tends to slow them down and may limit their effectiveness or stifle their creativity.

Of course, one also has to note that a new form of philanthropy may be emerging — the "for-profit" model, such as the one recently announced by Larry Page and Sergey Brin, the founders of Google. They plan to create a philanthropy, with a $1 billion endowment, that will be structured as a for-profit organization. It's mandate will include funding start-up companies and forming partnerships with venture capitalists, all with the aim of serving the public good. For example, one project they've suggested they want to tackle is developing an ultra-fuel-efficient hybrid car. I applaud that kind of thinking; it fits the times.

**FC:** What, if anything, does the emergence in the field of people like Bill Clinton, Bill Gates, Michael Bloomberg, and former Senator Tim Wirth say about the field of philanthropy?

**VG:** It's noteworthy that an idea conceptualized by Andrew Carnegie more than one hundred years ago is still influencing modern-day philanthropists. It was Carnegie, in his famous 1889 essay, "The Gospel of Wealth," who articulated the belief that all personal wealth beyond that required to meet the needs of one's family should be regarded as a trust fund to be administered for the benefit of the community. Many individuals and families have followed Carnegie's example, reflecting just how deeply the philanthropic spirit has taken root in our country. In that connection, it's interesting — and heartening — to note that contrary to conventional wisdom about who gives the most, Independent Sector reports that low-income people give disproportionately larger percentages of their income than do the wealthy. Fully 70 percent of American households make charitable contributions. In 2001, for instance, that amounted to $239 billion in giving.

In terms of today's major philanthropies, such as Gates' and Bloomberg's, or those who are creators or dispensers of philanthropy, such as Clinton, Wirth, and others, it's interesting to consider how many of them are politicians or former office holders. Clearly, those who have based their careers on public service and/or have amassed private wealth feel that it is important to continue to serve the public in new venues such as philanthropy.

**FC:** Another powerful force, globalization, is impacting philanthropy by, among other things, creating new philanthropic networks and driving more resources toward transnational issues such as health and the environment. Do you expect globalization to have a long-term impact on organized philanthropy? And what, if any, are the implications for democracy and civil society should that turn out to be the case?

**VG:** Unfortunately, while challenges such as the state of our environment and access to basic health care have a global impact, many foundations still shy away from addressing international issues. This will probably continue to be the case because finding solutions to the problems facing the United States is an increasingly urgent concern. Issues such as the hollowing out of the American workforce; meeting the needs of an entire new generation of immigrants; trying to cope with the collapse of pension funds; the deterioration of so many elements of the social safety net; the need to ramp up America's ability to be technologically and scientifically competitive; the need to increase levels of adult literacy; the many pressing improvements that need to be made throughout the K–12 educational system; and so many other needs that must be addressed will probably continue to attract most of the resources of American philanthropy. However, what this also means is that more money will probably be spent to address international issues that are likely to have an impact on our country — an example being the spread of infectious diseases.

> **We need new ideas, new thinking, and imaginative solutions to problems; organizing the resources to address those problems is also critical, but ideas have to come first. . . .**

**FC:** When talking about such large-scale challenges, it can be difficult to measure the impact of philanthropic dollars, which, after all, are relatively modest. Is philanthropic effectiveness a function of the amount of resources available to solve a problem, the quality of the ideas behind those resources, or both?

**VG:** Money has often been used as an excuse for a lack of ideas or imagination. If amounts of money spent on problems were an indicator of success, countless federal programs would already be successful many times over! We need new ideas, new thinking, and imaginative solutions to problems; organizing the resources to address those problems is also critical, but ideas have to come first. After all, ideas are what animate philanthropy; the ideas that a foundation has identified, supported, and nurtured will be its lasting legacy.

**FC:** Given the scope and magnitude of the changes and forces we're talking about, does the philanthropic sector have access to metrics that can adequately measure its effectiveness?

**VG:** During the past few decades, almost all of us in the philanthropic sector have been struggling to find the necessary mechanisms to measure the effectiveness of the work of our grantees. After all, if you cannot measure what you do, you cannot evaluate it. What is apparent is that we need solid data rather than anecdotal information or approximations to help us make informed decisions. In the absence of solid data, we often end up, instead, making decisions based on trends. Hence, one of the most critical challenges facing foundations is to determine what, in fact, constitutes solid and reliable data, how to collect that data, and how to use it wisely and effectively, in ways that will stand the test of time.

**FC:** Ford Foundation president Susan Berresford's recent announcement that she plans to retire in 2008 is a reminder that the vanguard of the baby-boomer cohort is approaching retirement age. Given the over-representation of boomers in the nonprofit and foundation worlds, is that a cause for concern for the nonprofit and philanthropic sectors?

**VG:** No, not at all. The philanthropic spirit and Americans' dedication to strengthening the nation, enriching its civic life, and improving conditions for their fellow citizens transcends generations.

**FC:** How long does it take to bring an idea from obscurity into the mainstream? And which of the "unfashionable" ideas currently championed by you and your colleagues are most likely to be mainstreamed over the next ten years?

**VG:** Ideas have not been hiding in obscurity. Ideas are formed, not discovered. However, what sometimes happens is that organizations and institutions in need of money try to implement new ideas that are presented to them — but which they do not have the ability or the resources to serve properly — because they need the grant funding that will come along with the idea. In such cases, some organizations may even accept grants even though they don't actually believe in or support the cause that the grant is intended to advance. Nonprofit organizations should be able to refuse conditions imposed by foundations on their grants if the conditions are likely to distort an organization's mission or put an undue strain on their resources, because then the organizations may come out worse than they went in because of accepting the grant. So the right fit is necessary: the right idea, the right time, the right leaders, the right grantee.

In terms of important ideas that the Corporation is focused on, we are concerned about Americans' declining enthusiasm and support for our public institutions — particularly public education — and about the pernicious notion that excellence can be achieved only in the private sector. I am a firm believer that in a democracy equality and excellence are compatible. To strengthen and transform our common bonds, we must strengthen our public schools, not abandon them. That is one reason we have supported urban high school reform, as well as efforts to improve schools of education — after all, excellent education begins with excellent teachers, and the schools of education at our nation's universities need to do a better job of training those who will become the teachers of America's next generation of leaders. Incidentally, the need to improve the quality of K–12 education, even of higher education, is a problem not only for the United States but for Europe and the rest of the world, as well.

> **In an age of specialists, we need to learn how to chart a course that does not duplicate outmoded approaches to problems but rather encourages different perspectives. . . .**

**FC:** The diversity of issues addressed by foundations — and the strategies employed in addressing those issues — would seem to offer more than a little hope of finding solutions to some of the world's most vexing problems. In terms of specific problems or issues, where do you see the best chance for breakthroughs over the next ten to twenty years?

**VG:** "Problems" have been with us forever, though they do seem to be increasing in complexity nowadays. There are more people in the world, the issues we're dealing with seem to have tendrils that grow from many sources, both domestic and international, and there is a kind of fatigue about confronting what needs to done. We are overwhelmed by information, but all that information does not necessarily get translated into knowledge. And even if by chance some of it does, the knowledge does not often get translated into wisdom — and even less rarely does any of this turn into effective action. In an age of specialists, we need to learn how to chart a course that does not duplicate outmoded approaches to problems but rather encourages different perspectives, different approaches, and a lively competition of ideas. This is one of the great strengths of the structure of American society: the ability to support and promote independent thinking and innovative ideas.

How well this diversity has served the nation can be seen in the example of Vannevar Bush, science advisor to President Franklin D. Roosevelt, who argued that the nation's large network of universities were, by their very nature, best suited to take the lead in conducting basic research, which pioneers the frontiers of human knowledge to the benefit of society. Public funding, he said, would promote competition among researchers, and projects could be selected on their merit through a peer-review process. The National Science Foundation has been doing this job since 1950. Competition, experimentation, and creating models is critical because, when that process is applied to the problems we face, the entire nation does not have to undergo the stresses and strains of trying to implement a solution and then finding out it doesn't work. That's one of the most important ways that foundations can be of incalculable value: they can support different models, different ideas, different ways of addressing issues that can then be disseminated widely when, and if, they prove useful.

**FC:** A final question: What is the current era of philanthropy most likely to be remembered for?

**VG:** An important notion that has enriched philanthropy in recent years is the formation of partnerships. More foundations are now working together in order to decrease replication of their efforts and increase the impact of their grantmaking. The Corporation, for example, works collaboratively with a number of other foundations on both domestic and international issues. Building networks is good for foundations and good for grantees, because networks can continually expand their strength, add new resources, and bring in new participants — as the Internet, which may be the greatest network of all, has certainly shown. But perhaps most importantly, I think today's philanthropic sector will be remembered for its outreach to the rest of the world — it's happening slowly, but it is happening. We're trying to transcend borders, work with different governments, different nationalities and different ideologies in order to begin to address the common problems affecting humankind.

**FC:** Well, thank you, Dr. Gregorian, for sharing your thoughts with us.

**VG:** It was my pleasure.

*Mitch Nauffts, editorial director of* Philanthropy News Digest, *spoke with Vartan Gregorian in October 2006.*

# Index

Aaron Diamond AIDS Research Center (ADARC), 63–64, 67–68
Aaron Diamond Foundation, 63–64, 65, 68–73, 206
accountability
    changes since 1950s, 188–189
    in disaster response, 144–145
    efforts to improve, 7–8, 11, 163
    legal changes, 166–168, 191–192
    need for, 75, 139–141
    recommendations of Panel on the Nonprofit Sector, 168–170, 174
    support for, 41, 42
    *See also* outcomes measurement; regulation; self-regulation
ACR. *See* Alliance for Charitable Reform
ADARC. *See* Aaron Diamond AIDS Research Center
advocacy. *See* public-policy advocacy
Africa
    education programs for girls, 110, 111–112, 114, 118
    Gates Foundation programs, 141
    Riders for Health, 108
AIDS research, 63–64, 66–68, 71
Alliance for Charitable Reform (ACR), 52–53
American Red Cross, 144, 174, 206
Andrews, F. Emerson, 1–2, 3–4, 5, 6–7, 187, 190
Anheier, Helmut, 88, 119, 172
Annenberg Foundation, 70
annual reports, of foundations, 5, 8–9, 189

architecture, sustainable design, 85–87
arts programs, 70
Ashoka, 105, 109
Asia Foundation, 109
audit committees, 169
AVINA Foundation, 109
Aviv, Diana, 164–174

baby boomers, retirement of, 128–129, 211
Baucus, Max, 168
Benetech, 117
Ben-Horin, Daniel, 147–161
Bereuter, Doug, 183
Berkshire Hathaway, 142, 143
Berman, Melissa, 37–45
Bernstein, Carol, 65
Bernstein, Daniel, 65
Berresford, Susan, 211
Bill and Melinda Gates Foundation. *See* Gates Foundation
Blecher, Taddy, 118
Bloomberg, Michael, 199, 209
boards. *See* trustees
Bono, 34
Bornstein, David, 117
Bradley, Bill, 140
Bradley Foundation, 34, 54, 58
Branson, Richard, 208
breakthrough groups, 50–51
Brin, Sergey, 209
Broad, Eli, 183–184

215

Buffett, Warren
  donation to Gates Foundation, 22, 57, 115, 143–144, 171–172, 178, 195–196, 198
  family, 22–23
  investments, 142
  philanthropy, 22–23, 142, 183–184
  support of estate tax, 144
buildings, "green," 85–87
Bush, George W., 176
Bush, Vannevar, 213
business leaders, 183–184, 199, 209
  See also entrepreneurs
businesses
  corporate giving programs, 180
  social responsibility, 142
  venture capital, 11–12, 113, 196

California
  Central Valley and Inland Empire, 93, 94, 96–97, 101–102
  demographic diversity, 96
  economy, 93
  ethnic media, 77
  Irvine Foundation mission, 95, 97–100, 103–104
  poverty, 93, 96
California Wellness Foundation, 149
Campaign for Female Education (CAMFED), 110, 111–112, 114, 118
Canales, Jim, 93–104
capitalism, 22, 199, 203
Carnegie, Andrew, 16–17
  creation of foundation, 196, 197
  "The Gospel of Wealth," 203–204, 209
  libraries funded, 114, 204
  wealth, 13
Carnegie Corporation, 58
  annual reports, 8
  assets, 195, 208
  behind-the-scenes work, 192
  collaborations with other foundations, 213
  criticism of, 196
  deed of gift, 197
  education programs, 70
  establishment, 197, 204
  founding of Foundation Library Center and, 5, 7
  leaders, 6, 204–214

program areas, 212
Carson, Emmett, 120–131
Carter Center, 109
Center for Effective Philanthropy (CEP), 32–33, 173
challenge grants, 81, 83
charitable gift funds, 41
charitable giving
  for disaster relief, 165
  distinction from philanthropy, 180, 207
  historical trends, 51
  by individuals, 142, 170, 209
  regulations, 205–206
  tax incentives, 51, 52, 206
  use of Internet, 206
  See also donors
charitable organizations. See nonprofit organizations
Chernow, Ron, 13, 14
CIDA City Campus, 118
civil society, 8, 9, 116–117
Cleveland Foundation, 197–198
climate change, 29, 77–78, 114
Clinton, Bill, 183, 199, 209
Coca Cola Company, 89
Cohen, Rick, 134–146
Coleman, Andrea, 108
Coleman, Barry, 108
Collins, Dennis, 94
Collins, Jim, 113
Commission on Private Philanthropy and Public Needs (Filer Commission), 10, 133, 135
community foundations, 120–121, 124–125, 127–128, 130–131, 176, 197–198
competition in philanthropy, 57–58
CompuMentor, 147–151, 152, 153, 157–158, 159
computers. See technology
Congress
  charitable reforms, 52–53, 166–168, 169, 176–177, 191, 192
  estate tax issue, 44–45
  investigations of charitable practices, 3–5, 42, 163, 177, 187, 190–191
conservative foundations, 34–35, 54–55, 60
corporate giving programs, 180
Cotton, Ann, 110, 111–112, 118

216

## Index

Council on Foundations, 10, 175, 176, 178, 180–182, 184–185, 189, 192, 194
Cox, Eugene, 3, 4–5
Cox Committee, 3–5
Craigslist, 154
creative philanthropy, 172

David Rockefeller Fund, 20
Davis, Susan, 105
Dean, Howard, 154
democracy, relationship to philanthropy, 135–136, 138, 200
Democracy Alliance, 35
Detroit, 87, 88
Diamond, Aaron, 65–66
Diamond, Irene, 63, 64, 65–67, 68, 69, 70–71, 72
Diamond Foundation. *See* Aaron Diamond Foundation
directors. *See* trustees
disaster response, 144–145, 165
   *See also* Hurricane Katrina
DJB Foundation, 64, 65, 66
Donee Group, 133
donor intent
   respect for, 48, 49–50, 136, 197
   spending-out strategies, 63, 68–73, 178, 196
donor-advised funds, 38, 121, 176, 177
donors
   advice for, 78–79
   advisory services, 38
   cultural influences, 44
   gender differences, 44
   giving during lifetime, 72, 196
   individuals, 142, 170, 209
   low-income and working-class, 142, 209
   motives, 44
   risk-taking, 43, 123
   services for, 60–61
   *See also* charitable giving
Drayton, Bill, 105

eBay, 154
Edna McConnell Clark Foundation, 172
education
   in California, 97–98
   Diamond Foundation programs, 70
   of low-income children, 51
   programs for girls in Africa, 110, 111–112, 114, 118
   reforms, 55
Einstein, Albert, 32
endowments, 50, 195
Engelhardt, Sara, 188–202
entrepreneurs, business, 105, 115
   *See also* social entrepreneurs
environmental issues
   global warming, 29, 77–78, 114
   "green" buildings, 85–87
   impact of business activities, 114
estate tax, 44–45, 51–52, 144
European Foundation Centre, 185
evaluation. *See* outcomes measurement
Evangelical Council for Financial Accountability, 54

family foundations, 95, 206
Federal Emergency Management Agency (FEMA), 144, 145–146, 165
Ferry, W.H. "Ping," 65
Fidelity, 121
Filer Commission, 10, 133, 135
financial services firms, 121
Ford Foundation, 2, 4, 8, 9, 206, 211
Foundation Center
   contributions, 189
   data collection, 7
   founding, 1–2, 5–7, 187, 188
   goals, 6, 187
   publications, 189, 193–194, 208
   roles, 192, 193
   staff, 188
*Foundation Directory*, 189
foundation field
   changes since 1950s, 8–11, 187–189
   as distinctive sector, 8–10
   infrastructure organizations, 10, 192
   malaise in, 88
   in 1950s, 1, 2, 187
Foundation Library Center, 1–2, 5–7, 187
*Foundation News*, 189
*Foundation Yearbook*, 208
foundations
   annual reports, 5, 8–9, 189
   arguments for increased spending, 140

217

assets, 1, 2, 140, 171, 187, 195
collaborations, 50–51, 125–126, 198, 213
collection of data on, 1–3, 5, 7
communication by, 76, 193
cultures, 73–74
failures, 33, 76
large, 171, 195–196, 208
leadership in, 183–184
limited-term, 63, 178
mission statements, 49, 123
number in United States, 1, 6, 187
perpetual, 63, 178, 197, 206
public perceptions of, 11, 180, 193–194
relations with governments, 11, 59–60, 191
relations with grantees, 74, 89, 100–101, 126–128, 170–171
small, 171
societal roles, 22, 187–188, 207–208
staff, 103, 130
structures, 206–207
*See also* donor intent; grants; philanthropy; private foundations; regulation; trustees
Freechild, 154–155
Friedman, Thomas, 25
Fruchterman, Jim, 117
future of philanthropy
    areas for improvement, 42–43
    challenges, 35–36, 89, 101–102
    community foundations, 130–131
    grassroots organizations, 116–117
    growth, 184
    influence of globalization, 184–185, 199
    leaders, 211
    program areas, 77–78, 212–213
    regulatory change, 184, 191–192
    Rockefeller on, 22–23
    roles of individuals and institutions, 160
    social change goals, 11, 43–44
    types of organizations, 197–198

Gallagher, Brian, 173
Gardner, John, 8, 11, 111
gatekeepers, 156–157
Gates, Bill, 22, 23, 34, 123, 143, 171, 183–184, 199, 209
Gates, Frederick T., 13, 16, 18, 38
Gates, Melinda, 22, 23, 34, 123, 143, 171

Gates Foundation, 45
    Buffett's donation, 22, 57, 115, 143–144, 171–172, 178, 195–196, 198
    education programs, 70
    grantees, 115–116
    health programs, 141, 172, 201
    risk-taking, 129
    size, 143, 171, 195–196
Gellhorn, Alfred, 67–68, 70
gender differences, of donors, 44
*Giving in America* (Filer Commission), 133
global warming, 29, 77–78, 114
globalization
    challenges for philanthropy, 28–31, 180
    economic effects in California, 97–98
    equity issues, 29–30
    importance, 25
    influence on philanthropy, 22–23, 60, 184–185, 199, 209–210
Google.org, 45, 208, 209
governance. *See* accountability
government
    comparison to philanthropy, 179
    program cuts, 178
    public faith in, 77
    relations with foundations, 11, 59–60, 191
    roles, 59–60
    *See also* Congress; regulation; taxes
Grameen Bank, 107
grantee perception reports, 32–33, 173
grants
    amounts, 1, 179, 187
    information on, 189
    proportion of nonprofit revenues, 170
    refused by nonprofits, 74–75, 128, 211–212
    social benefits, 140
    for social change, 121–123
    strategic approach, 98–99
Grassley, Charles, 166–168, 176
grassroots organizations, 77, 116–117, 135
    *See also* nonprofit organizations
"green" buildings, 85–87
Gregorian, Vartan, 204–214
Gund, Agnes, 70
Gunderson, Steve, 175–185

# Index

Hale, Victoria, 115
Harlem Children's Zone (HCZ), 172
Headwaters Foundation for Social Justice, 130
Heald, Henry, 8
health services programs, 108, 115–116, 141, 172, 201
    *See also* AIDS research
Heintz, Stephen B., 25–36
Henderson, Lance, 109
Ho, David, 63, 68
Hoffman, Paul, 4–5
House of Representatives
    Un-American Activities Committee, 4
    Ways and Means Committee, 3
    *See also* Congress
Humane Society, 206
Hurricane Katrina, 144–146, 165, 177, 180, 206

ideological diversity, 56–57, 137–138
    *See also* conservative foundations; liberal foundations
immigrants, in Minnesota, 129–130
Independent Sector (IS), 10, 163, 164, 209
Indian Ocean tsunami, 144
Individual Retirement Accounts (IRAs), 177
Inglis, William O., 13
innovations
    diffusion, 110
    by foundations, 198
    by social entrepreneurs, 51, 111–112, 115
Institute for Educational Affairs, 48
Institute for One World Health, 115–116
institutions
    building, 42
    future roles, 160
    philanthropic, 196
    public faith in, 77
    societal role, 21
    successful, 45
intellectual property, 157–158
Internal Revenue Service (IRS)
    approval of disaster response funds, 145
    audit rate, 174
    990 Forms, 2, 4, 7, 170, 189
    oversight role, 163, 169
    *See also* taxes

Internet
    blogging tools, 155
    charitable giving through, 206
    use by nonprofits, 148, 149, 152–156, 158–160
    virtual communities, 155–156
    *See also* Web sites
Interplast, 155, 159–160
IRA rollovers, 177
Irene Diamond Fund, 64, 65
IRS. *See* Internal Revenue Service
Irvine, James, 95
Irvine Foundation. *See* James Irvine Foundation
IS. *See* Independent Sector

James Irvine Foundation, 93–104
Japan Center for International Exchange, 185
John M. Olin Foundation. *See* Olin Foundation
Joint Tax Committee, 53
Joseph, Jim, 194
Joseph, Stephen, 67

Katrina. *See* Hurricane Katrina
Keele, Harold M., 4
Kellogg Foundation, 8, 9
Kilbourne, Edwin, 68
Kresge, S.S., 81, 83
Kresge Foundation, 81, 82–84, 85–87, 88, 89–91

leadership
    of board members, 83–84
    in foundations, 183–184
    in nonprofits, 90, 91, 99–100, 128–129, 211
    roles, 33–34
    of social entrepreneurs, 117
Leat, Diana, 88, 119, 172
LEED Program, 85, 86
Leffingwell, Russell, 6
liberal foundations, 35, 55, 137
Lieberman, Joseph E., 26
limited-term foundations, 63, 178
L.J. and Mary C. Skaggs Foundation, 149
Lynde and Harry Bradley Foundation, 34, 54, 58

Machel, Grace, 20
Machel, Samora, 20
Magsaysay, Ramon, 19
Mandela, Nelson, 20
March of Dimes, 173
Marshall, John E., III, 81–91
Mazow, Seth, 155, 159–160
McConnell Clark Foundation, 172
McGee, Vincent, 64–79
media
    ethnic, 77
    films, 108
    lack of coverage of philanthropy, 207
    television series on social entrepreneurs, 109
media scrutiny of philanthropy
    benefits, 61–62
    celebrity factor, 34, 178, 193
    increase in, 31, 42
    portrayal of foundations, 193–194
    reports of wrongdoing, 163, 164, 165, 177
    watchdog role, 165–166
Mercy Corps, 206
Meyerson, Adam, 47–62
Midwest, economic conditions, 87–88
Miller, John J., 47
Minneapolis Foundation, 120, 121–125, 127, 130
Minnesota
    immigrants, 129–130
    Northwest Area Foundation, 141
    restoration of voting rights to felons, 124–125
Minnesota Meeting, 124
mission statements, 49, 123
Morris, Emory, 8
Mottola, Maria, 196

Nasaw, David, 204
National Center of Charitable Statistics, 171
National Committee for Responsive Philanthropy (NCRP), 133–134, 135–136, 137, 141
National Institutes of Health, 59
National Science Foundation, 213
Nature Conservancy, 173–174
NCRP. *See* National Committee for Responsive Philanthropy
Nesbitt, John, 184

Net Tuesday, 155, 160
NetSquared, 148, 154, 155, 160
New America Media, 77
New York Foundation, 196
Nielsen, Waldemar, 56, 61
9/11 attacks, 27–28, 144, 145
Nonprofit Finance Fund, 86
nonprofit organizations
    burnout of executives, 100
    capacities, 127–128
    as customers or vendors of foundations, 126–127
    fraud and abuse, 5, 52–53, 144, 145, 168
    grassroots, 77, 116–117, 135
    growth, 84–85, 165
    leadership, 90, 91, 99–100, 128–129, 211
    public charities, 60, 197, 198
    refusal of grants, 74–75, 128, 211–212
    reinvention, 173–174
    relations with foundations, 74, 89, 100–101, 126–128, 170–171
    revenue sources, 170
    use of technology, 148–150, 152–156, 158–160
nonprofit sector
    academic study of, 41, 58, 108
    congressional investigations, 3–5, 42, 163, 177, 187, 190–191
    distinction from for-profit sector, 114–115
    health, 164–165
    intermediary organizations, 60–61
    public confidence, 163, 167–168, 193
Norris, Ruth, 109
Northwest Area Foundation, 141

Olin Foundation, 34–35, 54
Omidyar Network, 45
Open Society Institute, 57–58
operating foundations, 206
Osberg, Sally, 105–118
outcomes measurement
    approaches, 58–59, 123–124
    difficulties, 141
    grantee perception reports, 32–33, 173
    growing emphasis on, 31–33, 140–141
    impact assessment, 41
    metrics, 103, 210–211
    need for, 74

return on investment, 182
of social entrepreneurs, 113–114
Oxford University, Skoll Center for Social Entrepreneurship, 108

Page, Larry, 209
Panel on the Nonprofit Sector, 163, 166, 168–170, 174
Participant Productions, 107
payout rates, 138–139, 177–179, 192
Payton, Robert L., 133
Pension Protection Act of 2006, 52–53, 176–177, 191
Perkins, James, 5–7
perpetual foundations, 63, 178, 197, 206
Persico, Joseph, 14
Pew Charitable Trusts, 192
pharmaceuticals, 115–116
philanthropy
  alternative vehicles, 196, 198, 205, 208, 209
  competition in, 57–58
  deconstruction, 208
  definitions, 39
  distinction from charity, 180, 207
  effectiveness, 39–40
  engagement, 39–40
  freedom of, 56–57
  public perceptions of, 34, 194, 207
  societal roles, 61, 179–180, 190
  strengths, 42
  surfer theory, 194–195
  types of organizations, 40–41, 45
  *See also* foundations; future of philanthropy; grants
Philanthropy Roundtable, 47, 48–54, 56–57, 59, 60
Pifer, Alan, 103, 119
political activity
  of foundations, 200
  role in social change, 201
  *See also* public-policy advocacy
political leaders, 183–184, 199, 209
Porter, Michael, 140
power dynamics
  within boards, 72
  within foundations, 73

between funders and grantees, 100–101, 126–128, 170–171
press. *See* media
private foundations
  advantages of form, 198
  behind-the-scenes work, 192
  collaboration, 198
  debates on, 133
  future challenges, 101–102
  mandatory payout rates, 138–139, 177–179, 192
  perpetual, 206
  restrictions on political activity, 200
  *See also* foundations
progressive foundations. *See* liberal foundations
public charities, 60, 197, 198
  *See also* nonprofit organizations
public health, 77–78, 201
public-policy advocacy
  approaches, 55–56
  role of philanthropy, 30–31, 200–201
  roles of foundations, 11
  *See also* social change

Ramon Magsaysay Awards Foundation, 19
Rapson, Rip, 90
RBF. *See* Rockefeller Brothers Fund
Red Cross, 144, 174, 206
Redford, Robert, 107–108
Reece, B. Carroll, 3
Reece Committee, 5
regulation
  of charitable giving, 205–206
  enforcement, 139, 163, 165
  existing, 138, 168
  in future, 184, 191–192
  mandatory payout rates, 138–139, 177–179, 192
  need for, 41, 42, 139
  opposition to increased, 53
  Pension Protection Act of 2006, 52–53, 176–177, 191
  recommendations of Panel on the Nonprofit Sector, 168–170
  restrictions on political activity, 200
  tax laws, 9, 190, 191, 192, 200
  *See also* Internal Revenue Service; self-regulation

221

responsive philanthropy, 135
return on investment, 182
Revenue Act of 1950, 2, 3, 5
Riders for Health, 108
Ridings, Dot, 139
risk-taking
    avoiding, 122–123, 138
    by foundations, 33, 129
    by individual donors, 43, 123
    in philanthropy, 31, 43
Robin Hood Foundation, 58
Rockefeller, David, 14–23
Rockefeller, John D., 13–14, 16–18, 38, 45, 143, 196
Rockefeller, John D., Jr., 13, 14, 17, 18–19
Rockefeller, Laura Spelman, 16
Rockefeller Brothers Fund (RBF)
    endowment, 22
    founding, 17
    leaders, 15, 19–20, 25, 26–27
    program evaluations, 32–33
    risk profile, 31
    tagline, 28–29
Rockefeller family, 14, 15–16, 19–20, 38
Rockefeller Foundation
    annual reports, 8
    behind-the-scenes work, 192
    endowment, 22
    establishment, 16–17, 206
    grants, 3, 14
    influence, 22
    objectives, 18
    program areas, 18
Rockefeller Philanthropy Advisors (RPA), 37, 38–39, 43, 44
Rockefeller University, 14, 21
Roelofs, Joan, 137
RPA. *See* Rockefeller Philanthropy Advisors
Rusk, Dean, 8
Russell Sage Foundation, 2, 4, 8, 9, 187

Sage Foundation. *See* Russell Sage Foundation
Salole, Gerry, 185
Santorum, Rick, 166
Sarbanes-Oxley bill, 53
Scaife foundations, 34, 54
Schwab Foundation, 109

self-regulation
    accreditation, 54, 56
    inadequacy, 139–140
    opposition to, 53–54, 56
    recommendations of Panel on the Nonprofit Sector, 168–169
    support for, 6
    *See also* accountability; regulation
Senate Finance Committee, 53, 166–167, 176
    *See also* Congress
September 11 attacks, 27–28, 144, 145
Six Apart, 155
Skaggs Foundation, 149
Skoll, Jeff, 106, 107, 109, 111, 117
Skoll Awards for Social Entrepreneurship, 109–111, 112–113, 118
Skoll Center for Social Entrepreneurship, Oxford University, 108
Skoll Foundation, 105–118
Sloan Foundation, 11
Smith, James Allen, 187–188
Smith Richardson Foundation, 34, 54
social change
    philanthropy and, 191
    social Web and, 153–156
social change, foundations and
    barriers, 122–123
    business perspective, 113
    in future, 11, 43–44
    grantmaking, 121–123, 140
    public-policy advocacy, 11, 30–31, 55–56, 200–201
    roles, 119, 121–125, 136–138, 139
Social Edge, 116
social entrepreneurs
    celebrating, 109–111
    connecting, 109, 116
    definition, 106–107
    examples, 107–108, 115–116
    experimentation, 44
    identifying, 109
    importance, 105
    innovations, 51, 111–112, 115
    leadership, 117
    outcomes measurement, 113–114
    personalities, 111
    relationship to philanthropy, 108–109
    stakeholders, 113

sustainability, 112
television series on, 109
social venture capital, 11–12
social Web, 153–156, 158–160
socially responsible business, 142
Soros, George, 199
spending-out strategies, 63, 68–73, 178, 196
Standard Oil Company, 13, 17
Starr, Kevin, 96
strategic philanthropy, 98, 194, 195
surfer theory of philanthropy, 194–195
sustainable design, 85–87
Synergos, 20

Tax Reform Act of 1969, 9, 190, 191, 192, 200
taxes
    estate, 44–45, 51–52, 144
    incentives for charitable giving, 51, 52, 206
    *See also* Internal Revenue Service
technology
    foundations and, 151–152, 197
    future, 78
    product donations, 148, 149–150
    social benefits, 117
    use by nonprofits, 148–150, 152–156, 158–160
    volunteers, 148–149
    *See also* Internet
technology assistance organizations, 147
TechSoup, 148, 150, 152, 157–158
TechSoup Stock, 148, 150, 153
Thomas, Bill, 167
Thomas, Lewis, 67, 68
*Time* magazine, 34
tobacco companies, 142
Tocqueville, Alexis de, 91
Toffler, Alvin, 147, 173
Toffler, Heidi, 173
transparency. *See* accountability

Trott, Mena, 155
trustees
    diversity, 130, 135
    effectiveness, 83–84
    leadership, 83–84
    power struggles, 72
    selecting, 50
tsunami, Indian Ocean, 144
Turner, Ted, 45, 199
Twentieth Century Fund, 2

United Way of America, 170, 173
United Ways, 173, 198
U.S. Green Buildings Council, 85

Vanguard, 121
venture capital, 60, 113, 196, 209
venture philanthropy, 10, 11–12, 39, 196–197
Vincent Astor Foundation, 206
virtual communities, 155–156

Walsh Commission, 190
Web, social, 153–156, 158–160
Web sites
    of foundations, 189
    on technology, 148
    Wikipedia, 153–154, 157
    *See also* Internet
Wheeler, Katie, 95
Wikipedia, 153–154, 157
WINGS, 185
Wirth, Tim, 183, 209
workforce development, 183
World Bank, 184

Yamamoto, Tadashi, 185
Young, Donald, 4, 8
youth, social Web and, 154–155
    *See also* education
Yunus, Muhammad, 107, 110

**Alpena Co. Library**
211 N. First Ave.
Alpena, MI 49707